Ecovillages

Ecovillages

A Practical Guide to
Sustainable Communities

Jan Martin Bang

Floris Books

First published in 2005 by Floris Books
©2005 Jan Martin Bang

British Library CIP Data available

ISBN 0-86315-480-8

Printed in Great Britain
By Bath Press, Bath

Contents

Part 2   Design

6. Water and Sewage   155

7. Energy Sources and Alternative Technology   176

8. Alternative Economics   200

Part 3. Putting it all together

Acknowledgments

My first thanks must go to the community where I live and to my immediate family, for giving me the context where I could work on this book. Especially to Ruth for putting up with the many hours I have spent away from her doing the actual writing. Albert Bates and the inner core of the Global Ecovillage Network got me started on the serious road to learning and teaching Permaculture Ecovillage design. Oyvind Solum got me involved in the Kilden Ecovillage Group when we settled in Norway, and it was while teaching a Permaculture design course to them that the idea for this book emerged. Special mention goes to Roy Halvorsen and Kevin Reeder for valuable discussions during that seminal period. The people at Floris Books have made these wild ideas a practical reality: Christopher Moore, Hannah Phillips, Christian Maclean, Ulrike Fischer and Katy Lockwood-Holmes.

There are many other people who have helped me develop ideas and gain insight, I thank all of them.

Jan Martin Bang

How to use this book

The original idea for this book was that it would be a study tool for a group designing an Ecovillage project. It can still be used as such, but I decided pretty early on not to fill it with teaching notes, questions and little tests at the end of each chapter. You are all adults; read it, talk about it, take the notes you need to take. I would still recommend that the entire design group read each chapter in turn and spend a session discussing and commenting upon it. My aim here is to give the economist some insights into the technicalities of building and gardening, and to give the alternative engineer some insights into social relationships and conflict resolution.

You can just read it for fun. I tried not to be academic and long-winded, but give real life examples from things I have done. Some of these are fun stories and I hope you appreciate them.

The Living Examples I have included throughout the book are not all still alive and kicking! These are based on personal experience over the last two decades and many of them have undergone changes since I visited them. Some have closed down (e.g. The Harman Centre), some I have lost contact with (e.g. Bhole Baba), others have severed all contact with the rest of the Ecovillage world (e.g. Terre d'Enaille). This in no way diminishes their value as examples. Ecovillages are living entities: they sprout, grow, develop, change and sometimes die off. Each one is a compromise between what is desirable and what actually happens in practice.

You can read specific chapters for ideas and guidance. During the year that I cooked in the Kibbutz kitchen I read many recipe books, but never actually used a recipe while cooking. I have always found it valuable to read about other people's experiences to help order my thoughts about what I intend to do.

You can also use the book as a door stop, to prop up a bookshelf or maybe plaster it into your wall as an insulation brick.

1

Introduction

1. The Story of the Global Ecovillage Network

How I ended up in an Ecovillage and good reasons
why you might do the same!

Communists and communes

During my first week as an undergraduate at Nottingham University in 1969 there was a Student Fair, where all the University clubs advertised themselves and tried to capture as many new members as possible from the fresh intake of new students. It was a confusing concourse of stands, tables and notice boards covered in posters and pictures. There were lots of people milling around.

A year before, the students in Paris had joined with the workers and proclaimed a revolution. Mao's *Little Red Book* was everywhere. America's behaviour in Vietnam had made capitalism a 'bad thing' and revolution was seen to be 'the answer.' Che Guevara was fast becoming a saint. Television in Western Europe was still largely black and white, and at the age of twenty so was my view of the world! Of course I felt drawn to the communist and socialist stalls; these were going to be my comrades in arms! For me too, revolution was in the air, and I would not for a minute have thought of joining the Rugby Club or the Scrabble Society. This was not about filling your free time with enjoyable hobbies, this was the very stuff of life, looking for the most meaningful task, much more important than undergraduate studies. Many of us had applied to university not so much to graduate as to change the world! My own registration to study Geography and Archaeology was not so serious, what I really wanted to do was to take part in the student revolution.

Opposite the Socialist Society stall I saw the Peace Society stall, staffed by a pretty girl, clearly worth a quick visit, even if the literature being offered was not up to much. What caught my eye was not the girl, however, but a magazine — *Commune Journal*. From history lessons at school I knew about the Paris Commune of 1870. From newspapers and people I had met I had experienced the Paris Commune of 1968. Were there other Communes? Was this about the next one?

In the end I came away from the Student Fair with a copy of *Commune Journal*. It was well produced, good graphics and most of all, it was filled with ideas about a whole new way of creating a new society, an alternative society! Instead of doing battle with the ponderous dinosaur of the old society with all its faults and wrongs, we would just go out and create a new one. It all seemed so simple in those days, creating a new society. Communes were springing up like mushrooms after rain and collapsing at about the same rate. It was a time of optimism and experiment.

Organic gardening and alternative technology

A few years later I was still obsessed with the idea of the alternative society. I completed my studies in Geography and Archaeology, just, and even managed to study Education and qualify as a teacher. Up to then, as a student, I had shared flats in town with other students, but now we were wage earners, and renting a house out in the country with other people seemed to be 'the thing to do.'

So we moved to a small rural cottage, first three of us, soon to be four, two couples, quite respectable, really. We all had lots of friends and practically every weekend there was a party! The house had a garden, we installed a wood burning stove and talked late into the night about renewable energy and self-sufficiency. So at the age of 25 I began to garden: clearing land, hoeing out weeds and sowing seeds. I had to ask the neighbour, a local farmer, to come and identify what were weeds and what were vegetables that first year, when little green things came sprouting through the soil. We gathered wood from the hedge trees to heat the house. We borrowed all the books we could find in the local library on edible plants and mushrooms to identify what we could eat out in the woods. We kept chickens, gleaned beans and peas from the fields around the farm, baked date and walnut loaf, and felt ourselves to be true revolutionaries, living radical social change in our very lifestyles.

In my second year of teaching I reduced my hours and taught part-time. My head teacher warned me that I was jeopardizing my career. I felt it was more important to liberate two days a week! One of these I spent at the local agricultural college, reading in the library. When I explained to them that I wanted to study Organic Agriculture on my own, they looked a little confused, but agreed in the end that I could sit in the library and read what books they had on the subject. Not much! But I did find some stray volumes that had found their way there: John Seymour, stuff from the Soil Association and books from Rodale Press. I read, I took notes and learned about how plants grow in the soil.

My second free day I decided to devote to alternative technology. I found a few like-minded people in Nottingham and together we arranged working weekends out at our cottage. The best days we spent at the local rubbish dump, collecting useful things other people had thrown away. Then came the idea of an Alternative Fair in the main square in town. We organized ourselves into the East Midlands Alternative Technology Group and participated. We displayed Cretan Windmills made out of junk, a solar panel made out of a discarded radiator, a range of composting systems and our prize exhibit, a Solar Cigarette Lighter! A large lens from a lamp had been found and accurately set up with a piece of wire to find the exact focal point. It was amazing, when correctly aligned with the sun, (and we were blessed with good weather that day) we could light cigarettes as fast as any gas lighter!

Today, nearly thirty years later, this hardly seems very special, except maybe for the lighter, that would still be pretty radical! But believe me, in 1976, for the average Joe strolling through Slab Square in Nottingham, this was mind-bending stuff. Solar panels? Wind generators? Compost? Symbols of a New Age!

The Well People Group

Time went by, Ruth and I had teamed up during our time at Nottingham University (and we're still together!) and in the mid-70s had spent a year and a half on Kibbutz in Israel, jeopardizing my career even further, and finding out that a complete alternative society is possible. A society where money does not change hands, where no one has a wage, where members collectively own all the means of production. This was not just a few freaks in an old cottage in the country, but more than 100,000 people and for several generations! Quite an eye opener, that one!

Back to England in the late 1970s and early 1980s, we moved to deeper rural pastures, to Lincolnshire, to the undiscovered Wolds, where we lived in the hills with wide views and much more self-sufficiency. There we got involved in alternative health, Ruth working with a naturopathic doctor who was convinced that health was a positive attribute that needed cultivation. He had started something called the Well People Group which was devoted to promoting health rather than just treating disease. How to cultivate good health? Diet, exercise, supportive people around you, a good attitude, in short, an alternative lifestyle. We set up a wholefood co-operative, working together with other people to provide good food for a wider public. For me, all this reinforced the idea of the alternative, a complete package, a new society, a holistic worldview.

This was the time of heavy politics. The Cold War was at its highest. Greenham Common was surrounded by women living in benders in the rain, literally being pissed on by the police and the army. In Lincolnshire we lived between three RAF bases equipped with nuclear weapons. There seemed to be a Cruise Missile lurking behind every hedge! I was scared, I had nightmares about nuclear war, bombs raining down over the countryside. We had our first child, Jake, and decided to move back to Kibbutz, to the complete 'cradle to grave' alternative society. No kidding, in 1984, it looked pretty peaceful in the Middle East compared to what we feared might happen in the Cold War.

The complete world of Kibbutz

Life on Kibbutz was a true alternative. Here we were, deciding upon our lives democratically; every week there was a General Meeting. Equality, everyone had the right to speak and vote. But there was no real environmental awareness. I worked in mainstream industrial agriculture. Even organic food was seen as weird. We had our second child, another boy, Isak, and found ourselves missing the organic, wholefood diet we had had in England. After seven years we asked for a year to travel, to live in other communes in England and in Norway. We ended up for most of the year in a Camphill Village in Norway, where Ruth took time out to give birth to our third child, Sarah, our first daughter. I worked most of the time in sewage treatment, making Flowform water cascades (see p. 171, Flowforms) which activate the water to clean itself biologically.

The Camphill Network was created in the 1940s by a group of Austrian refugees from Nazism who were inspired by the spiritual science of anthroposophy developed by Rudolf Steiner. The Camphill Schools begun by working with mentally handicapped children, and subsequently developed to create communities where mentally handicapped adults worked alongside other people to support themselves. Throughout the world today there are 106 Camphill Communities in 21 countries.

Before coming to Camphill and meeting anthroposophy I had experienced the alternative life as a series of disconnected aspects. Organic gardeners were not really looking at alternative technology; communes did not seem to be hotbeds of natural medicine. Even though these different aspects had some crossover, I could not yet discern a unifying philosophy or worldview. It was there, hidden, but was not being expressed explicitly. The Findhorn people talked to the angels in their garden. Others were reinventing Shamanism and travelling in the spirit world. Christian communes were well organized and happy to connect with alternative types. There was a jumble of spiritual streams, much of it very weird. There was a vague New Age feeling that we shared, but no one really knew what it meant, and any definition was quickly dismissed as parochial and inappropriate. Anyway, what did we need a definition for? We recognized each other pretty quickly.

My suggestion to the anthroposophists in Camphill that this was the New Age philosophy we other alternative types had been looking for was not well received. They didn't want to be connected to all those long-haired freaks with their outlandish habits. However, my enthusiasm was not dampened and I have been reading anthroposophy ever since. I am more and more convinced that this is worthwhile for any person who wants to be part of a new, alternative society.

When we came back to Kibbutz in 1992 I asked to work in ecology as opposed to agriculture. I began to teach, first on the Kibbutz, then with visiting groups and eventually I worked for the Kibbutz Movement, setting up seminars and courses in environmental awareness.

Kibbutz in Israel is a unique phenomenon. It has over 250 villages, up to 150,000 people, spread throughout the land. A very strong movement, with lots of political and economic clout. Within this movement I was trying to create an explicitly environmental agenda. In 1993 a group of newly arrived Australian immigrants hosted a number of seminars with Bill Mollison (one of the founders of Permaculture) throughout Israel. Together we arranged for him to speak to some Kibbutz environmentalists. Over the following months I found more partners within the movement and together we set up an office, called the Green Room, at the beginning of 1994. Our agenda was to stimulate and co-ordinate environmental projects throughout the Kibbutz movement. A year later, in 1995, an American arrived at a conference I was involved in, looking for environmental activists within the Kibbutz movement.

The Global Ecovillage Network

Albert Bates was from the Farm in Tennessee in America and one of the founders of the Global Ecovillage Network (GEN). He told me he was looking for an environmental group within the Kibbutz Movement and had funding to train someone in Permaculture (see pp. 45, 49) and sponsor the first few courses in Israel. So it was that Albert arranged for me to attend a Permaculture design course at the Farm, to get a grounding in holistic planning. Afterwards I found myself at Findhorn in Scotland, at the starting point of GEN, looking for a Permaculture teacher to start a Permaculture group in Israel.

The Farm, Tennessee, USA:
an Ecovillage training centre

Date founded — 1971
Approximate number of residents — 350
Location — rural Tennessee
Spiritual or ideological affiliation — hippie
Visited — about 10 days in the summer of 1996

The history of the Farm is itself a lesson in community development, how it was set up, the first pioneering years, the crash, and how it overcame the trauma of de-collectivizing to become again a thriving community. Read more about that in *Voices from the Farm*, see Book List (p. 259) at the end of the book. When I visited, I came to participate in a Permaculture design course, and stayed at the Ecovillage training centre. This was what really impressed me, a demonstration site in Ecovillage techniques. We worked on mulch gardens, washed in solar heated showers, where the water ran into the gardens to fill a pond for wildlife. There were two strawbale houses in construction, one square and the other circular. We dug swales to allow the rain water to drain into the soil, we looked at the Shitake Mushroom business as an example of ecological economics. The building we stayed in was being fitted with solar panels for electricity while we were there, and we saw examples of solar cooking stoves. We built compost heaps for the garden using the kitchen waste.

Not only was it an active place keeping us busy learning practical techniques. People came from far and wide to learn different things there. Kids from depressed urban areas came to cool off in the country. People from other countries, from the West and from poor countries in the South. The training centre was a real two-way street. It reached inwards to look at the jobs that needed doing to create an ecological community, and it looked outwards to diverse groups in the world who needed to meet and create friendship and understanding. This combination of inner and outer work is vital for the Ecovillage impulse, it represents a kind of breathing impulse, a balance.

ABOVE. Photovoltaic collectors being mounted on the roof of the Visitor Centre.

BELOW. Solar cooker developed on the Farm being demonstrated.

ABOVE. Solar heated showers. The parabolic mirror on the roof concentrates solar energy on a black water tank. Showering is best done in the afternoon, when the tank has had all day to warm up, which fits in well after a day's work.

OPPOSITE. Drainage ditch from the showers, this is led past vegetable gardens and down to a small pond which encourages aquatic life in order to bring diversity into the gardens.

BELOW. Swales being levelled at the side of the road. These take the run-off and allow it to soak slowly into the ground, raising the water table and minimizing flooding.

This meeting confirmed an idea that Ross Jackson, the founder of Gaia Trust, had raised: that relatively small amounts of money could most effectively be used in getting the right people together to share ideas and inspirations, who would then go back to their projects more motivated and stimulated. This would then in turn produce greater results: 'The best money is often given to support meetings between people, for networking' (*And We Are Doing It!* By Ross Jackson).

The conference 'Ecovillages and Sustainable Communities,' held at Findhorn in the autumn of 1995, attracted over 400 people from over 40 countries. It was so well subscribed to that over 300 more had to be turned away for lack of space. Here the Global Ecovillage Network (GEN) was created, formally founded by a number of communities from around the world: Findhorn Community, Scotland; the Farm, Tennessee, USA; Lebensgarten, Steyerberg, Germany; Crystal Waters, Australia; Ecoville, St Petersburg, Russia; Gyurufu, Hungary; The Ladakh Project, India; the Manitou Institute, Colorado, USA; and the Danish Ecovillage Association. Three networking offices were organized: Lebensgarten covering Europe and Africa, the Farm covering the Americas, and Crystal Waters covering Australia and Oceania.

Here we were saying *Yes!* to a whole new society, a society which would create a way into the next century. This time it was not just a vague feeling: there were organized groups and an explicit agenda. Together we would work out what kind of tools we would need, what kind of buildings we should build, how we should live together, and how we should manage our finances and make our decisions.

A year later GEN was invited to participate in the UN Habitat II conference, held in Istanbul in June 1996. This was an important step up, GEN was able to present itself publicly for the first time and was formally incorporated as an association of autonomous regional networks. It had the best and largest NGO presence at the conference and presented a proposal for a 100 million dollar fund to build Ecovillages around the world as teaching centres and examples of the sustainable development aims that came out of the Rio 1991 Conference, known as Agenda 21. Despite continuous lobbying by Declan Kennedy, an Irish German former professor of Urban Architecture at Berlin University, this 100 million dollar goal was never achieved. But GEN did manage to reach out across the globe and initiate many projects and networks.

Burnout and the negative activist

One of the striking features for me about the people involved in GEN was the highly positive charge they gave to their work. I had for years been working with protest movements. We had said *No!* to nuclear weapons, *No!* to War, *No!* to pollution, *No!* to Nuclear power, *No!* to toxic substances on our farms and in our food. It was all getting a bit much, to get up every morning and say *No!* Here finally was a group who got up and said *Yes! Yes!* to human scale communities. *Yes!* To organic food, *Yes!* To economics as if people mattered.

This was a convergence of a number of elements I had been following for decades. Permaculture was the tool, GEN the inspiration, Kibbutz the setting. Here was the whole range of alternative features. A complete society incorporating all the varied elements I had been chasing for all those years. At last I felt I could help create the kind of society I had envisaged when I had first come into contact with communes. A society that incorporated alternative technology into its very fabric; that ate food grown without chemicals as a matter of course; that saw health as an ongoing feature of every aspect of life and that sought to work together with other like-minded people across the world, cementing ties of friendship and undermining the causes of war.

This positive, holistic vision was extremely effective in galvanizing people and creating an atmosphere where optimism generated its own energy. For myself, this meant access to a network of activists, most of whom had a background in Permaculture.

The Earth's condition today requires non-specialists: that is, people who know something from a wide range of disciplines, who are trained to combine these skills into a holistic understanding, and who are socially, ecologically and politically engaged. Permaculture seemed to me to address this issue. Ecovillages, or for me, Green Kibbutzim, would be places where these skills could be taught to anyone who wanted to learn. There is a Chinese story that advises the person who wants to plan for a year to plant rice. He or she will get a yield before the year is up. Those who want to plan ten years ahead can plant trees, they will be big enough within a decade to give shade and fruit. The person thinking a hundred years ahead should work in education, that is the way to change the world. Permaculture is education, teaching people to think and plan for themselves.

Ecotop, Germany:
a suburban housing development

Date founded — 1995
Approximate number of residents — hundreds
Location — on the outskirts of Düsseldorf
Spiritual or ideological affiliation — environmental
Visited — a short stop for about two hours in 1998

This was a complete suburb. It was a really large site, with many different elements. The housing was only about a quarter finished in 1998, but there were people already living there. Two courtyards with four-storey buildings around them, in the middle pedestrian squares with trees, grass, children's playing areas and communal sitting space had already been completed. More apartments were still to be added, and there were plans for detached houses. There was to be a mixture of different rental schemes to allow people with low incomes to live there, as well as the well-off. The idea behind this was to create a community of diversity. The houses were being built of natural materials, passive heating and cooling was planned, wastewater was already being treated biologically, and community services such as child care and shops were part of the plans.

Next to the project there had been established a complex of community gardens for some years. This was integrated into Ecotop to allow for the growing of vegetables by those living there. In addition, these gardens created a social space that was already developing an interaction between people. These gardens were circular, with an open common space in the middle, with each private garden like a slice of cake reaching out to the periphery. They were already well established, with a striking variety of little sheds for tools and lots of trees and shrubs.

Ecotop took the Ecovillage idea and applied it in a big scale to a whole suburb. The ecological idea provided a focus which integrated gardening, celebrating together, housing, living together and providing a sense of community for a variety of different groups of people.

ABOVE. Inside the first building complex. Here are gardens and sitting areas, safe areas for children and adults well away from traffic.

BELOW LEFT. South facing sun catcher in a brick wall. By creating a warmer microclimate at this point more exotic species can be planted, as well as breaking up an otherwise boring straight bit of garden wall.

BELOW RIGHT. Entrance to the first building complex.

ABOVE. The centre of the communal gardens, showing gates into three private gardens.

BELOW LEFT. Handmade secluded bench in the Ecotop gardens.

BELOW RIGHT. Biological treatment pond for wastewater. This handles the waste from the first building complex.

What is an Ecovillage?

Ross and Hildur Jackson, who had set up the Gaia Trust a few years before, had been looking for wise ways to use the money they had made available for ecological projects. They had asked Diane and Robert Gilman to write a report on Ecovillages, and it was this that had created the thinking that eventually led up to the creation of GEN. Diane and Robert had defined an Ecovillage as follows and this definition has more or less followed GEN's thinking since then:

— *Human scale, usually thought of as somewhere between 50 and 500 members, but with exceptions.*
— *A full featured settlement, in which the major functions of life — food provision, manufacture, leisure, social life and commerce — are all present in balanced proportions.* They were careful to point out that this should not mean that Ecovillages be totally self-sufficient or isolated from their surroundings.
— *Human activities harmlessly integrated into the natural world.* By this they meant to imply that there is an ideal of equality between humans and other forms of life. In practice this means that a cyclic approach to resource use should be aimed at, rather than the linear, throw-away lifestyle which has become the norm in western society.
— *Supportive of healthy human development.* A balanced and integrated approach to fulfilling human needs — physical, emotional, mental and spiritual — was envisaged, not just for individuals, but for the community as a whole.
— *Successfully able to continue into the indefinite future.* This is the principle of sustainability; indeed, in many cases Ecovillages and Sustainable Communities are terms that are used interchangeably.

Their report went further, to define a number of areas in which Ecovillages would have to create new situations. This list in itself can serve as a planning list for Ecovillages and does not look very different from some of the Permaculture courses which I have been involved in:

— *The bio-system,* where the relationship between the Ecovillage and its ecological environment is as low-impact as possible.
— *The built environment,* where building technology, materials and design are looked at holistically.
— *The economic system,* where fairness and non-exploitation would be hallmark features.

Sunrise Farm, Australia:
a pre-GEN Ecovillage

Date founded — 1978
Approximate number of residents — several families at the time
I visited, today 28 adults and children
Location — eastern Victoria, north of Buchan
Spiritual or ideological affiliation — self-sufficiency, back-to-the-land
Visited — about a week in 1984

When I visited Sunrise Farm, it was still ten years to go before the Global Ecovillage Network was launched, and at a time when Permaculture was still largely confined to Australia. It was at Sunrise Farm I found the books *Permaculture Two*, and the *Earth Garden Books*. This was the context where Permaculture grew.

Sunrise Farm was really a wide valley out in the bush, where a group of families, couples and single people had bought in to a large acreage, each one getting a plot to build a house, establish a garden, and have forest enough to be more or less self-sufficient. Each unit was responsible for doing their own thing, making their own living and paying their bills. The sense of community was fostered by planning together, accepting new members, and celebrating festivals in their community building.

I remember them as pragmatic, straightforward back-to-the-landers, welcoming, fun to be with, and good at getting their houses and gardens together. They used their natural resources, built their houses out of local timber and mud brick, and grew their own food. The couple that we stayed with had a solar electricity system which delivered lights and music. They used junk imaginatively.

They are still there twenty years later, still largely living off the land, still sharing their community planning with each family responsible for its own economy. They are open to new people joining, and clearly are part of that larger, rural community movement which is not making any news but getting on with a low impact, alternative lifestyle. There are thousands like them, and they're here to stay.

ABOVE. Reused windows; car windows in the door, creating a very aesthetic arch.

LEFT. Upstairs sleeping area in a wooden round house. Access is by the ladder.

ABOVE. *Small tool shed or shack built out of junk materials.*

OPPOSITE. *Pot belly wood burning stove made out of two large lorry brake drums set one on the other. Immensely heavy and massive, it kept the heat for hours.*

BELOW LEFT. *Tool tidy rack at the communal workshop.*

BELOW RIGHT. *Interior of a family house.*

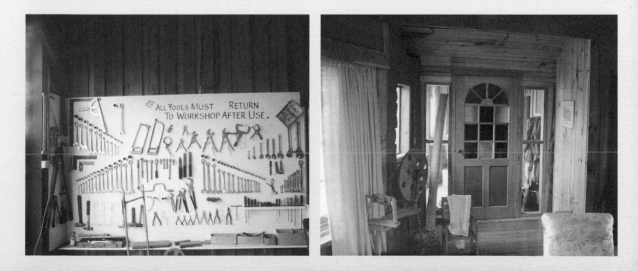

— *The governance of the community,* democracy, conflict resolution, leadership and the relationship between the Ecovillage and its neighbours, would all need to be redefined.
— *The 'glue.'* This is a term which has come to mean something hazy in one sense, but something that is very real and fundamental. How do communities keep together? What is it that binds us together as a group of people? We enter here into the realms of the spiritual and ideological.
— *The whole-system.* All these ideas just mentioned need to be integrated and understood as being parts of a greater whole, that work together in symbiosis. For me this is where Permaculture becomes relevant as an integrated planning system and it's this thought that prompted me to go ahead with writing this book.

Ecovillage training centres

These definitions of Ecovillages do not give a strong enough emphasis to one aspect which to me is fundamental: the relationship between the Ecovillage and the rest of the world.

There are some communities that are into self-reliance and self-sufficiency, that hoard food and supplies, are well armed and, in the event of total social disaster, will defend themselves against all comers. There are groups who pursue aims which are in conflict with my sense of rightness. There are yet other communities that are happy to have established a good lifestyle for their residents and the rest of the world can go hang!

There is an ever-present danger that we think we are the only righteous ones and that all other groups are less worthy. We live in an existentially questioning age. Do we have a future? Can we overcome the technical problems of pollution and resource depletion? Can we escape the social and spiritual nihilism so prevalent in our western society? If we can, where do we look for the answers we need? Where are the solutions being tested out?

It has become clear to me that to create a viable future society we need action on many fronts. There is no single solution that has all the answers. When I look back at what we have in our society in Western Europe, it seems that we owe a lot to radical innovators several generations ago. People who were prepared to experiment, to test out their ideas in real living situations. Often this was hard and many, if not all, of the radical collectives of the nineteenth century have disappeared, some more quickly than others.

It is my firm belief that it is in intentional community, specifically in Ecovillages, that these solutions are being sought. They are today some of the

Camphill Solborg, Norway: my own home!

Date founded — 1974
Approximate number of residents — 45
Location — southern Norway
Spiritual or ideological affiliation — anthroposophic
Visited — I live here

In the community where I live at Solborg Camphill Village in Norway we have a biodynamic farm, extensive vegetable gardens, a bakery, a weavery, a large forest for timber and firewood, herb growing and drying, and a carpentry workshop.

The farms and gardens in Camphill Villages produce food of the highest quality while nurturing both soil and wildlife. Generally the organic waste from the kitchens is composted, usually by a village compost set up. Horse transport is quite common, being very efficient and low cost at a village scale. Villages in England have pioneered wastewater treatment using ponds, reedbeds and Flowform water cascades (see p. 171, Flowforms). These are now standard in the Norwegian villages. Buildings, both communal halls and chapels, and the usually large residential houses, are largely constructed out of natural materials, and avoid the use of poisons and plastics as much as possible. There is a great deal of self-sufficiency.

Most of us live in large extended families, co-workers (both long-term people with their families, and young temporary volunteers) and villagers (mentally handicapped or otherwise in need of help), sharing our lives, our meals, our living rooms and bathrooms. There may be as many as fifteen people or more gathered round the dining table three times a day. Each house has its own budget, and is run more or less autonomously by a couple of responsible co-workers, the house father and house mother. In the morning and the afternoon everyone goes to work, in a variety of workplaces. Everyone has a workplace, and contributes something useful to the running of the village, according to his or her capability. No money changes hands, and work is seen to be something that is freely given within the fellowship, recognizing that some people have higher capabilities than others.

Solborg is in southern Norway, an hour from Oslo, on the edge of an extensive wilderness area. Within the village we have a Steiner school with over 100 pupils, and the Bridge Building School. This school offers courses in Camphill theory and practice, and in ecological building, specializing in strawbale construction, and in Permaculture.

BELOW RIGHT. Wenche, Ruth and Lone. The basis of village life is to create a social space where every member of the community feels useful and wanted.

RIGHT. Kitchen waste being taken to the farm for composting. Outside the house there are eight different garbage bins for sorting and recycling waste.

BELOW. Morning meeting in high summer. Every morning most of the village gathers to sing a song and go through the programme for the day.

ABOVE. The independent Steiner School lies within the village and creates an additional centre of life, and gives the village greater contact with people from outside.

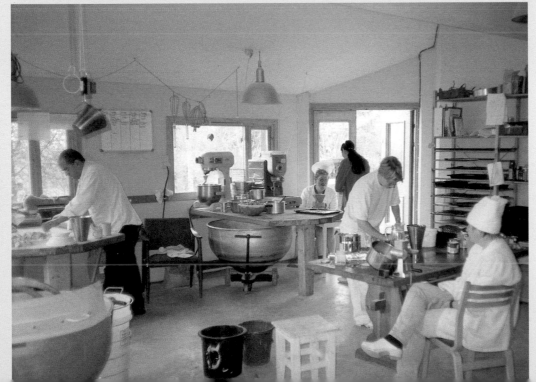

LEFT. The bakery supplies the village with bread, pasta, muesli and, once a week, pizza. It provides meaningful work and sought-after products.

most fertile areas for innovation, experiment and problem solving. This does not mean it is easy to live in an Ecovillage, indeed, the opposite is true. It's hard to bear the intensity, the responsibility and the tension. It's a hothouse. But it is here that we are developing the techniques and technologies which will eventually give birth to a truly sustainable society, caring for the environment and the people.

For an Ecovillage to have relevance into the future — and for me to want to co-operate with it and feel that we share some worldview — it is essential that it be outward-looking and open. To develop a training centre is one way to express this in concrete terms. Inviting people to join for longer or shorter periods, to learn alongside each other and then go back into the larger social context with new ideas and techniques.

That is why it is so important to develop Ecovillage training centres, something which was pictured right from the beginning of GEN. If we only build Ecovillages that are an escape from the problems of the larger society, we will have achieved very little. Only by engaging with the society around us, inviting people in to us, can we hope to achieve change in the larger society. I was mightily inspired when I read Vinoba Bhave's autobiography and found that he had anticipated the Ecovillage impulse by many years:

> I walked through India for a full thirteen years ... in the course of these journeys I established six Ashrams. I call these Ashrams experimental laboratories. The thinking carried on in the Ashrams will energize the work outside, and act as a source of inspiration and guidance. Our Ashrams must serve as power-houses for the areas in which they are placed. Let the power be felt throughout the neighbourhood, the power to build the kind of society to which we are committed: a society that manages its affairs non-violently, is unified by love and stands on its own feet, self-reliant and co-operative. Such a village society provides the best education, both spiritual and scientific, and takes care that every household should have full, productive work. Our chief task is the creation of a whole non-violent human society — non-violent, strong, self-reliant, self-confidant, free from fear and hatred.

On to Camphill

As we reached the end of the millennium it became clear to us that our Kibbutz was not going in a direction that we could reconcile ourselves to. Every community has its life-cycle and Kibbutz Gezer was in a phase we did not want to share. So in the summer of 2000 Ruth and I, with our three children, moved to Norway, to Camphill Solborg. A strong attraction for me was the newly established school for ecological building (the Bridge Building School) where I could carry on teaching Permaculture.

I soon became involved in the small but active Norwegian Ecovillage Group, Kilden (the Source), and we set up a Permaculture design course aimed specifically at the group of activists who were designing their first Ecovillage at Hurdal. It was during that course that the idea for this book emerged.

2. Patterns in Nature

The idea of Permaculture ecological design: reading nature's book

A very short history of the development of human consciousness

We all have our various points of view, in our everyday lives and also in our deeper consciousness. We might experience the same events, but we often interpret them completely differently. In a similar way different eras throughout history have also seen the world from different points of view. There is a popular idea that our knowledge of the world has grown and developed during the course of our history. That in the beginning we knew very little and that now we know a lot. That we have developed from ignorance to knowledge. But when we look closer we find that people just experienced the world differently in past ages and that our development is not simply a straight line ascending.

In the age of Mythology our experience of the world was full of meaning and significance. The ocean, for example, was enormous, changing, deep, wild or calm. It reflected our own mind, it was an experience of a personality, Poseidon to the Greeks. Everywhere in nature there were faces and personalities. The natural world around us was a reflection of ourselves and we could gain insight into ourselves by observing it.

About half a millennium before Christ there occurred in the West, in Greece specifically, a change from Mythos to Logos. A change from the mythological consciousness to logical thinking and rational thought. The philosophers began to ask questions about the nature of the world. Where does it come from? What is it made up of? One of their starting points was the idea of the four elements, earth, water, air and fire.

Hippocrates laid the foundations of western medicine around 450 BC. He was obsessed with process and how the temperaments related to various substances of the body. Air was related to blood and the sanguine temperament, water to phlegm and the phlegmatic. Fire was clearly choleric and had to do with yellow gall, while earth was melancholic and related to dark gall.

This system of thinking continued and was developed without structural changes for the next two thousand years. Alchemy continued the aspect of process in a strong way, relating various elements, such as mercury, sulphur and salt, to the four elements already defined by the ancient Greeks. Process was still seen as the most important aspect of the world and the human being. Paracelsus, 1493–1541, was an alchemist and is still regarded as an important figure in medical history. Alchemy today is widely regarded as some kind of medieval superstition, but today's chemistry is actually mostly alchemy without the spiritual bit, 'Alchemy Lite.'

With the Renaissance there came a complete break from the traditions of the ancient world. Copernicus discovered the heliocentric nature of our solar system, Luther broke with the venerable and dominating Catholic Church and eventually Descartes declared that anything that cannot be measured is not worth considering. Materialism gradually came to dominate our western thinking and this began to spread around the world with the so-called Age of Discovery. Art, Science and Religion had until then been regarded as an undivided trilogy; gradually they drifted apart. Today they seem to be completely unrelated.

Since the Renaissance we have taken apart the world. We have become caught up in a reductionist science that removes the spiritual component as unmeasurable and therefore irrelevant. For Descartes nature was dumb, there was no spirit in sticks and stones, nature was *res extensa*, a dead thing, while *res cogitans* was the thinking component which was the foundation of our existence: 'I think therefore I am.'

Surely we are much more than just thought. We walk, talk, intuit, feel and act. 'I walk, therefore I am,' or 'I talk, therefore I am,' or even 'I intuit, therefore I am.'

In our era, having completed the journey from the whole to the part, our task is to put both the world and the human being together again. We need to reintroduce the wholeness of the world and the creatures within it.

Writing something may be taken as an analogy: I have an idea; to begin with it is a complete whole, but I analyse it, break it up into manageable components and begin formulating chapters, paragraphs, and finally compose sentences made up of words and letters. I hope that someone will read these letters and words, understand the sentences and eventually come to share my understanding which initially inspired me to write. In our view of the world we may now be at the stage of being obsessed by its letters. But the idea of writing is that what I write should be read by someone. Now that we are able to read the letters of existence, surely the next step is to read what is written.

This is the immediate task for us at this point in the development of our consciousness, to read the book of the universe we have been given. To arrive back at the Big Idea by laboriously making sense of the letters, getting the understanding implied by each sentence and finally comprehending the universe by the flow of ideas we perceive in the paragraphs and chapters given to us by nature. This is what Permaculture sets out to do.

Earthaven, North Carolina, USA:
a Permaculture Ecovillage

Date founded — 1995
Approximate number of residents — *ca.* 60 people
Location — Appalachian Hills of North Carolina
Spiritual or ideological affiliation — Permaculture
Visited — a couple of days in the summer of 2004

Earthaven was planned by a group of Permaculture designers including most of the teachers who taught the first design course I attended, at the Farm in Tennessee. It is spread out in the forests along a valley in the steep Appalachian Hills, with several neighbourhood clusters, a co-housing building housing several families, a seminar centre offering courses in Permaculture, and several small businesses.

The forest is natural re-growth after clearing in the early years of the twentieth century, and is again being cleared, used for construction, and replaced by either buildings, gardens or fruit and nut trees.

Many techniques of ecological building can be found there, strawbale, mud, timber and junk. In many ways Earthaven can be seen as a showcase for Permaculture techniques, and there are courses run by many of the residents in building, gardening, planning and social aspects. Some of the vigour of the community can be seen by the activities going on within. The editorial office for both *Communities Magazine* and *The Permaculture Activist* are at Earthaven and there are two Permaculture teaching businesses. There is a regular tour of the community every Saturday morning for visitors, and a large seminar centre with resident apprentices and courses. Many of these activities reinforce each other, with courses being advertised in the magazines, and one of the Permaculture teachers, Chuck Marsh, also running a tree nursery and consultancy business.

ABOVE. Strawbale house, mud plastered and with a solar collector on the roof.

LEFT. Within the larger community there is a co-housing group.

ABOVE. One of the small businesses is a shop serving the community and the many visitors.

BELOW LEFT. One of my first Permaculture teachers, Patricia Alison, giving a Saturday morning tour to a group of visitors.

BELOW RIGHT. The garden belonging to one of my first Permaculture teachers, Chuck Marsh, showing mulching within a border made of bottles.

ABOVE. Construction using local, natural materials.

BELOW. Co-housing apartments with shared balconies.

Mollison, Holmgren and Australian bush freaks

In the mid-seventies Bill Mollison was teaching ecology at the University of Tasmania and he formulated the idea of Permaculture together with one of his students, David Holmgren. It was first thought of as an interdisciplinary earth science with a potential for positive, integrated and global outreach. The first book, *Permaculture One*, was published in 1978 and the first design course was taught in January 1981. By this time the concept was already sweeping across the western alternative world and Permaculture groups were gathering in many places.

Australian alternative types were gripped by a 'return to the bush' fever in the mid-seventies. How many of them there could have been in a country with such a relatively small population I don't know. Keith and Irene Smith started the *Earth Garden Magazine* in 1972 and in their *Earth Garden Book*, published in 1975, talk of thousands. The *Second Earth Garden Book*, published in 1978, is a companion volume and both books describe various ways of gardening, gathering wild foods, building houses and managing small farms and home-steads. The material is based on experience, accompanied by crude drawings and fuzzy black and white photographs, and is a treasure trove of self-suffi-ciency advice. Nowhere could I find a single mention of Permaculture, but most of the articles could have come straight out of *Permaculture Magazine*. This was clearly the mulch out of which Bill Mollison grew the ideas of Permaculture.

Mollison called Permaculture 'a complete agricultural ecosystem' in the introduction to *Permaculture One*, also 'a pioneer effort in perennial agricul-ture.' He goes on to say that it was aimed at small groups, living on marginal land, cheaply available. Clearly he was in Keith and Irene's world, the Earth Garden freaks.

From homestead gardening to community economics

Whether Mollison and Holmgren could have foreseen the direction that Permaculture subsequently took I can't say, but there is a hint at the end of that introduction. They talk there of creating a tool for development in urban and rural areas, a model which integrates ecology, energy conservation, landscape design, urban renewal, architecture, agriculture and the location theories of geography. In *Permaculture Two*, published in 1979, there is a section on Permaculture and Community, but it is only just over two pages and introduces the topic very generally. Permaculture is not yet taking on the subject system-atically, but social issues are already on the agenda.

In 1986, Max Lindegger and Robert Tap published a collection of articles harvested from various Permaculture magazines: *The Best of Permaculture*. It contains a number of pieces relating to urban Permaculture, applying the concept to city situations, but very little reference to social and economic solutions. Ten years later Ross Mars in the *Basics of Permaculture Design* devotes a whole chapter to 'Community' and another to 'Permaculture In School.' (This book, by the way, is the best short introduction that I have found yet. Clear, concise, well written and well illustrated. If you can only take one light book with you, take this one!) Graham Bell, in his *Permaculture Way*, published in 1992 was already applying Permaculture to a much wider spectrum, as we might infer just from some of his chapter head-ings: 'The Value of People,' 'Real Capital,' 'Universal Aims,' 'Your Community' and others.

Within a couple of decades, Permaculture had developed from a better way of farming and gardening, to a design tool which could be applied to virtually any human situation.

Permaculture is about designing sustainable human settlements. It is a philosophical and practical approach to land-use integrating microcli-mate, functional plants, animals, soils, water management and human needs into intricately connected, highly productive systems. It presents an approach to designing environments that have the diversity, stability and resilience of natural ecosystems. It seeks to regenerate damaged land and preserve environments which are still intact.

The most radical element in Permaculture is not stated explicitly in these early books, but is implicit within their pages. The systems that are suggested and described are based not only on working with nature, but on analysing how natural systems work and imitating these as much as possible. Within the garden this might seem obvious to most people; make your garden as much as possible like a natural forest, just populate it with food-bearing plants. Then all you have to do is wander round foraging every day! No problem in sub tropical Queensland, but might be a challenge here, where I live right now: Norway, in November minus ten outside, thick snow, and our next prospect of the thermometer rising above zero is some time next spring, five months away.

By adapting to widely different ecosystems Permaculture became a set of principles rather than a recipe.

Kibbutz Lotan, Israel:
Permaculture field school

Date founded — 1984
Approximate number of residents — 150
Location — Arava Desert, southern Israel
Spiritual or ideological affiliation — Reform Judaism
Visited — I worked with their Permaculture Field School
as an advisor and teacher from 1994 until 2000

David Holmgren visited Lotan in the mid-nineties and conducted a workshop which involved setting up a herb mulch garden next to the clinic. I got involved a year or two later, and by then a larger kitchen garden had been established next to the dining hall. This was not so successful, and was cramped by other buildings and parking lots, so the vegetable garden was moved a few hundred yards away, called the Eastern Garden, and became large and productive. Groups came and went in connection with a developing tourist business, and Permaculture was integrated as one of the subjects that was taught, as workshops and as features of festivals and gatherings. The garden expanded, a compost demonstration was set up, gathering places for groups were built, garbage sculptures were created, and alternative technology was incorporated. A biological toilet was built, water sculptures inspired by Flowform water cascades (see p. 171, Flowforms) were plumbed in and strawbale and mud building techniques were used all over the place.

In 2000, just before I left, we had a design course for some of the members, and talked about setting up a Permaculture Field School, offering work experience for volunteers, and courses for students. In the course of a few years, a few square metres of herb garden had grown into the largest Permaculture demonstration site in the Middle East!

ABOVE. Homemade recycling centre. Here, garbage is turned into resources by being sorted into groups, and made easily available to anyone who needs it.

BELOW LEFT. Daniel Greenberg of Living Routes after having used the homemade composting toilet. The whole structure was handmade from local or recycled materials.

BELOW RIGHT. A herb garden being prepared by mulching with kitchen waste. This is situated just outside the dining hall, close to the kitchens.

ABOVE. Raised beds constructed from local rock and clay. This gives access to handicapped people, is much easier to work by anyone, retains moisture and stops compacting. The vegetables are supplied to the community kitchens.

BELOW. Soil sample showing several centimetres of soil built up by mulching on top of sand. This is making the desert bloom!

The idea of taking ecological cycles and using them as design patterns may seem obvious when it comes to gardening and farming, a little less so when we build a house, and probably quite foreign to those designing a business, an economic system or a process for group decision making. It was when Permaculture began to address these problems that it became more relevant, more international and of interest to people involved in Ecovillage design education. Perhaps it was the simultaneity of the Ecovillage idea emerging just at the time of Permaculture reaching this stage, or perhaps it was because many of those who founded the Global Ecovillage Network were themselves Permaculture designers. Whatever the reason, we found ourselves with a powerful design tool, at the right time and in the right place. Not only a tool that gave results, that gave us designs for food production, landscape modelling and house building, but in addition one that we could use for designing alternative economic systems and village democracy. This design system did not limit itself to the mechanical and materialistic, but also gave direction to the individual in a personal and positive way.

Permaculture looks for the patterns embedded in our natural world as inspirations for designing solutions to the many challenges we are presented with today. Permaculture encourages individuals to be resourceful and self-reliant and to become a conscious part of the solution to the many problems which face us both locally and globally. Permaculture means thinking carefully about our environment, our use of resources and how we supply our needs. It aims to create systems that will sustain not only for the present, but also for future generations. The idea is one of co-operation with nature and each other, of caring for the earth and its people.

When looking at the development of Permaculture, it is important to mention three influences from which Mollison drew heavily. The first was Eugene Odum, who taught ecology at the University of Georgia in the United States in the 1950s. His books, *Fundamentals of Ecology* and *Ecology*, were groundbreaking texts laying the foundations of a new science. This is focused on the idea of seeing things in their contexts, of coming to an understanding of the world by looking at the individual pieces within their surroundings. When I went to school, Nature Studies were very much concerned with individual bits. We looked at the Rabbit, we drew and found out about the Starling, the Wolf and so on. Today, thanks to the work of Odum, children look at the rabbit in its habitat, surrounded by woodland and hedges.

The second major influence in Permaculture was Wes Jackson, who taught at the California State University at Sacramento in the 1970s. In 1976 he founded The Land Institute in Kansas and in 1980 he published *New Roots For Agriculture*. This book called into question the whole practice of plough agriculture and called for a new sustainable agriculture based on crops that act like a natural ecosystem.

The third great innovator to whom Mollison often refers is Masanobu Fukuoka, a Japanese agricultural scientist who developed the so-called 'no till agriculture.' His book, *The One Straw Revolution*, swept the West from 1975 onwards with a message that one could obtain good yields by cutting out the plough, chemicals and weeding. His work was based on research carried out over 25 years on his own farm and was rooted in an approach that combined the insights of Zen Buddhism with the rigorous agricultural science of the twentieth century.

It was no coincidence that these people were all heading in the same direction at the same time. We call it synchronicity, the phenomenon that a given idea is right for its time.

Deep ecology

The Norwegian philosopher Arne Naess conceived the idea of deep ecology, which was further developed by a number of other writers. The key to understanding deep ecology is being aware of the difference between what is called shallow and deep ecology. Shallow ecologists are everywhere, they are concerned about the world, active in conservation and protection, but they regard the world as somehow being for the benefit of mankind, that humans stand central. We protect the rain forests to maintain the atmospheric balance so that *we* can breathe easily. Deep ecologists are relatively few and far between, and regard human beings as merely one of an enormous number of created beings, all of which are woven together in the vast tapestry of life. All things are of intrinsic value themselves and protection is extended to all beings for the value of the whole.

This core concept of deep ecology has created quite a stir, especially for Christians, who see themselves as God's appointed stewards of creation, and for anthroposophists, who see the development of human self-awareness as the highest pinnacle of freedom yet achieved in the physical world. A little bit of controversy is of course healthy and good and we all welcome a good discussion. For me as a Permaculture designer, it is the process of deep ecology which has value. Whether deep ecology is 'true' or not and what kind of value we attach to 'deep' or 'shallow' is not really of interest to me.

Arne Naess was a skilled climber, as well as being the youngest appointed Professor of Philosophy in Norway. As a climber he was well aware of the effect of being exposed to stupendous nature and his starting point for deep ecology was the deep experience. This he describes as spontaneous, a realization of the wholeness of nature as a *Gestalt* and an experience of the smallness of the human individual within the vast web of nature. This experience leads to deep questioning: where ultimate norms are looked at, where one's own lifestyle is reconsidered and where concrete decisions are taken. This questioning has led to the development of the deep ecology platform and to deep commitment:

— Deep experience

— Deep questioning

— Deep commitment

— Deep ecology platform

— Beyond the platform

The deep ecology platform has subsequently been worked and reworked, and ardent followers of this path have now gone 'beyond the platform,' exciting new paths being forged here in the thinking world. The deep commitment is for me the philosophical underpinning of the Permaculture process, where change in behaviour is the result of thinking about the world and understanding how it works. This is a serious philosophical foundation for Permaculture for those who find that important. In practical terms it slows down those impatient technical people who rush in and want to 'get on with it.'

Reading nature's book

Which brings us back to where we stand in the development of human consciousness. Having now managed to reduce the whole world to small and understandable units, we should be able to read it and make sense of it. When I was living in Israel and first teaching Permaculture, I was inspired one morning to write about this:

It is dawn in the land of Israel. First a gentle lightening of the velvet dark, then a slow spread of colour rising into the eastern sky. Deep vibrant colours, which gradually fade as the light increases. It is already clear daylight as the sun slides over the rim of the horizon. A flash and there it is, hard, shiny, sparkling. Another hot summer day is on the way, but at this moment the heat is anticipated, the actual temperature is very refreshing.

From our campsite we look over gentle rolling hills, some clothed in pine, others bare and wild, and in between there are fields and orchards, vineyards and olive groves.

Feeling at home is a complex set of emotions, but still a recognizable feeling and common to most of us some time in our lives. 'Feeling at home' is composed of familiarity, memories, upbringing, deliberate decisions, religious or political convictions, and elements of knowledge and understanding.

This feeling of being at home is not static. It is a process, which builds up slowly like the dawn and is reinforced by each new experience of itself. It is a relationship between the individual person and his or her surroundings. It is a natural way of being. If we are deprived or somehow lack this feeling of being at home, we are no longer a complete human being and our consequent behaviour can become irrational or destructive.

In our fast-paced modern world problems seem to loom up threateningly on the horizon, and the next moment they are upon us, intractable and often tragic. We seem to be determined to pollute our world, create disasters with terrible human consequences, make incessant wars which kill large numbers of innocent people. There is obviously something wrong with us, but how can we cure it?

I would not suggest that feeling at home is a sure panacea and that if we all felt at home for a few minutes each day the world's problems would all be solved and we would find ourselves back in the Garden of Eden again. And yet ...

Now I am in the full dawn of a summer day, surrounded by carob and fig trees, olives growing slowly among their silver and green leaves, clusters of grape forming on the vine. For a few minutes I am part of the solution, not part of the problem. Quietly, unobtrusively I sense connections to all of these things around me: the stones, the soil, the plants and the trees, and the ancient city mound about a mile away.

As I look around me I see all the elements that fill this landscape, and I begin to ask why and how. Why is that orchard in that particular place? How did that road come to turn up that valley instead of the next? The landscape is like a book and I try to read it. I recognize the plants, their parts, the leaves and the branches, trunks and root systems, fruits and flowers. I can also see groups of plants, communities of plants interacting with each other and the animals which graze here. I see how the landforms influence drainage and water behaviour. Just like in this book, the total message is composed of letters, spaces, words, sentences, paragraphs and chapters, so nature is composed of leaves and fruits, stems and roots, geology and landscape, irregular tracts of complex ecologies involving many species of plants, animals, insects and human management. Just as in a book, complex ideas based on written material can be built up from relatively simple elements, so nature can build up a staggeringly complex ecological web from the simple elements of mineral, vegetable and animal.

Unlike this book, the information presented to us by the book of nature is displayed all at once, not linearly. We, the readers, have to make our own way into this book, moving from object to object and from idea to idea. Patterns emerge and, just like in a book we learn to recognize words and whole expressions, so we see patterns in nature.

These patterns are reflected in each other, and in our own lives and thoughts. Getting to know these patterns is part of this feeling of being at home, of feeling the familiarity and security of our surroundings. It is based partly on observation of what is around us and partly on learning about these things from reading, thinking and talking to other people. Seeing how these patterns are reflected in our own behaviour, we see how clearly we are related to our surroundings and how grounded we really are in our own world.

Reading nature's book is what Permaculture is all about.

Some patterns from nature

When we observe natural systems around us, we see reflected in them other patterns, reminders of other truths; and the ability to see this is one of the faculties we need to train as Permaculture designers. Our creativity is dependent upon developing this faculty of perceiving patterns and using them in diverse situations.

In the unfolding of evolution we can trace certain patterns emerging. Even if we may not subscribe to the idea of life resulting from the division of cells in some primeval soup, we can discern sequences, some beginning with the simple and leading to the more complex. Somewhere along this line sex appeared on the scene. In the Ecology Park where I worked in Israel we were lucky enough to have this demonstrated for us by a pair of carob trees standing discreetly a few metres apart, but obviously reaching out towards each other.

The male carob tree is an insignificant looking fellow, with small leaves and of correspondingly small stature, but then not a lot is demanded of him. At the right time of year he has to produce a certain amount of pollen, spray it over his partner and then relax; his job done. This pollen is so fine that only those of us with allergies usually notice it. The female, on the other hand, is a stately tree when fully grown, often four or five metres high, with a thick crown of dark shiny leaves. It is often possible to walk about under the tree and to pick the thickly clustered seed pods during the winter and spring.

She has to work hard, this female tree: growing tall enough so that grazing sheep and goats are deterred from eating the whole tree, and giving a large crop of highly nutritious pods. These are not only useful to grazing animals, but are tasty for us also — for those of us who like carob chocolate or carob honey!

This is a different view of the role of the sexes than the one that prevails in western society, where the man is traditionally thought of as the breadwinner. He is the taller, stronger partner and this has given rise to a whole social pattern, which often discriminates against women and has even created an ownership pattern where men own most of the earth and, in some societies, even own women themselves. Even among birds and animals, it is often the male who has the most striking displays. In our Judeo–Christian–Islamic tradition, we have the story of the creation of Adam and Eve; Eve was created from one of Adam's ribs to be his mate.

By contemplating the patterns we discern in a tree, we can be led along many paths of thinking.

We can also look at the tree from the technical point of view, as a unit that collects and stores solar energy.

The trunk brings the tree up off the ground and into the light. It sends out branches which in turn send out twigs and here the leaves grow, either seasonally in a deciduous tree or all year round. It is these leaves which capture the sun's energy, using it to give life to the tree and making it capable of utilizing the food stores in the soil. This energy also builds up biomass in the form of wood, thickening the trunk and branches year by year, adding new leaves and new twigs as required. These small green solar panels, these leaves, are much more efficient than anything we have come up with in our laboratories and workshops. As they get older and less capable of absorbing solar energy, they wither and fall, providing a leaf mulch around the tree which in its turn will decompose and add nutrients to the soil.

The cycle is completed, from soil to leaf and back to soil again, all powered by energy from the sun. But we must not forget the wood, the timber that is so painstakingly built up year after year. We can chart its progress in the tree rings and appreciate it in the grain of the wood. This we can use for construction or for decoration. When burnt, this wood will release the stored energy and give it back in the form of heat and light. A lesser version of the sun itself. When we light a fire, we are enjoying again the sunlight that fell upon some forest maybe a generation or two ago. The firewood is like a torch battery, waiting for us to turn it on.

In addition to this purely mechanical view, the tree is a spiritual being, an object which has been worshipped and venerated in various ways from the very beginning of our religious experience. It forms a pattern which unites earth and heaven. The roots reach down into the dark moist soil, drawing up its nutrients. The crown reaches up to heaven, catching cosmic influences in its leaves. I often think I would like to use the tree as my role model, my feet firmly anchored on the earth, my head reaching up to heaven. The tree is a bridge between the physical and the spiritual.

A tree is all these things. As we meditate quietly, holding it in our consciousness, applying our knowledge of it, we come to discern different patterns and we can relate these patterns to other areas of our lives. This I call the essence of Permaculture.

Reading meaning in the things around us

The aim of science is to explain how our world functions, to help us understand the universe we are born into. The last few hundred years of reductionist research has certainly broken things down to their component parts, but does not always do that well when explaining how it works. Permaculture and other holistic methods try to set things in their context and look at processes. In this, they owe a debt of gratitude to the work of Johann Wolfgang von Goethe, 1749–1832, who tried to establish a more holistic scientific worldview, but who was eclipsed by the dominant form of reductionism so prevalent in his time. His work was taken up, after lying fallow for nearly a century, by Rudolf Steiner and forms the basis for much of the spiritual science of anthroposophy.

In the methodology of Goethe, we can find two approaches which are relevant to us. One is to place things in their context, to look at the relationship between the object and its surroundings: 'things in the world.' This is very different from mainstream science, which attempts to isolate things in sterile laboratories in order to study them.

The other approach is to look for patterns, to study 'things' in different ways in order to look at how they develop and to try to discern an underlying form in what seems like chaos. This Goethe demonstrated best in his metamorphosis of leaf shapes which still forms the introduction to many who study anthroposophy today. Whether Mollison studied Goethe or anthroposophy I can't say; I certainly have no evidence for it, but it is clear that there is an affinity in the approach.

Permaculture is based on an approach that has clear and solid foundations in the philosophical sense. Permaculture is also about practice, it is a design tool that demands implementation to be complete. Most of this book is devoted to just that.

Permaculture is right for our time. It is one way to help solve the problems of our runaway society.

2

Design

3. Modelling the Ecovillage: the Social Aspect

The three-legged stool

At the Ecovillage Conference held at Findhorn in 1995, where the Global Ecovillage Network was founded, the idea of the three-legged stool was used by various people to illustrate how a healthy Ecovillage needed to be supported by three basic elements.

— One leg represents the *personal:* How do I relate to myself? What is my experience of the world? What spiritual or ideological stand do I take? How do I combine my experiences and my ideas with my upbringing and my traditions?

— The second leg represents the *social:* How do I relate to my fellow human beings, my family, my friends? What kind of relationship do I want to develop with them? What kind of social structures do we want to live in? How can we develop together the kind of relationships which might allow me to grow as a human being?

— The third leg represents the *ecological:* What is our relationship to the geology, the flora and fauna of our particular site? What kind of impact do we make upon the natural world? How do we supply our needs? How do we design our physical structures? What kind of materials do we use? What kinds of energy do we use?

These three 'legs', the *personal*, the *social* and the *ecological* also represent a path of development, from the individual outwards, to our fellows and ultimately to the world surrounding us.

Threefolding

The social aspects of anthroposophy are most developed within the Camphill Villages, where the threefold division of society is regarded as a basic tool for modelling the life and structure of the community. This threefolding was presented by Rudolf Steiner in lectures during the last part of the First World War and the years that followed. He traced how the three great ideals of the French Revolution, fraternity, equality and liberty, had been corrupted by the rise of nationalism and the development of the centralized nation state. Threefolding was presented by Steiner as a way of rebuilding Europe after the disaster of the First World War, but his ideas did not gain credence and were largely dormant until taken up by Karl König in building up the Camphill communities in the 1940s and 50s. König based his thoughts on his study of the development of European society over the preceding centuries. In England, he saw the industrial revolution as the modernization of economic life, leading to demands for fraternity, the development of trade unionism and labour party politics. In France under the French Revolution he saw a change in the legal life leading to demands for equality and in Middle Europe (later unified to become Germany) changes in the spiritual life leading to demands for liberty. König further traced how a failure to integrate these three ideas led to the insanity of Nazism, fascism and state communism after Steiner's death.

The basic idea of threefolding is very similar to what was presented at Findhorn as the three-legged stool:

We worship and philosophize, educate, create music and art in the **spiritual sphere**. Here we need our freedom to develop ourselves.

We decide amongst ourselves, regulate our lives together, in the **sphere of laws** and rights, and here we need to regard ourselves as equals, with equal rights.

We work, produce, buy and sell in the **economic sphere** and need the fellowship (brotherhood and sisterhood) of looking after each other; not necessarily as equals, for clearly, some have more capacity and some have greater needs.

These three spheres are always with us, they are not determinants of how we should or might behave, but an attempt to make sense of our every day lives and how we come together as human beings. One of the insights of this social anthroposophy is that we are at heart social creatures.

König was very inspired by three figures from history and has often referred to them as the 'three pillars of Camphill.' These three personalities illustrate in a human way the three spheres of society and often form the objects of study in Camphill villages in order to deepen our understanding of our social life.

Johann Comenius (1592–1670) was convinced that peace and understanding between people would be the result of a greater wisdom that individuals could strive for and that this needs to be based on a regard for the spiritual nature of others.

Ludwig Zinzendorf (1700–1760) was instrumental in forming the Moravian Brotherhood and was convinced that the social life found in community was vital to those who search for Christianity and a deeper spiritual life. The Moravian Brotherhood subsequently developed into the Hutterian communities, of which there are hundreds in the USA and Canada, and these in turn inspired the Bruderhof communities, a small network of ten communities in the USA, England, Germany and Australia.

Robert Owen (1771–1858) is perhaps better known to those who have studied the growth of labour ideologies and social reform over the last two hundred years. He founded a series of communities and economic enterprises which have had a great deal of importance in inspiring trade unionism, co-operation and other social innovations in the sphere of work and economics.

Finding patterns in the natural world and using these to illustrate, explain and design our own needs is a process well known to those of us who use Permaculture as a design technique. Applying the same exercise to the structure and development of the human being can lead to greater insights into the social sphere. Karl König developed this in depth in some of his lectures towards the end of his life and this has formed the basis for a great deal of study work within the Camphill world. It is quite usual for the villages to have extended study sessions and work through texts in order to arrive at a greater understanding. This has the effect of raising consciousness on social issues and ensuring that, as the social dynamics create a continuous series of changes, these take place within a studied framework. For those who want to immerse themselves deeper into these speculations, König in *Man As A Social Being* gives a good starting point with the alchemical processes of salt, mercury and sulphur.

Thinking machines

The term 'thinking machine' may seem a bit out of order today, trying as we are to get out of 'machine thinking' and into 'organic thinking.' Still, Permaculture can be thought of as a kind of tool and I will shamelessly add other tools to our toolbox, picked up from all kinds of places where I have come across them.

Patrick Geddes was a Scottish city planner who died in 1932 at the age of 77. His classic *Cities in Evolution* is still an inspiration for many and continues to be

Findhorn, Scotland:
the alternative university

Date founded — 1962
Approximate number of residents — *ca.* 250
Location — northern Scotland
Spiritual or ideological affiliation — New Age
Visited — Ecovillage Conferences in 1995 and 1998

Findhorn is one of the largest and most established of the New Age communes founded in the 1960s. It has already generated a mythological past inspired by spiritual revelation, its first great breakthrough was the growing of giant vegetables on pure sand. The Findhorn insistence on high quality in whatever they did has resulted in establishing a solid reputation in many fields. They are the only community I know of that has a direct relationship with the United Nations through their Ecovillage training programmes.

The impression I have from two visits and lots of reading is that Findhorn can be compared to a university. There seems to be a relatively small group of permanent residents, most of whom are experts in their individual fields. Large numbers of people pass through Findhorn, staying one, five or ten years, going on to found other communities or start projects in other parts of the world. These ventures keep in touch with each other and with Findhorn as the 'Circle of Light,' today being a global network which stays in contact via newsletters, a magazine, email and personal visits.

Organizationally the place has gone through many changes, and may be compared to an onion, with a small core group and many layers of commitment. It's hard to define where Findhorn ends. When I lived in Israel I had good contact with an ex-Findhorn resident who was initiating Permaculture projects both on the West Bank and in Gaza. Here in Norway Hurdal Ecovillage was initially inspired by Findhorn, and maintains regular contact with the place.

Technologically Findhorn has used many of the techniques described in this book. Handmade houses from natural materials, super insulation, energy from wind and sun, Living Machines clean their wastewater, barter systems, biodynamic and organic cultivation, earthships and strawbale houses can all be seen in use and form the basis of many courses and teaching projects.

ABOVE. Meditation house built by hand out of locally found materials.

ABOVE. *Community Centre with a round meeting room in the upper storey and an expanded communal dining room beneath.*

LEFT. *The original caravan and garden where it all began in the early 1960s.*

BELOW. *The original and first whisky barrel house.*

ABOVE. Inside the Living Machine, Nancy Jack Todd explaining how the wastewater is cleaned biologically.

ABOVE. The Living Machine being unveiled, the first of its kind in Europe.

LEFT. The Bag End neighbourhood; environmental housing with high insulation and solar heating of various kinds.

a rich mine of ideas, interpretations and practical suggestions. In the *Sociological Review* in 1930 he published *Ways of Transition, Towards Constructive Peace* and in it used what he called thinking machines. These are methods to arrange ideas in such ways that we see problems or situations from a new angle, so helping us to arrive at solutions. The thinking machine which I have been using was used by Graham Bell in his Permaculture design courses and illustrates that any three factors in social life have six sub relations. The thinking machine is a box of nine squares with the three original ideas arranged diagonally:

Personal		
	Social	
		Ecological

By cross-referencing the three original statements we get the following:

Personal	Personal Society	Personal Ecology
Social Person	Social	Social Ecology
Ecological Person	Ecological Society	Ecological

This gives us a list of topics which might be explored collectively, giving us a broad outline of the kind of community we are trying to establish. We have here an open-ended process, with no specific aim other than to raise questions that arise out of connections which we might otherwise not make. Comparing for instance Personal Ecology with an Ecological Person may help us understand how ecology and individuals relate to each other.

The usefulness of this thinking machine lies in its ability to make connections. It is ideal as an agenda for a group discussion, not held in a critical way, but deliberately allowing ideas to arise and be looked at. Any three topics can be selected and they can be written in any order. Don't be afraid, be innovative and select wildly different ideas. The aim behind this is to open up connections and bring up ideas that would otherwise remain hidden from our consciousness.

This kind of group discussion might lead to a blueprint, a manifesto or a mission statement upon which the group can base their development, attract new members and can be used as a foundation for design. In my experience of working with groups this is a powerful tool and a useful process towards shaping a group-identity.

The spiral of improvement

The International Standards Organization (ISO) has been developing Environmental Management Systems (EMS) for many years, culminating in the ISO 14,000 series. This is based upon previous international management experience with the ISO 9,000 and other systems. Couched in a highly professional language, it was written for mainstream managers within corporations and factories, many of whom are already using the ISO 9,000 management system.

The attraction of an internationally accepted standard is often clear to a factory producing for a defined export market. This is not always the case for a community, where there is little immediate commercial advantage. As I add new social processes to our planning toolbox, I keep stealing ideas from other places and however suspicious we might be of mainstream mechanistic management systems, there are gems to be picked up even there!

The ISO EMS sets out a structure for a management system and it is up to each company to create the details. It can be seen as a spiral of continuous improvement, each turn comprised of a number of clear steps:

1. **Environmental Policy** is the key to the whole process; this has to be comprehensive and state clearly what is hoped to be achieved. This requires a Mission Statement of ideals with clear goals.

2. **Planning** defines how the company or community can control the results of its operations, products and services, with readily measurable targets and objectives and a specific timeframe. Essentially we are taking the Environmental Policy and putting it into action. The Plan has to state clearly how this is to be done. This part should map out how the next three steps will be carried out.

3. **Implementation and Operation** involves assigning a manager as an official EMS coordinator who will ensure implementation, with regular reviews and reports to the overall management. Written procedures are required. A procedure also has to be developed to cover emergencies, including a review after the event.

4. **Checking and Corrective Action** follows on from the above to set up a system where key environmental characteristics are measured and recorded, a regular scheduled activity assigned to specific people. A Corrective Action Procedure identifies when to react, who responds and what actions need to be taken.

5. **Management Review** consists of the results of internal audits, reports on new requirements and regulations and a discussion on the strategic plan for the company. The management can then decide whether to modify or change the existing Environmental Policy to better meet changing needs and targets. At this stage the first turn of the spiral is completed and the whole process can be repeated with a new and improved Environmental Policy. Now that the managerial infrastructure is already in place, the repetition of the Planning, Implementation and Checking procedures should be much easier. This is why I like to use the image of the spiral, in that essentially the same process is repeated each time; because there should be improvements, the starting point is always at a higher level.

Even though this EMS was developed by people who had probably never heard of either Ecovillages or Permaculture, and was aimed specifically at mainstream business, it has many elements which make it highly relevant to the development and management of an Ecovillage.

First of all it is based on the pattern of the spiral, a powerful natural template that we find in the microstructure of DNA, in the shapes of shells and in cosmic galaxies. As Permaculture designers we have a natural affinity for patterns familiar to us from the natural world, especially such an archetypal pattern as the spiral.

It also follows a familiar pattern in beginning with an assessment of our ethics and ideology, continuing by setting out a plan for action and subsequently carrying it out. This follows the Permaculture principle of design as a result of protracted and thoughtful observation rather than immediate and thoughtless action.

Finally the built-in process of monitoring and reviewing the initial ideology in the light of experience carries within it an approach that suggests flexibility and a willingness to learn.

There are two factors which can help to make this more effective:

— It should become a habit for all groups to agree upon the next meeting at the end of the previous one. In this way there is an inbuilt continuity. There is nothing so sapping of energy as one person running around trying to coordinate a number of disparate people into an agreed meeting which as yet has no date or time.

— The other factor is the writing of minutes or conclusions, and getting these printed, copied and out to the relevant people. We often forget what we talk about and think we have agreed upon something when in fact we haven't. Writing things down helps us along.

Democracy or dictatorship?

In a recent discussion here in the Camphill Village where I live a topic came up amongst the short-term volunteers that had been discussed for some time among the long-term members. We long-termers had not arrived at any clear decision. There had been some polarization and disagreement amongst us. A few of us felt strongly negative about the suggestion. We had decided to shelve the question, to spend some months dealing with other issues and either take it up again or let it die. At this meeting with the volunteers, one of them bravely suggested: 'Why not just take a vote, the majority decides and that will be the end of all this talking?' Democracy seems so simple, let's just get on with it and decide something.

When I lived on Kibbutz, many things were decided by voting in the General Assembly and a majority of one was often enough to carry the day. This led to a great deal of political manoeuvering and often resulted in disgruntled losers.

Before democracy human societies had various forms of tyranny, hierarchical models where individuals or small elite groups ruled over the majority. In the development of western society, the struggle for democracy was indeed a brave and heroic one; growing up in the middle years of the twentieth century, I was inspired by this recent struggle. Having experienced democracy over the last few decades in various forms, I can see that it is vastly preferable to the old-style tyranny, but I also realize that there lies something beyond. Winston

Zegg, Germany:
the Social Forum, a tool for
community building

Date founded — 1991
Approximate number of residents — *ca*. 80
Location — northern Germany, not far from Berlin
Spiritual or ideological affiliation — social creative
Visited — Communal Studies Conference, about 4
days in the summer of 2001

Creating peace implies that we begin with a conflict. The founding group at Zegg bought an old Stasi training camp in East Germany after the collapse of the Berlin Wall. The site has a harsh history which is being turned around in the search for new relationships between people. The energy built up by Zegg has already led to the setting up of an affiliated community at Tamera in Portugal, where Permaculture and youth projects form the basis for conflict resolution work with people from conflicts in the Middle East.

Zegg has been busy retrofitting old buildings, a challenging task given the lack of ecological awareness in the East German building tradition. They have also set up a Permaculture project which provides vegetables, fruit, cleans their wastewater and gives them a basis for courses.

Perhaps their most radical innovation is the Social Forum. This is a tool for creating sociability and preventing and solving conflicts. This is not a technique readily taught in books, but requires a facilitator and an experienced group. One person volunteers to be the focus, and the facilitator guides the group and that person through interactions in order to reveal conflicts, bring them into the open, and give guidelines to their solutions. Given that Zegg does not practise monogamous relationships, but rather encourages openness amongst its members, this tool has been remarkably successful in resolving jealousy and other complications arising from members pursuing a number of sexual relationships.

ABOVE. Earth cob building: detail.

ABOVE. Air-inflated meeting dome; not much privacy, but plenty of space!

BELOW LEFT. Rehabilitated ruin, creating a semi outdoor café space.

BELOW RIGHT. When the weather is good, the communal dining room spills out onto the terrace.

ABOVE. In a large marquee specially erected, Zegg hosted the International Communal Studies Association conference in 2001. About 150 delegates from all over the world attended.

BELOW. Achim Ecker, Permaculture teacher, explains the wastewater treatment system.

Churchill is supposed to have said once that democracy is a bad way to lead society, but the alternatives are even worse. Now I'm no big fan of old Winnie, but on this one I used to be in agreement with him. However, my experience with other forms of decision-making in small groups has led me to realize that there is a world of decision-making beyond democracy, one which we might sum up under the name of consensus. So there are alternatives to democracy and some of them might actually be better.

We might see this in the context of a scale, where tyranny is at one end, the least desirable, and we move through democracy towards consensus. The danger of consensus is that one person can effectively veto a process, but if we remember that a part of consensus is to get to know and trust each other, this tendency may be overcome. In any case, the process of decision-making in a situation which demands getting to know and trust each other, is itself valuable for us as human beings.

The process of working together at a common task is not easy. How does the group function? How do we tackle conflict and problems? How do we generate enthusiasm and nurture creativity? All of us who are familiar with group processes know well how fickle groups can be, how the mood changes, seemingly without reason.

If we take as our starting point that individuals have a spiritual side to them and that spirituality is something that is embedded in our world, it is only a small step to understanding that groups have their own collective spirit, their own development and that moods and changes often occur in the spiritual sphere. Karl König states this quite bluntly:

> A state, a people, a community, a village or a town is not merely the sum total of all the people living there but ... is a higher organism. It does not consist of flesh and blood, however, but is created and formed by soul and spiritual powers. (Fohrenbühl, March 29, 1964)

We are not dealing with mechanical processes, or merely using clever tricks developed by modern group psychology. Obviously these have their uses, but overall we need to appreciate the wholeness of the group, its group soul. The question is: how can we nurture this? How to keep it alive and fresh, and see that it develops through the various stages of youth, maturity and perhaps even old age. How do we help a group soul to rejuvenate when it gets too old and tired of life? It's hard to give direct answers to these questions, they require an inner work that can't be led by precise and specific guidelines.

The co-ordinating leader

In my experience, most groups of people tend to have some kind of leader, but this word has become very loaded, with lots of connotations. I like the word focalizer or co-ordinator, words that describe which function this so-called leader takes upon him or herself. In a healthy group dynamic, it's often the person who can express what the group agrees to and who can be trusted by the group. Of course this role can be taken by a number of people, but often it falls more on certain individuals than others. Let's keep the word leader, for what it's worth and compare the old style leadership to a more healthy group coordination.

The traditional hierarchical leadership model:
1. Authoritarian leadership
2. Patriarchal domination
3. Social class divisions
4. Ethic: duty and responsibility
5. Work for gain
6. Organizationally fragmented
7. Internally divisive
8. Lack of identification with the group
9. Lacking vision

Authority can be based on coordination and care. The leader's task is to create participants, not necessarily to create agreement. It is the fruitful disagreement between co-workers which creates life, change, development and creativity. There is nothing so fruitful as to be disagreed with, so instead of protecting truth, the leader should inspire to new thinking. The leader should represent a human fellowship underway and by nurturing positive human relationships make an organization into a living organism.

The co-ordinating leader:
1. Authority based on coordination and care
2. Equality between the sexes, based on variety
3. Equality between all
4 Ethic: cooperative development of social quality
5. Work: self-realization within social value creation

Clil Ecovillage, Israel:
a community of smallholdings

Date founded — *ca.* 1973
Approximate number of residents — 170
Location — Galilee
Spiritual or ideological affiliation — loosely ecological,
spiritual, peaceful
Visited — several short visits in the 1990s

Clil is not a village in the traditional sense of the word. There does not seem to be any kind of centre: just a broad valley with scrub-covered slopes on each side and spread-out homesteads scattered in a seemingly haphazard way. This is clearly not a community where people come to live together and explore issues of togetherness. Inspired by Gandhian pacifism, organic food production, independence, spirituality and self-sufficiency, the residents have shaped a way of life that allows them to be collective and individualistic at the same time.

At Clil it's the details that reveal the deep commitment to ecological design. The houses are hand-built from local, natural materials. Vines provide shade in summer, grapes in autumn and the sun can shine through the bare branches in winter. There are solar panels for electricity and stacks of firewood for heating and compost heaps to nourish the vegetable gardens. Here are people really living off the land in a gentle and respectful way.

OPPOSITE TOP. One of the homesteads of Clil.

OPPOSITE BELOW. Solar panels powering one of the houses at Clil.

ABOVE. Homestead among the shrubby hills of the Western Galilee.

RIGHT. Vine-covered porch in Clil. Shade during the summer, giving sun access during the cooler winters.

OPPOSITE TOP. The valley of Clil, homesteads spread out with lots of space in between each one.

OPPOSITE BELOW. A hand-built house of local stone.

6. Dynamic systems thinking
7. Integration of the different functions
8. Personal identity in the group
9. Visionary

Leadership functions can be taken on by a small group within the community. This has the advantage of spreading the load; a certain amount of rotation can lead to many people in the group gaining experience of leadership.

Quality circles

This is a method which has arisen in mainstream industry to make it more humane and efficient. Much as we might be critical of high-tech industry and management, we don't need to reinvent the wheel, when others have something useful to offer us. Quality circles are problem solving groups where participants prioritize and solve their own experienced problems in their own workplace. The typical quality circle has the following characteristics:

1. A group from the same workplace
2. An agreed-upon leader from the workplace
3. Voluntary participation, during work time
4. Regular meetings, weekly or fortnightly
5. Self-prioritizing
6. Identification, analysis and solving of problems
7. Oral or written presentation of solutions

This is a fairly simple recipe and does not need a lot of elaboration. Put it into your social toolbox and get it out when you think it fits. You might consider problems as challenges, opportunities for the group to grow and develop. Rather than be overwhelmed by problems, perhaps it might be useful to welcome them as the next step in group growth. After all, in Permaculture we talk about growth happening at the interface between biotopes, where different systems meet and interact. Could this also be true of groups that we grow and develop through meeting new ideas?

Within the space of the group life, there is no reason why people with different views cannot work together. Indeed, in the future, it is vital that we achieve the tolerance and open-mindedness to meet different people in that space, and not just be a comfortable club where those of the same conviction meet to wallow in their sameness.

One of the dangers of taking social tools from mainstream society is that they are generally very mechanistic; we need to balance that by introducing a spiritual element. Here is an example of how a potential conflict was solved some years ago.

As a gesture and step towards peace in the Middle East a Jewish–Arab, Israeli–Palestinian, Christian–Moslem community was founded in the 1970s on the border between pre-1967 Israel and the West bank. The founder was a Roman Catholic priest whose vision was a community where people of the three religions would create a common space to help reconciliation and peace. After a few years the community was growing and thriving, but it was not as spiritual as his original vision. So one day he came to the General Assembly with the idea of building a chapel. But, he explained, 'it must be triangular, so that each religion can have its own corner to pray in!' There was a silence, broken finally by a question: 'And where do the atheists go to pray?'

The chapel was finally built, but built round, with nothing in it and called the Place of Silence. The spiritual dimension is not a monopoly of the conventionally religious, but a meeting place of people who work out of strong inner convictions.

Ecovillage auditing

Ecovillage auditing provides a measuring rod for existing villages and communities to compare their current status with ideal goals for environmental, cultural and social sustainability. It was developed early on in the Global Ecovillage Network as a way of measuring Ecovillage performance. The Ecovillage audit is based on the four elements of air, earth, water and fire. To these four elements has been added a fifth dimension called quintessentia:

— *Air* covers cultural events, rituals, customs, openness, service to others, communal space, in short, the cultural side of the community.
— *Earth* encompasses the physical environment, food, buildings, restoration of nature, solid waste management, place and size.
— *Water* includes the physical infrastructure of water sources, wastewater, energy, transport and the information infrastructure.
— *Fire* covers the social and economic environment, including health, democracy, decision-making processes, the mixture of dwellings and workplaces, services, and the relationship with society outside the Ecovillage.
— *Quintessentia* is largely a product of balance in the previous four, adding in vision and commitment.

The audit is couched as a questionnaire which is meant to be repeated periodically in order to chart progress. These questions go into a great deal of detail, such as demographic profile by age, gender, ethnic origin, percent of recyclable building materials from the local bioregion, diversity of species increasing yearly, both flora and fauna, total electricity use for domestic heating and cooling, sources of electricity and lots more. This requires a good deal of painstaking research, at least in its first application. In a similar way to the spiral of improvement (see p. 67), once the first exercise has been completed, it will be much easier to do it again a second time.

The Global Ecovillage Network developed two versions of this audit, a short one and a long one. The short one is to be found at the end of the *Directory of Ecovillages in Europe* (see Book List, p. 260). The longer version can be accessed through the GEN website, it is several pages long and can be quite daunting as a project.

The audit is a tool to assess the health of a community, much like a full medical examination will assess the health of a patient.

Footprint analysis

In 1996, Mathis Wackernagel and William Rees published a book called *Our Ecological Footprint*. Working at the University of British Columbia, they had developed a method of analysing our ecological impact by translating every resource use into how many acres it required. This was then divided by the number of people benefiting from that resource use, so they could arrive at a figure of how many acres it would take to support a person in his or her particular lifestyle. The analysis for Vancouver showed some interesting results: a city of 1.8 million people covering about 1 million acres, they found that when you add the land that their food is grown upon, the materials and energy needed to build and support the city, as well as the land used for garbage and affected by pollution, the total amount used by the city of Vancouver, its ecological footprint, was about 19 million acres. This translates into about 10 acres per average Vancouverian. In the United States, the average rises to 12.2 which results in a further interesting figure: should everyone in the world consume resources as voraciously as does the average American, we will need three times the available useful land on the planet. Or to put it another way, we will need three planets!

The footprint analysis requires a good deal of careful research and calculation, but most of the figures would be available by doing the Ecovillage audit mentioned previously. As yet I do not know of any Ecovillage which has used this to assess its footprint, but it would make an impressive statement about our environmental impact and of course it has tremendous educational potential.

Whether footprinting had something to do with this or not, the University of Vancouver developed a computer game for city planning which leads one to similarly fascinating and insightful results. Published as a game on the web (*www.basinfutures.net*) by the university's Sustainable Development Research Institute in 2001, it listed variables such as transportation, energy consumption, waste disposal, residential, commercial, industrial zoning and more. As these are adjusted, it reads back what life would be like in 2040. Clearly city planning is much more complex than Ecovillage planning, but a session or two might give a planning group some interesting experiences.

Social ecology

We began this Part by looking at threefolding and I want to finish by going back to it, looking at a real-life application of this theory. There is an ever present danger that we lose sight of the spiritual dimension in all these clever group processes.

Threefolding is not just a neat theory, but has real applications to everyday social life. In Scandinavia this theory has been used in a practical way to help Steiner schools, other institutions and businesses to develop management structures and solve conflicts. This consists of a specific process of group building, a process which needs to be carried out in a particular order. We have seen similar processes in the spiral of improvement and in quality circles, and this is something that is also fundamental to Permaculture design: useful action as the result of considered observation, thinking and planning. Here, social ecology in action has defined a three-stage process: starting with the vision, going on to planning and ending up with action as a final result. Whether you like it or not, in some cases the linear approach is unavoidable!

1. **Aims and visions**. We need to define our vision and to come to a general agreement. Here the spiritual process is really important. During this phase widely different points of view can emerge and these need to be presented positively and objectively in order to preserve the creative qualities. We need not go into lengthy discussions; here it is important to listen, to create a dialogue, to create the room we need to listen to each others' point of view. It is always good to have a written presentation, where we will end up with a mosaic of differing points of view. These aims and visions need to be taken up again and again in order to keep them fresh and dynamic.

Old Bassaisa, Egypt:
local future study centre

Date founded — initially perhaps 5,000–10,000 years ago!
Approximate number of residents — maybe a few hundred
Location — Nile delta
Spiritual or ideological affiliation — Muslim, agricultural
Visited — a whole day in the summer of 1996

My first glimpse of Bassaisa was across one of the sluggish Nile canals, an irregular clump of flat-roofed houses surrounded by flat fields that have been continuously cultivated for thousands of years. It was the second day of my first visit to Egypt, the first day having been spent in police stations and embassies after having my passport stolen. However, I realized straight away that it was not the usual thing for a virtually unmarked peasant village to have at its village square a Future Studies Centre with solar panels on the roof and a range of computers hooked up to the internet inside.

They went much further than just thinking and introducing modern electronics. We saw a methane gas producing unit, which used the manure from the cows. After the gas was extracted, the slurry was used as manure, and the gas saved on precious firewood for fuel. They were also consciously building upon their traditions of co-operation by working their fields together, and utilizing every part of their land. We noticed that paths were very narrow, and had no verges.

Inspired and mentored by Professor Salah Arafat at the American University in Cairo, villagers at Bassaisa had spent over a decade looking at how they lived and how they could improve their lives. They soon realized that the high birth rate, combined with the non-availability of agricultural land, would compel them to expand elsewhere or expect a gradual lowering of their standard of living. They formed a co-operative, pooled the little money they had and bought land on the western edge of the Sinai Desert. This they called New Bassaisa which we visited next day.

ABOVE. The village seen from across one of the irrigation canals of the Nile.

BELOW. View across the flat-roofs thickly covered with straw and chaff to insulate against the summer sun.

ABOVE and RIGHT. Computer link inside the Future Studies Centre.

BELOW. Team of Bassaisa residents planting rice into irrigated fields.

الملتقى الفكري
حول
حاضر ومستقبل الجمعيات الأهلية
في مصر

ABOVE. Small group meeting in the Future Studies Centre.

BELOW. Irrigation water from the Nile spreading into one of the rice fields.

To get through this group building process, to create a shared vision, is a demanding exercise and we can define some of the qualities we need as human beings for this to be successful. Here there is no definite order of procedure, neither is one more important than another. In fact, I would maintain that all are equally crucial, like the four wheels of a car. If one is missing, whichever one, the car cannot move:

— The quality of *balance*, harmonizing, tying together. This is characterized by Sun qualities.
— The quality of *listening* to both people and to time. Social listening, what lies behind the question? Dialogue, those who want to carry out action also need to be able to listen. Venus qualities.
— The quality of *flexibility*, the possibility of improvising. Are we flexible enough to carry out our vision even when things change? Mercurial qualities.
— The quality of *organization*, delegating tasks, clear mandates. Is our organizational capability good enough for our overall aim? Moon qualities.

2. **Short-term aims**. We need to plan the tactics which can realize the aims and visions we shared to begin with. This is a planning phase where we take hold of the future. We create the rules of play, which need to be considered carefully. All the facts that are relevant need to be gathered, especially economic ones. We need to create a map for us to follow as we progress. This requires a process imbued with warmth.

We can start this with a series of questions:

— Who will decide? Why precisely that group or that individual?
— How long do we have to decide? Is there a deadline?
— Who will be affected by this decision? Should they be able to give their opinions? Do we need a longer investigation?
— Who leads the process? It can certainly be different groups or individuals during different parts of the process, but it is useful to map this out now.
— Are there hidden agendas?

3. **Energy and action**. We need to carry out the actions which we've planned. The will is important in this phase, and clear and honest talk between co-workers is essential. Much of the rest of this book is about carrying out change in the physical world, the result of thinking and planning.

Conflict resolution

Another aspect of social ecology looks at conflicts and the forces of destruction. Our times are characterized by two polarized tendencies: individualism and interdependence. This dichotomy causes conflict. To balance these opposites would help us to develop as people.

Conflict can be seen as a disease, with a diagnosis and a prognosis. Structural changes don't always lead to lasting solutions. We need to grow and develop as human beings in order to prevent the same problems happening in other situations. If we think of it as a disease, we might look for some social bacteria: the Rumour bacteria, the Fixation bacteria and the Persuasion bacteria. Our first approach, following this analogy, might be a conflict diagnosis. Just like a doctor checks out his or her patient, it is important to see the situation as objectively as possible:

1. What is the basic issue?

2. What has happened up to now?

3. Who is involved in this conflict?

4. What are the personal and formal relationships between the partners?

5. Can these partners solve the conflict with their present attitudes?

6. The core question: is there something underlying this conflict?

If conflict is a social disease, or, talking about social ecology, a form of pollution, we might consider it in an entirely different way. First of all, it might not be a wholly negative thing. Disease and pollution are, like pain, signals we need to respond to. Something isn't right, we need to change the way we do things. My hand is painful, it is burning ... take it out of the flame! Our land is polluted ... stop throwing waste around indiscriminately and recycle it! Our group is wracked by conflicts, everyone is arguing and fed up with everyone else ... re-establish relationships and working methods!

The mechanism of conflict can be thought of as a descending staircase, where for each step awareness and judgment is reduced. Social ecologists define nine steps in three groups of three:

Bhole Baba, Italy:
religion as community glue

Date founded — 1979
Approximate number of residents — 7
Location — Apulia, southern Italy
Spiritual or ideological affiliation — Hindu
Visited — for two days in the summer of 2000

Bhole Baba became an Ashram in 1979, the first in Italy, and became the centre of a network of similar ashrams and affiliated individuals throughout Italy which recognize Babaji, the Mahavatar of the Himalayas, as their inspiration. Thousands of people have been to visit over the years, to experience this small community with a strong commitment to environmental living and spiritual growth. The land was cultivated biodynamically, with two cows giving milk and milk products. The diet was completely vegetarian, with orchards providing fruit and olives for oil.

At the time of our visit the community had dropped to seven people, several of whom were soon to leave. The farmers had gone, the cows had been sold, and the land was largely uncultivated. Some of the fruit was collected, herbs were still growing in profusion, and there was still one vegetable garden in use. The main inspiration and founder of the Ashram, Lisetta Carmi, had left some months previously. Despite the falling number of residents the ones who were there were busy preparing for a major festival and conference a few days ahead, where they were expecting over 150 visitors.

Bhole Baba is situated in Apulia, an area known for its peculiar housing tradition of Trulli. These are limestone cones, dry walled, a building tradition which no doubt stretches back for thousands of years. I have seen pictures of similar stonework from bronze age Malta, and from the Mycenaean Greek burial tombs. It was a place of unlikely combinations: the Trulli, a Hindu temple, biodynamic gardening and a tremendous potential for being a learning centre. Anyone who wanted to till the soil, live off its produce, follow a simple lifestyle and a spiritual path would be well rewarded here. Permaculture and Ecovillage design courses would attract a wide variety of people, some of which might well be motivated to stay and make a commitment to the Ashram.

It was an inspiration to me that there exist these potentials, places which are open and offering a real alternative life.

LEFT. Biodynamic vegetable gardens still being cultivated.

BELOW. Abandoned Trulli near the Ashram.

ABOVE. Inside the shrine, located within a rehabilitated Trulli.

RIGHT. Meditation room within the grounds of the Ashram.

ABOVE. Rehabilitated Trulli as part of the Ashram complex.

LEFT. The temple, an exact copy of a temple from the Himalayas.

1. One-sided notions

— *First step:* discussion and argument; points of view harden; tension and bull-dozing; talking past each other; fortuitous sympathy groups.

— *Second step:* debate and polarization; strengthening one's own position by tactics and verbal power; ridiculing the opposition; impossible to think new ideas; groupings around points of view.

— *Third step:* overrun; no longer any point in talking; misunderstandings; negative expectations; lack of trust; hardened groupings and roles; the end of compassion.

2. The opponent is the problem

— *Fourth step:* stereotypes; self-fulfilling prophecies; rumour-mongering; positive view of self — negative view of opponent; strong groupings, authoritarian leadership.

— *Fifth step:* losing of face; formal attacks; building up of myths; casting out and isolation; scapegoating.

— *Sixth step:* strategic threats; using force to remove opponent; total fixation; the opponent is no longer human.

3. Destruction

— *Seventh step:* limited destruction; damage the opponent; willing to accept damage to oneself if the opponent is damaged more.

— *Eighth step:* attacking nerve centres; paralysing and dividing the enemy's defences, destruction of important systems; collateral damage.

— *Ninth step:* total annihilation, no way back; a battle of life and death.

Working with conflicts using this nine step analysis can be made a lot easier if we try to ascend just one step at a time. Often, we try to sort out conflict too fast: we have high expectations and think that reasonable people can just sit around, talk it through and it all works out OK. If we see that conflicts deepen as we go down each step, leading to annihilation, maybe we can solve the conflict by painfully hauling our way back up the stairs, step by step.

It is often easier to have a third party come in and help with such a process. Depending upon the specific conflict in hand, there are certain ground rules which we could keep in mind. First of all the role of the third party:

1. To make observations as objectively as possible.
2. To be neutral and not to moralize.
3. To try to see the situation from a distance.
4. To be accepted by both parties.
5. To develop trust.
6. To awaken the desire to take responsibility.
7. Raise awareness.

Once the two 'enemies' have accepted that there is a need to resolve the conflict and that a third party should step in to help them, the work of conflict resolution has three phases:

1. *Briefing.* This phase is over when the third party has gained some understanding of the situation, and when the conflicting parties have met and accepted the presence of the third party. An understanding of roles, ethics and working methods will have been laid down.
2. The way of information is based on observations, concepts and insights which lead to a *diagnosis.*
3. The way of choice is based on aims, means and the first step which leads to *resolution.*

Just as disease can be seen as a signal for improving health and pollution as resources looking for a use, social conflict might be regarded as an opportunity for self-growth. In social ecology this has been recognized as the eightfold way of training through fellowship. Parallels are to be found in Buddhism and in the Sermon on the Mount. It is a way of developing what we might call social skill. The art is to see oneself with an outsider's eye.

The eight activities we need to be aware of are:

— My ideas: where do they come from, are they my own?
— My decisions: how do I make them, if at all?
— My way of talking: how do I say what I say in any given situation?
— My actions: how do they affect my surroundings?
— My patterns of habit: why do I use my time in the way I do?
— My strivings: can I lift myself up over the everyday, where am I going?
— My capacity to learn from life: from my own and others' experience?
— Being aware of the part of my individuality which can pose these questions.

Qualities that we could develop from this kind of training would include listening with loving interest, creating a common picture, a common point of departure and the ability to act in freedom. We need to develop the capacity to observe, to evaluate and be able to take free actions. All this demands work upon the self, not in isolation, but in the context of social interaction. These are not lists to be followed slavishly or memorized by heart, but rather ideas and processes which can be observed, understood and put into practice.

If we look back at the ideas of social ecology, we can see a progression from building up a group identity, through working with conflicts, to training oneself as a human being to gain more freedom. Any group planning to build a new community out there in uncharted territory, looking for new relationships with oneself, with one's fellow human beings and with the world around them, would be well equipped if they take this social map with them.

4. House Design and Building Techniques

What do we live in?

Spiritual aspects

It probably would not be a good idea to build an Ecovillage, or any other living place for that matter on an old native American burial ground! On the other hand, to have a sacred spot in your community, where perhaps Neolithic people worshipped and set up standing stones, might be quite an asset. Clearly, specific places have spiritual qualities; some seem to be intrinsic in the place itself, others we give them by usage. It would be foolish to ignore this.

Everything has a spiritual aspect, including place and building. We also know that we feel better in some places than others. If we could only cultivate this intuition consciously, something that isn't so difficult, we can soon find ourselves being more aware of it. One way to access into this is to have a meditation in the place where you want to build. Open up to the spirit of the place itself and ask open-mindedly what that spirit would like you to build there, or what kind of usage it might envisage. The group can then go through the ideas that individuals come up with, regard each one uncritically and arrive at a series of ideas in conclusion. This is an exercise that we have used in many design courses.

The key to this kind of planning process is openness. We are dealing with creativity and with sensitivity, and these qualities require a special kind of nurturing. The one sure way to kill them off is to wade in with criticism and negative states of mind. Allow each vision to expand, observe it as a picture for what it is, allow it to be put aside as another takes its place. Each one can be recorded with a few key words and afterwards a critical evaluation can take place. As a group process, the quest for a spiritual quality specific to a certain place has tremendous value in building up a group soul. Within a planning group it is obviously necessary that you have experts on the physical aspects of construction, of farming and gardening, of finances and planning regulations. The great danger is that these people tend to dominate, are often full of their own importance and sometimes have little regard for the more subtle aspects of group dynamics, of the spiritual and social processes at work.

In *The Teachings of Don Juan*, Carlos Castaneda tells us about his initiation with a Mexican Indian Shaman. One of his first tasks is to find his place on the back porch of Don Juan's house, something which takes him all night, but sure enough, he eventually finds that one specific place has an altogether different effect upon him.

It is not easy to tackle this question in a hard scientific or even organized way. So much is up to our feelings, our immediate experience and our intuition. But our common sense tells us that we feel better in some places than in others and that we can reflect upon this experience. Our common sense also tells us that it's important that we feel good in the house where we live and the place where we work. Time spent finding out how to create that good feeling is time well spent.

Feng Shui

In the eastern tradition of Feng Shui, this aspect of place is the essence of the art. If we compare this with acupuncture, we may get some idea of what this system means. In acupuncture, which is fast becoming accepted now, we assume a series of energy flows on and through the human body. When these run freely, the body is healthy. If they are interfered with, we feel unwell. If we manipulate these energy flows, with needles, with massage or with herbs, all in the right places, we can in turn work on the health of the body. In Feng Shui, it is assumed that the planet has a similar set of energy flows. People who work with ley lines are aware of this. Dowsers and people who are sensitive to these forces can locate them and trace them across the land. Where these energy flows intercept there are places of stronger energy. Sacred places are often located upon such intersections and the flow of underground water is crucial.

Feng Shui works with this, defining places in terms of their energy and manipulating space by building structures which can tap into the energy already there. Places with negative energy, or where the energy flow has a negative effect upon the human being, can also be changed by rearranging doors, windows, access or putting in such things as mirrors, wind chimes, plants, bells, etc.

This is a traditional Chinese practice and was suppressed fiercely during the communist era in the last half of the last century. Feng Shui survived in Taiwan and especially in Hong Kong, and is now fast becoming accepted throughout the western world. You have to train with a master to become a Feng Shui practitioner, and there are schools and courses in many places in the West.

For some years now there has been a recognized phenomenon known as the Sick Building Syndrome. Especially prevalent among large office blocks and shopping centres, it seems to be the result of a combination of toxic materials and poor ventilation. Some designers, wishing to create the so-called Perfect Human Environment (!), have found it necessary to eliminate windows and all that untidy, shifting natural light and distracting views. Interestingly enough, a partial cure for the Sick Building Syndrome can be effected with running water and green plants. Feng Shui is especially effective in curing this syndrome, but it can be avoided to a great extent by good design.

Siting and zoning

It's no good having a great house and nowhere to put it. It might seem banal and obvious that we check out the site before we design the house, but often this is not done. Modern architecture often seems to regard the environment as a nuisance which needs to be changed and which just costs money. I have walked around brand new modern housing areas which are made up of two or three standard house designs, all repeated in great numbers, scattered around like the houses and hotels you get in a game of Monopoly with no regard for either prevalent wind or sun direction. The same house can be repeated at 180° turns, thus either revealing one side or the other to the southern, sunny side, as if it did not matter at all which side collected the sun's energy, or guarded against a cold wind in winter.

Finding the right site for a house is one thing, finding the right site for a village is a much bigger challenge. There are so many constraints that it seems to me more a matter of luck and happenstance than that old romantic dream of going into unspoiled and uninhabited land and choosing the right bend by the stream where the hill protects you from the cold north wind and the lion lies down with the lamb! Today most of the world has been settled and what hasn't been settled is largely protected; we want to keep it that way. Old deserted villages are probably the best bet and some of the Mediterranean countries seem to abound in them. Get in there while you still have a chance!

In other European countries existing villages and farms might provide good opportunities; in urban situations you are often confronted by interesting and challenging social conditions. Whatever the precise site happens to be, the idea of zoning will be a help in organizing thoughts around what should be where. This is based on common sense: the principle that the location of activities that you do most frequently should be closest to where you live. Compare that to the folks who commute to work for an hour each way every day!

When it comes to planning on the ground, Permaculture uses the idea of zoning, further modified by sectors and vectors:

Zone 1 — Homes and food (security) gardens. This includes the house itself and workshops that are in daily use, as well as gardens for herbs and intensive vegetables, especially those that can't be stored. Trees would be limited to those giving shade for the houses or providing regular and frequently used fruits.

Zone 2 — Closed spaces and orchards. This is still an intensively maintained area, the irrigation should be controlled, and egg collecting and daily milking can be located here. The actual sheds for these might be on the border between zone 2 and 3 giving access for the animals to range in the next zone. This area would also include pruned trees and mulch gardens.

Zone 3 — Larger open spaces and gardens. Water would be available in ponds and streams, but otherwise unmanaged. Trees would not need pruning, but would give yields in the shape of annual gatherings of nuts and fruits. Animals would be able to range freely.

Zone 4 — Reserves, fuel forests, windbreaks, etc. The managed, designed space that we surround ourselves with gradually gives way here to the semi-wild. From this area we gather from the wild; typically we use this for firewood and timber, and for those who eat meat this would be where we might hunt small animals.

Zone 5 — Wildlife corridors, native plant sanctuaries. We stop designing and let nature take over freely. We need to see nature in action, partly to see how things operate and partly to nurture our own spirits by connecting to the natural world in a quiet and meditative space.

These zones are, in theory, concentric circles, but need modifying with two more factors:

Sectors are parts of these circles, having specific attributes, such as the sunshine generally coming from a southern direction in the northern hemisphere, the prevailing wind direction and fire risk areas adjacent to the site. Occasionally zone 4 or 5 might be brought quite close to the house in a wedge, giving wildlife the opportunity to move across the site, or the location of a barn, shed or workshop might extend zone 1 or 2 further away than the perfect concentric circle.

Vectors further modify the pattern by creating dynamic flows cutting through the site, such as water courses, existing or planned roads and tracks, wildlife corridors and the hills and slopes of the site. While sectors can be regarded as direction specific, vectors are often more serendipitous and move more or less where they want.

In the planning of any specific site, these three ideas are further modified by the things that we find there, existing buildings, roads, streams, hills and forests. It is said that Permaculturalists work with what they get. Sometimes there is a need to make major landscape changes and we'll look at that later; but generally it is better to make do and not move hills or major watercourses. This means that each design will end up as a unique exercise, applying the theory outlined here to that specific location. It might be said that understanding the theory is the science of Permaculture, while applying it in practice is the art.

When we apply these ideas to Ecovillage design I would like to emphasize that the collective ideology of the community in question must first determine the physical layout. Let's look at what this means by comparing briefly the planning of the Ecovillage at Clil in Galilee in Israel with the planning of a Green Kibbutz.

Clil is a small village of 170 people settled originally about 25 years ago. It was inspired by ideals such as Gandhian pacifism, organic food production, independence, spirituality and self-sufficiency. The members did not want to use the existing rural community models then available in Israel and they have been extremely successful in developing their own style. Each family is responsible for building and maintaining their own smallholding, and the focus of community planning has been reduced to roads, a kindergarten and overall decision-making, such as the size of the village and admission of new residents. The Permaculture zoning concept only has relevance at the household level, while the location of each household is largely dependant upon the availability of land. Clil may be thought of as a cluster of zones with a deliberate refusal to apply any overall planning concept to the village.

In the Kibbutz the planning of the community as a whole has always been paramount. The individual family has been of less importance. Indeed in much of its history children were housed and educated separately from the parents and even today most meals in most Kibbutz communities are eaten in the communal dining hall. Apart from a few square metres of personal garden by the front door of each house, it would be inappropriate to apply the zoning concept to the family home of the individual Kibbutz member. The zoning concept has to be applied to the community as a whole. Given the extremely

Twin Oaks, Virginia, USA:
a modern American commune

Date founded — 1967
Approximate number of residents — *ca.* 70 people
Location — an hour east of Charlottesville, Virginia
Spiritual or ideological affiliation — a collective founded
on behaviourism
Visited — a day in the summer of 2004

Twin Oaks was founded by a group of psychology students, inspired by the behaviourist theories put forward by B.F. Skinner in his novel *Walden Two*. It was established before the environment was a central issue within the alternative movement, long before Permaculture was thought of, and the Ecovillage concept was still a couple of decades away. To them, social and psychological issues were paramount: their aim was to produce better socialized human beings through patient education of the children.

The model closest to their ideal way of bringing up children they found in the Kibbutz education system and they named their children's house Degania, after the first Kibbutz. Like the Kibbutz, over the decades their rigid system of child-rearing gradually became more flexible, and by the time I managed to visit, Degania was no longer operating as a kindergarten, but had become a house for a family of residents.

As the years went by, environmental issues crept into the community, as they did throughout the western world, especially the alternative sector. Each house they built contained more environmental strategies, and older houses were often retrofitted with solar panels and other features. It would make a fascinating study of the rise of environmental consciousness to chart their building progress.

Today, nearly forty years on, the community is still income sharing, still operating a work point system that has changed relatively little from what was established in the late 1960s. The members still eat communally and share their vehicles. Twin Oaks has had the strength to inspire a number of other communities, East Wind and Dandelion to name just two. They are the focus of the Federation of Egalitarian Communities, host regular meetings and conferences, and have the main office of the Federation. They have much to teach in terms of social planning, conflict resolution and communal decision making.

LEFT. This building was retrofitted with a solar collector. As the ecological awareness gradually increases, changes can be seen, older buildings are modified, newer buildings contain more ecological techniques.

BELOW. Composting toilet, showing the doors where the finished compost can be taken out in wheeled bins. This building was called Pooh Corner!

RIGHT. Firewood stacked up for the winter. Being in a forest, there is no shortage.

RIGHT. As each building is constructed, it contains more ecological strategies. This building shows arrays of solar collectors on the roof.

ABOVE. Community herb and vegetable gardens.

BELOW LEFT. The car board. A community that pools its cars needs information to be accessible to anyone at any time. If you can figure out how it works, you might be well on your way to joining!

BELOW RIGHT. Lots of laundry to be done, here showing the solar/wind drying mechanism, known as the Clothes Line!

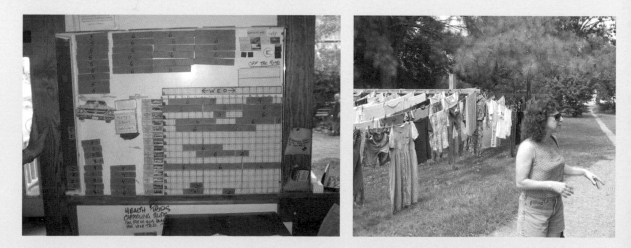

radical starting point of Kibbutz society, even with the changes going on today, we must regard the Kibbutz as one large household, with the concomitant zoning implications that this has.

I use this as an example to illustrate the simple point that before we can begin with such physical planning that is implied in the zoning concept, we must first define our ideals, aims and social parameters. These will then be reflected in structures on the ground.

Materials

Most houses being built in the western world today rely on industrial materials: steels, alloys, plastics and wood that has been shaped and impregnated — often chopped up and put together again — as well as various forms of artificial stone. These materials often represent an enormous energy cost in terms of production and transport. Aluminium, for example, might be mined in South America, transported by ship to Scandinavia where it is refined in factories using hydro-electric power, then transported again to North America where it is made into window frames. David Pearson gives us a comparison of energy costs in *The Natural House Book*. If we take as our starting point the cost of felling, sawing and transporting timber, estimated at 580 kWh/tonne, we can compare other materials:

Timber	580
Bricks	2,320
Cement	2,900
Plastic	3,480
Glass	8,120
Steel	13,920
Aluminium	73,080

Add to that the fact that impregnated timber and many plastics are toxic, these figures might make you want to use just old-fashioned logs straight from the forest!

I've often felt that our building traditions can be traced back to two of our earliest structures for shelter: **the Mineral** and **the Organic**, the latter based on vegetable and animal components.

The cave is essentially a massive structure, created by a hollow within a largely mineral matrix: heavy, immobile, stable in temperature, safe and secure. All stone and earth buildings reflect this tradition; I call this the **Mineral tradition**. This includes bricks and adobe, indeed all forms of earth building. Today's artificial stone, bricks and building blocks, come from a healthy tradition. In the past that's what they were, just burnt clay. In the industrialized world all kinds of substances were added to make them either cheaper, lighter or more effective (whatever that might mean). Here lies an interesting and cautionary hush-hush story. In Israel most electricity is generated by burning coal and oil; the ash from the coal-fired stations used to be dumped in the Mediterranean. A seemingly good solution until all those annoying environmentalists found out that this was polluting the sea and, after many years, managed to put a stop to it. What then to do with the ash? Some bright spark found that it could be mixed in with building block materials to make breeze blocks. Seemingly a good solution, until some other bright environmentalist found that this ash was mildly radioactive. Now radioactive is bad, whether mild or not, and the people working with it were found not to be adequately protected. Not to mention that living within four mildly radioactive walls might not be so attractive! No-one thought to market them as self-illuminating, think of the savings in lights ...

Our industrial world is full of materials that we have recently discovered, many of which have not been adequately researched. Impregnating timber with arsenic is for example a really good way to prevent fungus and insect attack, but makes it dangerous to chew or burn. Probably my scientific friends would call for years of research before I make the following assertion, but I stand by my firm conviction that part of the reason for the massive increase in allergies we are experiencing in the western world is due to the fact that we are surrounding ourselves with mildly poisonous materials, eating food that contains many interesting and new preservatives, flavourings and colourings. It may well be that when we investigate each one, that it's not so bad. Just a teeny amount of radioactive dust in a building block doesn't do very much harm. But when we add it all up, it represents a massive attack upon our health.

The second tradition in our building history, **the Organic tradition**, comes from when we lived in tents made up of sticks and skins. From here we have the long and varied history of wooden houses. This is the tradition of the nomad, the light structure which provided only minimal protection from the outside world, which responded rapidly to the changes in temperature and

Wilhelmina, Holland:
reuse of buildings

Date founded — early 1990s
Approximate number of residents — several hundred
Location — Amsterdam
Spiritual or ideological affiliation — none, urban radicals maybe?
Visited — one afternoon in the summer of 1998

Wilhelmina was built as a hospital many decades ago, and as technology changed, gradually became too old-fashioned to be useful as such. Amsterdam City Council had by the 1990s built much better, modern hospitals to replace it, and decided to knock the old buildings down to make way for some urban improvement, such as a parking house, shopping mall or luxury apartments. Homeless urban squatters had moved into the empty buildings, found that they were ideally suited to their requirements, and petitioned the city authorities to let them take over, rehabilitate and live there. After some initial to-ing and fro-ing, this was finally agreed to, and Wilhelmina was turned into a co-operative housing project. Shared apartments with communal spaces for cooking, eating and relaxing were organized in the old wards, and cafes, workshops and other enterprises were opened.

The value of this lies not only in the reuse of old buildings, but also in the self-help, co-operative organization of the residents. Urban renewal does not need to be a 'big brother' effort by distant city authorities, but can be a real grass-roots enterprise, activating and empowering residents to take control over their lives.

RIGHT. Façade of the old hospital complex.

LEFT. Inside one of the apartments, which consists of a communal corridor, a communal room and a number of private rooms.

BELOW. Main entrance to the Wilhelmina complex, with café, childcare centre and small workshops.

humidity, a dynamic tradition reflected today in self-adjusting buildings and smart technology. Calling this Organic doesn't necessarily mean that it's organic, as we just noticed, pumping wood full of arsenic can hardly be called environmentally friendly. The terms Mineral and Organic refer more to where materials come from and how they behave. But here I go, slipping into Permaculture and looking for patterns, when I should be looking at building materials ...

Stone

The pyramids are built of stone, which just goes to show how long-lasting this material is. Because of its weight, it hardly justifies transport over long distances, but if you have stones lying around on your site, you're lucky and can save lots of money. Stone is hard to work with, you need to be pretty skilful to shape and lay stone. And that's a skill that is pretty uncommon these days. You need to be aware of the geology of your stone; some of it, especially younger, sedimentary stone, can weather badly, and is especially prone to frost and acid rain. Others, slate for example, are excellent for roofs and floors, but are often expensive and require transport and processing. Stones can be collected from the surface, or from a pile should you be so lucky, and used for rough, often thick walls for both buildings and around courtyards. Unless you are an experienced dry-stone wall builder you need to use a cement matrix to hold the stuff in place, and stone requires a lot more cement than brick walls. However, if your stone is free for the collecting, it should still save you money. I have built bridges, benches and walls with stone and cement with unskilled labour, and achieved great effects by incorporating all kinds of tile and strangely shaped stone into the surface.

The easiest and most effective way of using rough stone is to build a box of wood and fill this with stones, cement and reinforcing. These wooden boxes can be built in sections which are dismantled as the cement sets, and which can then be moved along to make the next section. Build a small tool shed first to gain some skill before you start on your dream house for the family!

Plaster and cement

These are really just artificial stone. A mixture of various processed powders made of ground up stones or clay is mixed with water and often other liquids, and spread while it is still wet and soft to form bonding between stones or bricks, or coverings over walls made of other materials. Eventually this dries and will become more or less hard, more or less waterproof, all according to which ingredients we include. The simplest plaster I've used was just a mixture of earth, sand and a little cow dung to make it hard to cement together old tin cans and plastic bottles to make a rough wall. Not terribly waterproof, but otherwise perfectly serviceable and, to those who are sceptical about the use of dung I assure you, absolutely odourless. When it had done its job, after a couple of years, we knocked it down, pulled out the cans and the bottles, and turned it into a garden! There's recycling! The choice of ingredients will be determined by criteria like: what is available, what do you need this structure to do and how expensive or environmentally friendly do you want to be? Earth plasters, made of local materials, are often very good. You can make a test of your particular earth by taking a sample, shaking it up into a jar full of water and letting it settle for a few hours. The coarser material, sand, will settle at the bottom, the finer in the middle and the organic matter on the top, even floating in the water. Ideally between 50–70 percent sand, 10–20 percent clay, (the finest particles) and a good addition of chopped straw (horse dung is the best!) is good for an all-round plaster. Builders who use earth plasters usually work from experience, test all the time and get a feel for it. If you can find one, work with him or her for a bit, otherwise just start doing it and build up your own experience.

Earth

This is one of the really old, traditional and widespread materials. There is so much written about it and so many traditions, that it seems ridiculous to try to cover this in just a short paragraph! Adobe and pisé are two words that are used for this. Adobe is usually taken to mean a method where we make bricks, dry them in the sun and cement them in place, using the same earth mixture as a bond. Pisé involves building a framed box, ramming the earth in hard, letting this dry and then moving the box upwards to then ram in the next layer and so gradually building up a wall. Earth is a great material. Pretty much readily available; you excavate a hole for foundations and site placement, and there you have your material! It is very plastic, so you can make any shape you want, curved walls, insets of other things. Some friends of mine made a small earth house, just one room, a few square metres (not so square really!), but large enough to hold up to twenty people sitting comfortably. They set in coloured glass dishes and cups for a window effect, and even an old-fashioned sieve with a wonderful pattern of holes as a light and ventilator. Bits of old cupboard were cemented (earthed?) into the walls. They had had no previous experience, just traced out the run of the walls, and got a pile of friends together and put lumps of earth on top of each other till they had walls the right height, then rafters across for the roof. With a nice earth plaster finish on the inside and outside, you have a heat retaining wall, thermal mass, breathing qualities to give good air and a healthy inner climate. Eminently recyclable, just take the roof off, pull out all the bits of junk you put into it and turn the whole thing into a garden! Earth can also be used in combination with a net frame of woven sticks, known as wattle and daub. You just weave the shape you want of pliable sticks, then slap on wet earth with a high percentage of clay and let it dry. Finish off with a smooth earth plaster and you have a durable wall. In the Middle Ages this was combined in the wood frame house and friends of mine live in houses like this today. These houses are several hundred years old and still functioning well.

Bricks and blocks

A step up from the adobe earth brick is to include a greater percentage of clay and fire the bricks, turning the material into a kind of stone. By adding cement and other materials, you can skip the firing and use the chemical hardening process instead. Ordinary bricks are standard sized, and you need skill and experience to lay good walls. You can make your own, but getting the 1,100°C needed to fire conventional bricks might be a little challenging and energy intensive. Building blocks are typically much larger, and shaped for things like corners, strengthening courses and door or window surrounds. You need much less skill to lay them, they often fit together like children's building blocks. Because they are bigger, walls go up much faster. Watch those industrial additives in the commercially made blocks though! Making your own cement blocks is pretty easy. In the 1960s the Appropriate Technology folks developed a lever operated press to make bricks from earth with a small percentage of cement added. The Cinva Ram, as it was called, has decades of experience behind it and tens of thousands of homes have been built with it. Once you have the idea, you might be able to build your own version, pretty simple technology, but effective. Also a good social way of doing things, needing relatively little skill, but can be fun and effective if a large group go at it for a while. Invite your friends to a brick-making party!

Tiles and pottery

Tiles for roofing can be made in the same way. Fired tiles are waterproof and will last for hundreds of years. Those old red pantiles used throughout Mediterranean Europe make very pretty roofs. Cement tiles can also be used, but the percentage of cement needs to be higher to get the waterproof effect.

In this category I am thinking also of glazed tiles, which have a long and honourable history and have been used maybe to their best effect in Islamic architecture. Mostly this is done in the same way that pottery is made, glazing square tiles in a kiln and using them as a covering for walls. Broken pottery can be used in a mosaic pattern with a good effect too. With the right bonding matrix, a wall can be waterproof. Glazed roofing tiles are also effective. One idea I have read about but never tried is to fire a clay building. Make the structure you want out of clay, let it dry, pile it up with brushwood and fire the whole thing. It comes out somewhat like Raku pottery and is supposed to be a good way of getting something hard and durable. I would imagine it can't be too big and the process could be a fire risk. Try it out if you live in the right climate and have access to the right materials.

Glass

I often wonder what life was like before glass! I read in the history books about stretching oiled skins across openings and wooden shutters which were closed at night. I think I would recommend using glass! There's really a lot of choice here. Some modern windows are very high tech, very expensive and utilize all kinds of techniques to minimize heat loss. At that end of the range, with aluminium alloy frames, triple plated, vacuum spaced, possibly photo sensitive glass, you need to consider the embodied energy and the processes that go into the components. At the other end of the range, scavenging windows and frames from houses about to be demolished, you can find the cheapest and most environmentally friendly solution. Bear in mind that if you do this it might be best to get hold of the windows before building the house, so that you can plan the window sizes right from the start rather than having to do a lot of bothersome retrofitting. Glass should absolutely be part of our building repertoire, letting the sun in when we need it, creating the greenhouse effect which will heat our buildings and greenhouses.

Metals

Today we use a wide range of metals in our houses, both for structural purposes, and for all kinds of fittings and connections. They are precious resources, mined out of the ground, heavily processed and often transported far, with all the embodied energy problems that this entails. On the other hand, with careful forethought, they can often be recycled quite effectively and that has an enormous bearing upon the energy use. David Pearson maintains that recycled aluminium uses only 5 percent of the energy used to produce new aluminium. Pipes, fittings and other components can often be salvaged from demolished buildings for a pittance. Even ordinary mild steel is usually about half recycled. It is worth bearing in mind that certain metals have health hazards: lead in pipes and in paint is perhaps most well known, but there are many others, mercury, nickel, zinc, silver, arsenic, etc. The amounts used in alloys are often so small as to be no problem, but it has to be borne in mind. Another effect we should be aware of is the creation of fields in the electromagnetic spectrum. A steel mesh box can become a Faraday cage, while the electric circuitry in a house can set up harmful electric fields. The increasing tendency to leave televisions and computers on semi shutdown might well show to have adverse effects upon the people living in houses filled with electric magnetic 'noise.' On the other hand, metals are usually chemically inert and can be preferable to the plastic stuff we are using more and more. In a fire, for instance, metals might buckle, but will rarely give off gas, which is something that plastics do in big amounts and with a very high toxicity.

Timber

For me timber seems the most accessible material, most user friendly and flexible. More so than stone, which usually requires some kind of bonding, involving dust, water and mud on my hands. Untreated timber is clean, can be shaped with fairly simple hand or power tools, can be fitted together with joints or pegs, usually ages well and can be recycled in many ways when we have finished with the building. But beware! Out there in the world of the builder are all kinds of hazards! Timber treated with arsenic to avoid fungus rot is highly toxic. I know we don't usually chew our houses, but burning building scrap on the fire can be a health disaster. Off-gassing can occur for years, turning your house into a mild gas chamber. In the old days here in Norway there was a method of naturally impregnating timber which I have always found fascinating, but it's a long-term proposition. You cut the very tops off fir trees and let them stand for a few years in this crippled way. The trees natural defence system then fills the trunk with pitch to minimize the danger of rot. When the tree is cut down the timber is literally dripping with resin and needs no other treatment. I have worked with such timber, and the only drawback is that your clothes and tools become covered with pine pitch, but on the other hand there are timbers still in usable buildings that are over 800 years old in many places here in Norway.

Different kinds of timber behave differently, some withstand water by their very nature, others split easily, giving us shingles for the roof. Others again are soft and easily worked into decorative elements. They come in many colours and often with delightful graining. Combinations of different timbers can be a real joy to live amongst. Trees are organic growths, responding to light, moisture and the contents of the soil they grow in. Trees have been revered as sacred objects since time immemorial. The bristlecone pine in California is the oldest inhabitant of the planet, living up to 5,000 years. The banyan tree in India can cover up to a square kilometre, surely the largest single living creature. The forests of the world are our lungs, maintaining a gas balance that we are totally dependent upon as living creatures. You can build a house entirely of wood, using pegs and wooden shutters. There is no other material I know of that could be used like that, except maybe steel. But who would want to live in a steel box? Of course there are environments that don't grow many trees, and in desert places, like the Middle East, stone, plasters and earth are much more relevant. But it would be difficult for me to imagine building a house today with no wooden components at all. With wood being a renewable resource, you might consider planting a few trees for every house you build, it would give your grandchildren something to build with when their time comes.

Grass and stuff

Canes, reeds, bamboo, grasses and straw all belong together. In one way they are the poorer cousins of the tree, similarly an organic material, renewable, flexible and with virtually no toxic properties. These materials got bad press with the story of the three little pigs, that nasty old wolf huffing and puffing and blowing their house away. Very unfair, straw houses are as old as the earliest shelter building and modern strawbale houses have been standing for nearly a century already. It's not so widespread in Europe or North America to use these materials today, but there are great examples of vernacular architecture from other parts of the world. If you ever need to fire up your imagination and creativity, take a look at the mudhifs of Iraq made of reeds, Balinese bamboo houses or the reed shelters used around Lake Titicaca in Bolivia. In our temperate climate thatching is perhaps the most well known use of this material. Long straw wheat or barley can be grown to provide the material. I have heard that the value of the straw can exceed the value of the grain, making me wonder which is the by-product. This technique is making a slow comeback in England at least and certainly is a material we should take seriously.

Strawbales (SB)

In a book on Permaculture and Ecovillages strawbale building requires a section by itself. This has become a kind of symbol of this particular niche culture, with SB building networks, magazines and projects all over the place. There is as yet, as far as I know, no industrial application here. Most people know each other by word of mouth, SB builders learn the techniques in informal ways from others and by experimenting. Most houses are custom designed, and built with a combination of self-build, help from friends and courses advertised through small networks. Excuse the pun, but this seems to be a real grass-roots movement, one which has potential and relevance to the future.

The whole thing begun over a century ago when Europeans moved into Nebraska and began farming wheat to be shipped back east with the newly laid railways. As the farming rapidly mechanized, the strawbaler was developed to get the straw easily off the fields. The plains of Nebraska are virtually treeless and stone free. So at some point some bright spark thought to stack up the bales, leave a gap here and there for doors and windows, and put a roof on this thing and live in it. A bit dusty inside and prone to be chewed by passing cows or horses, the next step was to put an earth plaster on the outside, and hey presto, we have the Nebraska style SB house! Today, this load bearing construction is being increasingly replaced by a post and beam structure where the bales are used as infill. Really a more flexible and easier solution. Whether SB houses are cheaper than other kinds is very difficult to say. One US builder estimates an overall 12 percent saving. Recently on an SB chat group on the web, someone reported a house in England built for £5,000. My recommendation is to establish the size of your building budget first, then consider the relative cost of materials. SB is certainly fun and has great social potential. It puts you into contact with a network, and most houses are built partly by groups of friends coming together to do the actual wall construction.

SB houses have the advantage of being built from an organic, renewable material. A material which breathes, depending upon the plaster you apply within and without, and which has an insulation far higher than that which is generally demanded by building codes. The actual wall construction, both bales and plaster, requires a group effort by people who need no special skills, though they do need an experienced guide.

Natural fibres
While caves solved the housing needs of some early people, tents did and still do cater for other, perhaps more mobile people. Today the tepee and the yurt have made a comeback, at least in certain alternative circles, and are viable forms of quick and relatively cheap housing. Even though artificial fibres have made great progress, the characteristics of wool and cotton are still hard to beat, and they have the advantage that you know you are dealing with safe materials. But beware! Cotton is often grown using a great deal of deadly poisons, and has not generally been associated with just and fair social systems. Both cotton and wool can be treated with chemicals such as formaldehyde, TRIS, dieldrin, DDT or sodium fluorosilicate. Check on labels or with producers. Other fibres, such as linen, silk, sisal, jute, rayon, kapok and coir are all vegetable derived and are worth considering.

Hemp has a special place today. It used to be produced in vast quantities in many parts of the world and was the basis for rope and coarse material for literally millennia. Due to the shenanigans of the American cotton interests, mixed with political considerations of a highly suspicious nature, the plant was banned in the US in the middle of the last century as the source of the drug cannabis. Weighty tomes have been written on it, and in the last decade there has been a renewed interest in its fibre potential, not to say a big interest in its mind-altering capacities over the last generation! Both as a crop, it requires very little protection against pests and diseases, and as a product, it would fit perfectly into a system which wants to grow and use organic, natural fibres. If you can get through the legal hassles of growing hemp, you would end up with a great addition to the farming cycle, a cottage industry of your own and a product that has a growing market in the West.

Generally, apart from the tepee and yurt dwellers, fibres would form components of your indoor fittings rather than the materials from which you build: curtains, carpets, wall hangings and lots more, not to mention clothes, bed-clothes, towels, etc. These are important in themselves, and make an otherwise empty shell into a place of comfort and inspiration. These fibres are usually the materials you sit and lie on, that you look at and handle from day to day. They are as important to your well-being as the planks, stones and bricks of your house!

Paints

Often the last thing you do to a building, whether it is newly built or old but newly bought, is to paint it. You choose the colours that you want to surround yourself with, and the finishes you want to see and touch. This area is a mine-field of dangers. Paints consist of a pigment floating in a liquid, either water or oil, and today can contain many compounds which are a hazard to our health. Often the quantities are minute and may not be significant in themselves, but taken together with impregnations in the timber, artificial fibres, plastics and other substances, produce a house that is a cocktail of undesirable chemicals. Beware, check labels, get a copy of David Pearson's *Natural House Book* for a comprehensive list of chemicals, surf the web looking for additional information, and in Western Europe find the suppliers of natural paints and varnishes. These suppliers exist in small numbers and are following a pattern not so different from the organic food market of a couple of decades ago. We might expect a similar expansion in this field and it would be good for us to help it along by supporting it with our custom.

Junk

Recycling of components has been mentioned in several other places. All over the world we are knocking down old buildings as fast as we can and often many usable components are simply being shovelled into land fills. Planking, beams, windows, doors, plumbing fixtures and furniture are all things that can be salvaged and used again. This idea does not lend itself to the mass produced modern industrial house, but rather to the individual, tailor-made, hand-built house. It takes a longer time and more intensive labour inputs to scavenge components, assemble them in the quantities a house demands, to design the house round the available materials and build it accordingly. We are getting away from standardization and mass thinking. At the Ecovillage level this is ideal. We can create our own cottage industry, collecting materials, storing them and using them, all at the local level. Often these things are virtually free for the taking, and require just a few hand tools to take apart and an old van to bring them home. This can keep people usefully employed and save vast amounts of money which would otherwise have to be earned in order to buy new materials. The ecological saving is significant and will bring down the embodied energy costs of building to an insignificant level. And the scope for creativity and inventiveness is vast! Some of my most enjoyable times have been spent wandering round junk yards, thinking about what I can use all these weird things for. The only limitations are our own heads.

'Earthships' is a building concept developed by Mike Reynolds in New Mexico during the late sixties and early seventies. He envisaged houses being self-supporting in energy, water and food, and he built them out of recycled materials that were easily accessible in his area. Old car tyres stacked up and filled with earth made up massive thermal walls, tin cans were cemented together with mud to make insulated interior walls. The idea of using junk not only makes our building cheaper, it also fills a need in getting rid of and making use of a resource. In Permaculture thinking there is no such thing as waste. Nature does not produce waste. Materials merely pass from one organism to another. Garbage is only a resource looking for a user. By simply changing the way we think, we can turn rubbish into resources and bring our creativity into play by finding out how to use it usefully. We can turn a problem into a solution. 'Earthships' are a classic example of Permaculture thinking in practice.

Plastics

For many environmental builders, this is real no-no area. 'Plastic people,' Captain Beefheart sang and bad mouthed a whole sector of materials. I think it was Amory Lovins from the Rocky Mountain Institute who once commented that the oil molecule is one of the most complex we know of and it's such a waste just to burn it up! Most plastics are made from oil today and once made can be recycled more or less indefinitely. This makes it a useful and flexible material which we might consider more carefully. The biggest drawback is that many plastics contain gases that leak out slowly, but with good technology this can be avoided. The other drawback is that plastics give off vile and noxious gases when burnt. Indeed, most people who die in fires today die not from the heat, but from gas poisoning. Given that we can eliminate or minimize these two problems, plastics have a place in our list of building materials. The only other consideration is that they are heavy industrial products. The extraction, refining and production of the actual materials demands a large and complex advanced industry. They are not cottage products, nor would most groups have much control over the process. However, plastics are hard to eliminate altogether. Plumbing and electrical systems rely heavily upon them, packaging of most other materials come complete with all kinds of plastics that we throw away even before we start doing anything. Most modern furnishings contain some of the stuff. It is a field where we need to check carefully and use a lot of common sense to balance what is desirable against what is feasible.

It might be good to finish off this section with a warning about fanaticism. Transport is a major factor in building materials. They tend to be massive and heavy, and the costs of moving them around are high, both financial and environmental. Therefore use what you have to hand. There is also a major consideration over time and money. If you have lots of the latter, but very little of the former, you will be employing people to build and will often have to use more standardized materials. There are very few commercial environmental builders around. If on the other hand you have lots of time but very little money, you will be well advised to spend that time looking for cheap, often unconventional, local materials. You can build your house out of junk! Discarded tyres, tin cans, reused doors and windows from demolished houses, earth, stones, straw ... all kinds of things can be pressed into service.

Design

Building a house is a process which used to be part of everyday life. In many cultures it still is, usually with other members of the community giving a hand and the whole construction becomes a partly social event. Anyone who saw the film *The Witness* might remember the barn raising episode, a powerful scene where seemingly hundreds of neighbours gathered, built and celebrated together in the Amish culture of Pennsylvania.

That this essentially vernacular tradition has disappeared from our culture is bemoaned by many and we resent the professionalization of building. I often wish myself back to a previous age, where building was not confined by law to a small group of state licensed architects, carpenters, plumbers and electricians. But I do see the sense behind setting up some kind of safeguard that your house doesn't fall on your head. Even with all the safeguards and controls we have built into our society, that does still happen.

Rolf Jacobsen, a Norwegian ecological architect, connected to Kilden, the Norwegian Ecovillage group, to the Bridge Building School and a member of the Gaia Architect Group, wrote in Hildur Jackson's book, *Ecovillage Living*, about the idea of building being like alchemy. The alchemist is not vernacular in the sense of practising a tradition that is part of a folk culture. He or she is an initiate, someone who has undergone long training at the hands of a master and who has gained knowledge of esoteric arts. An intriguing parallel! Just as an alchemist did in the past, today the natural builder uses raw materials from the earth (*prima materia*). With these materials he or she transforms space into a healing environment for the human being, realizing a vision by creating 'beautiful, natural buildings, fruitful Permaculture gardens, living Ecovillages and a sustainable and just society.'

Whether we learn from an esoteric master, an architectural college or a carpentry school, or if we just soak up a folk tradition, it is important to spend a long time thinking and designing before actually beginning to saw and hammer or whatever. During that period of contemplation and design we are first of all defining our vision: what it is we want, what is inspiring us, and how we get there. Permaculture is a series of questions, leading us along a path to some desired result.

How can our design reflect our spiritual, social and ecological lifestyle?

— *Spiritually* we need to reserve space for meditation, contemplation and sacred ritual. Is this a private thing or a group activity? Or maybe a combination of both. Maybe a quiet space in the garden is all that is needed, perhaps a special building, a chapel, where the community can gather to pray and where the individual can also find the silence to meditate.
— *Socially* we have already seen how important it is for us to decide if we all want to live together in one big room, or whether each individual or family needs to have their own house and garden. This is a big question which can keep an Ecovillage group discussing late into the night.
— Our *ecological* aims are also quite specific in their determination of our design. What kind of heating do we want? What kind of materials have we at hand? How do we deal with toilets and wastewater?

From my experience in community and with people, it seems to me that for most households it would probably be best to live in a group of around a dozen. We all can gather round the table and have a conversation over a meal. Often there are one or two away for some reason; so there is room for visitors. If people have their own rooms there is always the possibility of privacy, or intimacy with a smaller group. When the table grows to fifteen or more, conversations tend to split into subgroups and the noise level grows, often uncomfortably. It's crowded. Shared resources make sense, a washing machine is well- but not over-used. The kitchen does not have to be industrial, just large and well designed. Ecological living will in the future depend upon sharing our resources to a large extent. When every person on the planet gets their own car, house, washing machine, computer and television we'll need to go off to other planets to get raw materials and I'm not sure what we'll do about the pollution!

A house designed around a dozen does not have to be much larger than many large family houses in the affluent West. Designers can then ask the questions specific to the site. Where is the sun and the wind? Do we want sun in the dining room and in the kitchen for the morning time? Perhaps we orient the living room towards the west, so we can gather in the evenings and watch the sunset together. A back porch for sundowners? Storage of food and fuel can be along the north wall. Food stays cool and the woodpile will protect from those cold north winds. Large south-facing windows let in the winter sun. An overhang gives us a nice place to sit and shades from the hot summer sun. Work out the angle of the sun at various months and you have the amount of overhang needed. This is design in action, working with the realities of the environment and the needs of the human being.

Some years ago I was part of an internet chat group called the Ecobalance List. The Rocky Mountain Institute contributed a Check List of Sustainable Building which I modified and have used in nearly all my design courses:

Site Planning
1. Renovate if possible.
2. Evaluate site materials.
3. Locate building to minimize eco-damage.
4. Consider solar energy in siting and landscape.
5. Consider existing landscaping.
6. Consider transportation.

Design
1. Smaller is better.
2. Energy efficiency is top priority.
3. Optimize material use.
4. Landscape holistically considering energy and food.
5. Design for recycling.
6. Consider greywater recycling and use.
7. Design for future reuse of materials.
8. Avoid health hazards such as radon, EMF.

Job Site
1. Protect top soil.
2. Isolate chemicals from ground water.
3. Minimize job site waste creation.
4. Manage operations using eco-responsible contacts and partners.

Equipment
1. Efficient heating and natural cooling.
2. Efficient lighting, window placement.
3. Efficient water heating, consider solar.
4. Consider ventilation efficiency.

Materials
1. Avoid ozone depleting materials.
2. Avoid materials with high energy costs.
3. Utilize local material.
4. Look for locally recycled material.
5. Minimize use of old growth lumber.
6. Minimize materials that emit off-gas.
7. Minimize use of pressure treated wood.
8. Minimize packaging and resulting waste.

Design needs to be all-encompassing. William McDonough says in an interview that 'we don't really think of ourselves as designing buildings, we think of ourselves as creating an environment for a community. And we start with the idea of all species in that community.' (*Resurgence*, Jan/Feb 2002.)

Water and sewage

The provision of clean water and the treatment of waste are typically communal issues and merit a chapter to themselves. Here I just want to mention indoor toilets. Some people would not have toilets in their houses at all and sometimes in the early years of a new community, it would make sense to build a toilet and shower block for everyone. It does seem to me, however, that most of us want to be able to use a toilet in our own house, so let's take a quick look at what options we have.

Before we even begin there are a few basic questions we need to answer:

— Are we going to separate toilets from greywater systems and treat each one by itself? This is the most sensible approach; it is fairly easy to design from scratch but complicated as a retrofit.
— Are we going to buy a commercial system, or build one ourselves?
— Are we going to have a toilet that composts internally, or do we empty the container regularly and compost elsewhere?

Before you even begin to design your building, you need to address these questions, ponder them, discuss them and come to an agreement. Depending upon your answers, different design challenges will present themselves, having to do with space, access, height, etc.

Regarding water, your options are simpler. The only basic question here is whether you are going to catch rain water off the roof and store it, or only have it piped in from outside.

For a more detailed treatment of these aspects, turn to Chapter 6, Water and Sewage (p. 155).

Energy and heating

There is a whole chapter devoted to this issue (p. 176), but I want to mention a few design features.

As the sun moves across the sky from east to west during the course of the day, it will shine on different parts of buildings. In your house where you live, you might typically want it to wake you up in the morning, give a good strong light to the kitchen and to the main living room during the day, and warm your terrace in the evening. So you would design your house accordingly, bedrooms on the east, main rooms to the south in the northern hemisphere and the terrace on the west.

In a climate with hot summers and cool winters, an overhang would shelter the rooms inside from direct exposure to the high summer sun and give access to the warm winter sun, much lower in the sky, which would flood the rooms with heat.

The sun, shining through glass onto a dark surface, will heat up the surface, which will in turn heat up the air contained within the glass. This is the classic greenhouse effect and it's most noticeable for those who drive around in cars on sunny days. The car heats up like an oven in a matter of minutes. This effect can be used to heat buildings. There are three basic ways of approaching this:

— **Direct heating** allows the sun to shine in through the window and heat up floor and walls which in their turn will heat the room.
— **Indirect heating** allows the sun to shine onto a darkened wall which in turn radiates heat into the building, or which circulates warm air into the room behind it. This can be done simply by having a vented opening at the top and bottom of the wall. Hot air, warmed by the wall, rises and enters the room, sucking cool air into the space from the room at the bottom. A circulation is established and the room is warmed. This wall is often called a 'Trombe' wall.
— **Isolated systems** consist of collectors placed on the roof, on walls, or even adjacent to the building. These collectors warm up air, water or other substances which transport the heat into the building, releasing it where it is needed. The heat could be stored in an insulated water tank or a massive rock storage cellar. In some designs, this can be heated during the summer, taking several months to warm up and the heat released during the winter.

These three systems are not exclusive and good design could combine all three in a single building. Good design needs to be aware of these options. Even though most heating systems are best designed in a neighbourhood or cluster situation, there are tremendous savings that can be made just by designing the individual buildings with a sense for the sun and its heat delivering capabilities.

Social aspects

We are what we live in. When we plan our buildings, we are also planning what kind of society we want to create. That is the reason I put the chapter on social planning first. That is the key; without a clear idea of how we want to live together, it is impossible to plan and design buildings. When we inherit old buildings, we are also inheriting a social pattern and need to be very aware of this. Do we need to rehabilitate the buildings to reflect the new kind of social system we are creating?

Right now there is a wind of change sweeping through the Camphill movement. In 2002, we hosted a seminar in our village here in Norway to discuss architecture and society. The classic Camphill house is based upon the large extended family, house parents with their own children, a couple of younger co-workers and a number of villagers, people with special needs. We are often fifteen people round the table and we really share our lives, with one large living room, one dining room, laundry, kitchen and so on. This functions very well for most, but we are now realizing that some people don't fit in so well with this. As members get older, they might want smaller, quieter, groups. Families with children might want more time for themselves, more privacy. Therefore, as well as the family house we need other, smaller, different options, with a built-in flexibility so that bigger groups can get together from time to time.

In Norway traditional rural farm planning has involved building many small houses around a farm yard and we came back to this idea during the course of our exploratory seminar. We began to talk about the yard (called *tun* in Norwegian) as the basic unit of our community and how we could create a spread of different types of housing around this common, unifying feature. We are still in this debate, but can see quite clearly that whatever decisions we come to, they will end up as building plans requiring a building budget to put them into reality.

The year Ruth and I spent on Kibbutz in Israel in the 1970s was still the time that children slept in children's houses and spent quality time with their parents in the evening. Members' houses were small, meals were eaten in the communal dining room and washing was done by the Kibbutz laundry. During the 1980s, when we returned to live there as members, children were sleeping at home, and at the end of the 1990s the dining room was closed and many members began doing their own washing at home. Every one of these changes necessitated larger houses and this placed a large strain upon the Kibbutz economy. Sometimes the Kibbutz was unable to release capital for these changes: members felt frustrated and began looking for jobs off the Kibbutz, demanding to keep their wages instead of income sharing as we always had done.

Most Ecovillages that I have direct experience with favour nuclear family homes and often have single people making homes for themselves. This seems to be the pattern that Ecovillages in developed countries have inherited from the dominant culture. It's interesting to note that Ecovillages in other parts, like India, the Far East and South America, are working out of their own societies, coming up with different solutions.

I have been fortunate to live in communal villages that were and are trying to create radically different kinds of society, and have first-hand experience of how important the physical structures are that we surround ourselves with, and how they influence our social behaviour.

We make the buildings and the buildings make us!

5. Agriculture:
Soil, Plants, Gardening and Farming

Community food production, the Cartwheel model

Many years ago I was involved in a community project aimed at setting up a large Ecovillage in England. Part of my task was to work out a plan for food production. It covered four basic areas.

Allotment plots for individuals or households. There are always some people who like to grow their own food according to their own criteria on their own plot of land. Because of the intensive nature of this kind of horticulture, there is no need for large areas to be set aside for this and it lends itself best to small spaces between houses, close to where people live. This is typically zone 1 and 2 usage in Permaculture terms.

Market garden. This could be a commercially run venture, for several people their main income financially. Whether it would produce food for the village internally or be sold out is a question of how much the village wants to be self-sufficient, and how much it wants to integrate closely with the surrounding area. The basic principle would be to maximize yields within reasonable ecological limits. This gardening would produce vegetables and soft fruit outside and in greenhouses, and this would either be sold direct, or processed and sold at a higher price. The organization of such an enterprise would lend itself best to a Community Supported Agriculture (CSA) scheme, creating a new relationship between producer and consumer. This is covered more fully in Chapter 8 (p. 222).

Livestock. Some people want to eat animals and their products, and livestock forms a part of an integrated approach to working the land. For example pigs can be utilized as part of a garden rotation, clearing land of weeds, and manuring at the same time. Some households may like to keep a few chickens, but this is unlikely to cater for all the egg needs, and there is still the possibility of producing a surplus for sale. Many of these animals will eat waste products from the kitchen or the gardens, and this is a valuable way of turning waste into good food. Dairy produce would also be desirable, and I would think a mixture of goats and cows would be ideal in a temperate climate. Goats are less choosy about their fodder and utilize waste from the garden more readily. Cows would provide butter and more variety in cheese. Keeping of livestock is best done communally, as it requires frequent and regular care, which for one person or one small household might be very constricting. Milking, for instance, is best shared by a number of people, so that you get a lie-in occasionally, or an evening free!

Extensive arable crops. Crops such as wheat, potatoes, beans and peas for drying, animal fodder and many others are best grown in larger fields, and don't really suit the market garden approach. Here it is often fairly simple to produce far in excess of domestic needs, given that enough land and labour are available. Grain, such as wheat, barley and oats, can further be processed into bread and granolas or mueslis to create a higher value for sale. In contrast to market garden vegetables, arable crops store and transport well, and in many societies have formed one of the yardsticks of the economy.

Integration. All these four sections would be linked together, the animals providing manure for the land, and waste products used as fodder. Farming is a long-term process, requiring an overview in terms of years in order to be stable and efficient. It also requires careful co-ordination, so as to avoid shortages and surpluses. Anyone can raise a few vegetables on a patch of ground, but in order to make the best use of land and resources in a village situation, a certain amount of organization is necessary. There must also be the flexibility for individuals to expand into areas they are attracted to and to take on responsibilities.

Working groups. In a village situation we might think in terms of a specific number of groups who take on certain responsibilities. These might look like this:

1. Market garden planning.
2. Poultry co-ordination.
3. Pig farming.
4. Dairy farming and milk processing.
5. Arable crop co-ordination.
6. Experimental growing.
7. Machinery maintenance.
8. Marketing, sales and CSA.

Each group would have a focalizer or co-ordinator; this responsibility could be rotated. Individuals could easily work in more than one group and such lateral cross membership would be an aid to integration. All the groups would have to meet occasionally to make plans for the year or the season. Each group would keep some accounts of time and money in order to learn from their experience and be accountable to themselves and to each other.

What I have just described is an ideal model, a theory constructed out of my own imagination, trying to create a structure which would fit into a project. As with many designs for group situations, it is best to regard this as a starting point, an idea which the group can then change to fit in with their own ideas, a plan as a basis for change. Another approach would be to begin with a completely open agenda, a white piece of paper, and ask: 'What shall we do?' Personally I feel it's better to begin with something concrete and work from there.

When planning something so complex as an agricultural system for a village, it is best not to go into too much detail. Many things work themselves out as you go along. We set up a vegetable garden on the Kibbutz (actually as a result of a Permaculture design course). The location was not thought out too much, it was just a piece of ground between some houses which was not cared for. I never walked past this patch in my daily work and completely lost contact with what was going on there. A year later, during the follow up design course, we set up a similar garden next to the path to my office, where I went backwards and forwards several times a day. This garden I followed carefully and grew great vegetables.

Many small plots, located individually, can contribute significantly. This has to grow out of daily usage and personal habits. Location theories and detailed maps are great, but common sense and walking around the actual village is often just as good.

From PC to biodynamic to organic to chemical farming

We could see farming in terms of a spectrum, with classic Permaculture at one end and industrialized, mechanized and chemicalized hydroponics at the other. I'll be generous (though my gut feeling goes against this) and say that each kind of farming has its place and its appropriate application. I just hope no one gets offended if I don't spend much time on the chemical industrial end of the spectrum.

Somewhere round the middle of this spectrum you will find Integrated Pest Management (IPM). This is perhaps the most exciting and relevant approach developed over the last few years when it comes to the acceptability of change. It's fine to team up with a bunch of radicals and suggest the totally new approach of no-plough Permaculture cultivation. They might also buy the idea of linking up with the rest of the cosmos and with the spiritual world and going for biodynamics. But most farming in the western world is done by pretty conventional people; trying to promote things which are too radical will often generate conflict and rejection rather than positive change.

Which is where IPM comes in. You can start a conversation with a farmer who uses chemicals for weed and pest control by saying: 'Hey! Let's look at your pesticide and herbicide costs. How can we get them down? Maybe by using less! Great, let's look at how we can reduce the use of chemicals and still control weeds and pests.' By appealing to the economic sense, we might achieve co-operation and a reduction in poisons. It requires training to recognize and understand the weeds, pests, predators and parasites that plague all farmers. Don't for a moment think that organic and Permaculture gardens don't have these things.

It's important to understand that all things have their place and pests are indicators that something is out of balance — they require control, but not elimination — they have their place in nature too. It's ideal if you can control one pest by another, a predator, and try to keep damage at an acceptable level. The best way to do this is to set aside small pockets of wild growth, old rotting wood and tangled bushes with shelter; we call them Conservation Headlands. They don't need to take up any real space: a corner that's difficult to get into, a hedge, even a shelter belt from the prevailing wind. Let nature do the trick. Encourage birds, toads, frogs, lizards, centipedes and insects. Nature will regulate itself and adjust to a balance, but if the adjoining field where you are busy cultivating cabbages gets an attack of caterpillars, this is a veritable feast and free lunch for many birds. If you have already encouraged them in, they'll get rid of most of your problems.

You can go one step further and actively grow crops that repel pests and predators. Some of my favourites are marigolds, parsley, fennel, garlic and camomile. Try also chrysanthemums, aster, yarrow, anise and the Neem tree. There are mechanical techniques, such as barriers, traps, bands around trees and just plain hand-picking.

The principle here is to learn and study. Identify which kinds of pests and predators that are out there, find out about their life-cycles and their weak spots. If they go through a stage of being grubs, can they be picked off or eaten by a predator that you can introduce? Can you control them before they get to an egg-laying stage?

As a last resort, you might well reach for chemicals of one sort or another. Some are nature based, others less so. Some are recommended by all kinds of organic people, like derris dust, pyrethrum. Others are not so natural, but at the IPM level, the conventional farmer might carry on using them, but in smaller amounts. This is already a step in the right direction, if we can't eliminate the use of chemicals, at least we might reduce it. If a farmer sees this as working, he might be more open to going a step further, finding out about other natural strategies, and begin to look at organics and the use of compost and natural manures. This could be called the 'softly, softly' approach.

Getting back to our spectrum, we have begun more or less in the middle, but it might be useful to look at how it stretches out either side.

Biodynamic farming is based on the lecture cycle that Rudolf Steiner gave in 1924 to a group of farmers and scientists who were inspired and motivated by anthroposophy. Since then it has developed and grown, and can briefly be described as farming with a full cosmic consciousness, aware of the cycle of the stars and planets, and of co-operation with the spirit world. In *Farms of Tomorrow Revisited,* Trauger Groh summed up farming inspired by this system as follows:

— Remain in the realm of the living
— Different manures should be mixed and processed together
— Feeds for the livestock should come from the farm itself
— There should be a great diversity of plants
— Be aware of the carbon cycle, the circulation of organic matter
— Be aware of the silica cycle, encourage micro-biotic processes
— Create a harmonious balance between soil, plants, animals and landscapes
— Restore damaged natural environments
— Use biological insect and weed control

Work with the rhythms of the seasons, the earth, the moon, the sun and the planets.

One of the key ideas of biodynamic farming is to relate to the farm or the garden as a whole organism. One definition of an organism is something that has a defined boundary and is differentiated into several organs or departments. What is the boundary of our experience in nature? How far can we see and hear? Other senses come much closer: smell, touch, taste. We have in addition the concept of property with a clearly defined boundary. Within this boundary there is an identification with the land, we can work creatively with nature. The aim of biodynamic farming is to increase the fertility of the land and enhance the soil. The quality must increase and the surplus is a gift of nature. There should be as few external inputs as possible. The parts are to be of benefit to the whole.

While biodynamic farming is based on seeing the farm as a whole, and upon working with cosmic and spiritual forces, Permaculture is more aligned to mimicking nature as far as possible. Both of these we will find at the extreme end of our spectrum. Organic farming and gardening inhabit a place closer towards the middle. This is a farming concerned with doing away with chemicals, a reaction to the increasingly industrialized agriculture which spread world wide during the last century. With all respect to the organic farming movement — they have really done a terrific job — it can have tendency towards industrialization and can suffer from many of the larger problems that chemical farming does. It can be industrialized, and sometimes it can be difficult to see the difference between a chemical and an organic farm at first glance.

As we move through the centre of our spectrum, through IPM towards the heavy use of chemicals, we come to a system of farming of which the less said the better. Today the awareness of the problems created by chemical/industrial farming is growing fast, the demand for organic produce is expanding faster than the producers can keep up, and it's only a question of time and power struggles before organic farming becomes again the dominant force in farming.

It might be worth looking for a few moments at the extreme end of this spectrum, at hydroponics. This is possibly the least natural method of growing plants yet devised and furthest removed from the ideas central to Permaculture. A matrix of gravel, sometimes artificially produced, holds the plant roots, while nutrient-rich liquids are percolated through in a totally controlled environment, heat, light, humidity. There is a certain amount of pragmatism within Permaculture thinking, which says that in certain circumstances even the weirdest things make sense. While I lived in Israel I was in contact with a Permaculture centre in the Gaza Strip. I never got to visit the place, for political and security reasons, but I did see lots of pictures and talked to people who had been involved in setting the place up. Because of the situation there, lack of space, lack of land, pressure from the Israeli military presence, they had decided to set up their growing area on the roof of the house they were using. Throughout the Middle East, house roofs are used for lots of things. It really doesn't rain all summer long; the roof usually has a better breeze, cools down faster in the night, and is a generally useful space. Here the Gaza Permaculturists set up a greenhouse and built long tables filled with gravel. These were then flooded periodically with a liquid made from compost and manure, and plants were grown and harvested. This made a real difference to the nutrition of many people, and most of all raised awareness and positive hope among a whole neighbourhood. In the generally thawing political situation of the late nineties, this centre was to have been the springboard of a broad co-operative venture in organic farming between Israelis and Palestinians, one of the many co-operative initiatives destroyed by the Intifada that broke out in 2000.

The point of the story is to show that hydroponics has a place, however far removed from natural systems it might be. Rooftop gardening is a real strategy in urban situations and should not be dismissed. Permaculture is not just about having a subtropical plot and scattering seeds about and harvesting the haphazard results. It's about planning real life solutions to real life situations and helping people gain more power over their own lives. If hydroponics helps, do it!

Upacchi, Italy:
traditional crops as a basis

Date founded — 1990
Approximate number of residents — 40
Location — Tuscany
Spiritual or ideological affiliation — ecological
Visited — an overnight stay in the summer of 2000

The village was started in 1990 as a cooperative which bought the land, while the individual members bought houses privately. There was a strong ecological awareness right from the beginning and the houses were rebuilt with compost toilets, greywater reed bed treatment reused for irrigation, solar panels where affordable, and organic production both for home use and for sale. The community is made up of Italians and Germans, and in the late 1990s there had been some discussion and some disagreements about exactly which direction to take. When I visited, the cooperative had been dissolved and the land had been split up into private ownership, with two families owning most of the land and making their main income from its produce. The rest of the ten to fifteen families earned their main income through building work, teaching and as therapists.

Upacchi was the first Ecovillage in Italy, generating many articles and positive coverage in the press, especially the local press. Most of the buildings were built of local stone, using brick in some places, but keeping in character with the rest of the village. They were almost all rebuildings of the houses which existed from the previous village, which had laid abandoned for over thirty years. All the farming was organic: gardens, orchards and fields. There was an emphasis upon herb growing, with a large drying shed, using sun and wind. The herbs were bagged and sent to Germany for sale. There were also orchards of fruit and olive trees. Compost was made in large quantities, and the toilets were properly constructed compost toilets of the Clivus type, also generating acceptable fertilizer. The two farming families supplemented their income by renting a portion of chestnut forest, which they cleared and harvested annually. There were solar collectors for hot water, some photovoltaic generation, and several houses had large Kakelofen, which burn wood very efficiently and produce a large heat mass in the middle of the house. There was talk of setting up a wind generator. The site itself occupies steep land just west of Anghieri, and would be well suited to wind generation.

By upgrading traditional Italian 'peasant' crops to organic standards, and marketing them in Germany, the Upacchi members had found a niche which gave them a far higher cash return on their work than they would have otherwise got by selling to local middlemen.

LEFT. Reconstructed village housing.

BELOW. The village is situated on the top of a hill.

RIGHT. Village housing.

OPPOSITE ABOVE. Village housing undergoing reconstruction.

OPPOSIT BELOW. Herb drying shed.

BELOW. Herb gardens interplanted between trees.

Agriculture as power: advice to growers and consumers

Agriculture today is about power, not feeding people. It is an industry (really industrialized) which takes responsibility from people and makes them dependent and powerless, turning that power into profits for the few, essentially multinational corporations. In the US today only 10 cents of each dollar of disposable income is spent on food. Of that 10 cents, only 1 cent actually reaches the farmer, the producer. The other 9 are lost on food processing and food kilometres, transport. Big farms have expanded beyond their ecological and social niches.

According to Vandana Shiva, writing in *Resurgence* magazine in September 2000, wheat prices in the US dropped from $5.75 to $2.43 a bushel. In India, from 1999 to 2000, prices for coffee dropped from Rs.60 to Rs.18 per kg and prices of oilseeds declined by more than 30 percent. The farmers were clearly getting poorer. But the opposite was true of the companies that stood between the producer and the consumer. Cereal companies like Kellogg's, Quaker Oats and General Mills enjoyed return on equity rates of 56 percent, 165 percent and 222 percent respectively. A bushel of corn was giving the farmer less than $4, while a bushel of cornflakes was costing the customer $133! The cereal companies were 186 to 740 times more profitable than the farms.

No wonder the farmers are in trouble!

Even though we grow enough food to feed everyone in the world, there are 800 million people starving. Farming itself is producing enough, it is the economics surrounding farming that is incapable of getting the products to the right people in the right quantities. The picture that John Steinbeck portrayed in *The Grapes of Wrath*, of starving people watching the authorities burning food, is now repeated at a level so vast that it is difficult for us to comprehend.

We need to empower people to feed themselves. The techniques of farming are many and varied, and can be divided up into a spectrum of practices. We need first to look at the bigger picture, of how farming fits into our society, at the relationship between the producer and the consumer. In order to do this, let's divide up the world into two kinds of people, keep things simple. There are those who eat food and those who grow food. Let's look at what we can do in each case.

If you eat food (most of us are in this position I hope), you can try to grow your own, a few herbs on a windowsill, even just in a flower pot. Anyone can do this, even in an apartment in a high-rise block. In fact, starting small is a really good way of making a difference to yourself. If you have some friends (if you don't, this might be a way of getting some) get together and grow food as a group, find a small waste lot and get going. A community garden in a neighbourhood has a social function as well as being a good use of the land resource. What you can't grow, buy, but choose where you buy from. When you buy from an international corporation, you support that corporation, in the end they make their money from you and me spending what we have on what they offer. They make their profits by externalizing the costs of pollution clean-up, increased health care and social disruption. We pay the real cost of the product and they take the difference. When we buy organic and local it might seem, at first sight, to be more expensive, but as more and more people do so, they help to create more robust local communities which need less transport, less pollution clean-up and have less unemployment.

The friends you have made growing a few cabbages on a waste lot might be interested in bulk buying what they can't get round to growing. You could form a buying cooperative, a Community Supported Agriculture (CSA) scheme, or a Local Economic Trading Scheme (LETS). The easiest way to begin is to contact a local organic farmer, buy a few sacks of potatoes and divide them up amongst you. This cuts out the middleman and his expenses, giving the farmer a better price and the customer a lower one. When you avoid buying from multinationals, from chemical farms or from countries far away, you put your money into the alternatives. This makes a difference!

There are many different models of CSA out there being practised and we will go into more detail in Chapter 8, Alternative Economics (p. 200). What they all have in common is that they are setting up a new relationship between grower and consumer, and largely cutting out the middleman. This implies less supermarkets, less transport, less standardization, and at the same time more varieties, fresher vegetables, higher income for the producer and savings for the consumer.

Commercial market gardens often supply a distant market through one or more middlemen. This results in crops being grown so that vegetables are ready at the same time. The whole carrot crop will be lifted at one time, boxed up and driven to the wholesaler. There are some benefits to this, ease of planning, simpler labour organization, transport and so on. There are also drawbacks, which affect the consumer more than the producer. These have to do with freshness and which varieties are grown.

CSAs have evolved completely different growing cycles. Here the emphasis has become on supplying a box of mixed fresh vegetables to each household every week. The Garden Plan and the Garden Schedule (see Appendix, pp. 251–53) will need to be used in order to ensure a steady supply of a wide variety of different vegetables. The techniques of cultivation will need to be learned well, when people join such a scheme, they expect to get something in return for their weekly

contribution. It may well be best, if you are a group with relatively little gardening experience, to either hire or engage someone with that experience, or to go
through a few growing seasons just supplying yourselves before reaching out to
give a commitment to others. It's better to wait and do the thing properly, than
to rush into it and give the idea a bad name by failing to deliver your commitment. CSA is a two-way street. The community commits itself to supporting the
grower, but the grower also commits to supporting the community.

If you grow food, look for local markets to satisfy local needs. It might seem
lucrative to land a contract with a supermarket, but you might find that next
year they have found a bunch of poverty stricken Roumanian farmers to supply
the same vegetable at a much lower cost! As we know from following the media,
the international scene is fast moving and dynamic, which means in food terms,
unstable. This week the supermarket chain has landed a great contract for garlic
from Argentina, next week another container load arrives from South Africa.
You could grow it on your farm or market garden, and supply a steady amount
to your neighbourhood. If it is of good quality, and you create a relationship of
friendship and trust, those customers will keep on coming back.

You can link up with organized groups. There are growing numbers of veg-
etarians, organic growers and restaurants that specialize in vegetarian or
organic foods. Those people in your locality who eat food, but can't grow
enough, might be starting to organize a CSA or LETS scheme (see Chapter 8,
Alternative Economics, p. 200). Concentrate upon quality rather than quantity
— perhaps heritage varieties might be attractive to those who still remember
the taste of Cox's Orange Pippin and might even prefer them to the rather
bland and watery Golden Delicious apple. If you can find a steady local market, it might be worthwhile to consider varieties that yield for a longer time,
spreading their ripening time over weeks or even months, rather than a variety
that ripens all at once, giving you logistical problems by having to harvest the
whole lot in one go, while the fleet of trucks is waiting with their engines running.

Grow organic if you can. Within the organic sector, biodynamic produce is
in great demand, it takes more skill and training, but that's exactly the point.
Bring skill back into growing food, care for the soil, the plants and the environment. Farming is not just a technique, applying machines and chemicals
according to a timetable laid down by a salesman and presented in a glossy
brochure. Farming is a craft, a skill, ultimately an art. The farmer is an artist,
his canvas the land itself. The farmer who 'paints by numbers' is insulting his
own intelligence.

To increase the value of the food grown on your farm, you can try to add
value on site. Gherkins can be pickled and sold in jars, berries and fruit made

into jam, wheat baked into bread and milk made into yoghurt and cheese. Maybe this can be done together with the CSA or LETS group operating in your area.

Within an Ecovillage all this is much easier; you are already meeting each other for a wide range of reasons, and to add in a discussion of how you can grow things together and distribute amongst yourselves is no big sweat. If there is a possibility of having even a modest surplus of a few things, this is the big opportunity to connect with the local community immediately surrounding the Ecovillage. Buying things you can't grow from local organic farmers also creates that connection. You could galvanize a district into action by being the seed that creates a local economy, based around the production, processing and consumption of food.

With farming, it is important not to work too many hours, it is easy to get totally obsessed with the amount of work that could be done, that needs to be done. Time spent in contemplation is time well spent, and it's vital to achieve a balance between work and other activities. That's one reason why having several part-time people working at gardening and farming is so much more healthy all round. Another piece of general advice is not to buy too much from the outside world. Everything you buy costs money and that needs to be earned by selling produce, and usually in the process a certain amount of that cash gets lost in taxes, transport and other hidden things which push the price up. The secret is to be reasonable and pragmatic; it's a good idea to discuss things beforehand, asking questions like: Could we do without it? Can we make it/supply it ourselves?

During the farming year there are often little pockets of slack time in between the busy periods. It's a good idea to arrange a retreat for the farmers and gardeners once a year. A time to step back from day-to-day work, let some others tend to the absolutely necessary things, like milking the cows or watering the plants for a couple of days, and take the regular workers off to some place away from the farm to think and talk about what you have done, how you are doing it, why and what you might want to do in the future. When thinking about new initiatives it might be worth pondering the following angle: is this new venture inspired by the realm of the spirit or does it come from a motivation from the realm of money? This is not necessarily a loaded question, it's not certain that all things that are money-inspired are bad, but it's a good thing to be clear about why we do things, and it makes a difference how we can get other people involved. A spiritually inspired venture will often get others involved out of a motivation to contribute, whereas a money-inspired venture will get people involved because they can profit from it financially. Both options are OK, but it's good to be clear where we stand.

Kimberton Hills Camphill, Pennsylvania, USA: anthroposophical eco-architecture

Date founded — 1972
Approximate number of residents — 200–300 people
Location — east of Philadelphia in Pennsylvania
Spiritual or ideological affiliation — anthroposophical
Visited — overnight in the summer of 2004

The Camphill villages contain nearly all the elements that are included in the definition of Ecovillages that the Global Ecovillage Network began with in the early 1990s. In fact, it can easily be argued that the Camphill network was establishing Ecovillages fifty years ago, way ahead of anyone else!

In 1995, on his way to the conference in Findhorn that established the GEN, Albert Bates visited a number of Camphill villages in Northern England and Scotland. He still acknowledges the inspiration he received, especially in the field of wastewater treatment.

Joan Allen is one of the leading architects within the Camphill network, having designed houses, chapels and community halls for Camphill villages throughout the world for decades. She now lives in what is sometimes referred to as retirement, but seems to be as active as ever, at Kimberton Hills. She showed us her latest project, a care centre for the elderly, combining a residence, a nurses station and a retirement home built for an elderly Camphill sympathizer, which will be handed over to the village after she no longer needs it. A complex of houses, built around an open courtyard, facing the sun, with a water sculpture in the middle, and a wastewater treatment featuring Flowforms leading out into the woods behind. Natural materials throughout, colour schemes based on Goethe's theory of colour, and her latest discovery, light tubes. These are silvered tubes, connecting a translucent light catcher set into the roof, leading the light down into interior spaces. These then have a glow of light, enough to dispense with electric lighting during the day. Natural, cheap, simple and giving the interior of the building the rhythm of the day and the night.

In the few hours I had at Kimberton Hills, Joan made sure I saw their Community Supported Agriculture scheme. A classic veggie-box arrangement, with customers coming once a week to pick up their produce.

ABOVE. CSA pick-up point ready for a day's work.

BELOW. Community Supported Agriculture pick-up point with the first customer of the day already loading up.

RIGHT. Care centre for the elderly under construction. Rain water is collected off the roof and stored in the ground. Natural daylight is fed into the interior of the building via mirrored light tubes, saving electricity during the day.

BELOW. The bio-dynamic vegetable gadens supplying the CSA.

Structure and behaviour of soil

Good soils contain air, water, minerals and organic material. It is important that there is a balance of these things. We can talk about physical, chemical and biological elements. Average farm topsoil contains 25 percent air, 25 percent water, 49 percent minerals and 1 percent organic material. Virgin soils might contain up to 8 percent organic matter and some soils can go up to 20 percent.

Plants need a whole range of chemicals found naturally in the soil and in the air. From the air they need carbon, hydrogen and oxygen. For this reason it's really important that the structure of the soil allows air to penetrate and circulate. From the soil itself they need nitrogen, phosphorus and potassium, these are the three main ones, but without the trace elements of sulphur, calcium, iron and magnesium, the plants would be sickly and prone to diseases and pests.

Nitrogen is a main constituent of proteins; it gives dark green foliage, feeding the leaves, stalks and stems. Too much of it causes over-rapid growth and weakens the tissues. For this reason compost is best for the plants, for the nitrogen is released slowly and evenly over time. With chemically applied nitrogen there is a heavy rush, causing overgrowth, and then the nitrogen is often flushed away by rain, depleting the soil, leaving weak plants; the nitrogen then goes on into groundwater and eventually streams and lakes, which become over-rich and choked by algal growth.

Phosphorus stimulates root formation, giving a vigorous start to seedlings. It is highly sensitive to the acidity in the soil: above pH 7.3 and below pH 5.0 it becomes locked up and unavailable. It gives winter hardiness to crops that can stand some cold and frost.

Potassium forms and transports starch sugars and other carbohydrates. Root crops such as potatoes, carrots and beetroots respond well. Too much potassium results in excess water content, which makes crops susceptible to frost injury and pest incursions.

Bacteria in a compost rich soil will withdraw mineral ions, uniting with them to form organic molecules. This will form colloids which can be absorbed by plants. Thus trace minerals are incorporated into the plants. In vegetables grown without compost there has been found to be a general decline in trace minerals, whereas tomatoes grown organically can have up to 1,900 percent (!) more iron.

Magnesium shortage can be a problem on new land: a dressing of ground dolomite, not more than 1 kg per square metre will help and give a good long lasting supply.

If the soil is clay, add as much compost or organic material as possible to lighten it. Sawdust, leaf mould, manures, gypsum, even sand. A green manure such as rye, grass or a legume can be grown and ploughed in. Do not add coal ash! After the addition of green manures and crop residues the soil bacteria produce polysaccharides, which are glue-like materials which stick the soil particles into aggregate. This leaves space between the soil particles for air, water and roots to penetrate easily. Tremendous amounts can be produced. Decaying alfalfa or oat straw have been found to produce between 2,200 and 1,800 kg of polysaccharides per acre, a week after being added.

Too much potassium in the soil can block the uptake of magnesium, which is a very important trace element.

If the soil is too alkaline, that is, if the lime content is too high, add green manure,or any organic material you can lay your hands on. Aerate the soil with leaf mould, sawdust, wood chips or acid peat moss.

Whenever there is empty space, grow your own compost. The common annual sunflower is good, when 3–4 feet high, they can be pulled, soil dusted off and put straight onto the compost heap. Grow them a number of times rather than letting them grow too big. Mustard or lupins can be grown in the same way. The latter are very good, as they fix nitrogen and a few plants can be left in to give seed for the next year. Twig prunings can be burnt and the ash is full of potassium, as is most wood ash, and this can either be spread straight onto the soil, or incorporated into the compost pile. Leaves are full of lignins and hemi celluloses, which help with the moisture retaining characteristics of the soil. You can make a leaf bin, treading the leaves well down and leaving for at least two years, three years is even better. If you make one each year, you will have one ready for use every year after a three year period. Don't mix leaves and weeds, as the composting process of leaves is very slow and does not generate enough heat to kill off weed seeds.

Compost can be used for mulching instead of incorporating it into the soil. This keeps your weeds down, and the compost is gradually incorporated into the soil by micro organisms and large insect burrowers. Always think about what is living and working in your garden, and let them do the work for you.

Composting was worked out by the early organic farmers during the 1920s. Working in India, the most well known method was called the Indore method. This consists of building a bin with wooden sides to contain the material and spreading a layer of brush on the base of the heap. This was to allow air to be drawn in below, and putting stakes upright in the heap as it was built up allowed the air to circulate when they were pulled out after the heap was complete. Composting is an aerobic process, if air is excluded and an anaerobic process is initiated, fermenting and a kind of pickling will take place, resulting in a useless, evil smelling and wet material. Green matter, finely shredded, manure, soil and lime are added in layers, in a ratio of about 75 percent green matter and 25 percent of manure, with just a sprinkling of soil and lime. The heap is turned after three weeks and again after five. The compost should be ready in three months.

In our experience we did not find it practical to be so scientific and exact. With several years of experience behind us, we found a system that worked for us, giving us good amounts of compost regularly. We constructed three bins at the back end of the garden, the first was a large bin with an open front. Here went all the weeds and greens from the vegetable garden, whatever came out went in, often whole plants with roots and bits of soil still attached. Leaves swept up from paths in the autumn, together with the straw from the floor of the chicken shed whenever we felt moved to clean that out. Kitchen waste went first into the chicken run, to be picked over by them for any useful seeds or insects from cleaning vegetables. The centre of their run was pretty bare, and they scattered the stuff about while going through it. Once in a while we felt motivated to rake the stuff up, whatever was left, together with their droppings. This was then bucketed over into the first bin together with anything else that was going.

Next to the large first bin we had two smaller ones, also wooden, but with a front slat. All the sides and fronts were detachable. The first time we did this we merely turned the large pile over into the bin next to it and put back the wall between them. Now we had an empty first bin, ready for the next lot of weeds and stuff and a full second bin. By the time the first large bin was full again, it was time to take down walls, fork the second bin into the third space, the first into the second and we had again an empty first bin, a full second and third. Next time around, when the first bin was again full, it was time to get out the overalls, the wheelbarrow and the fork. Now the third bin was pretty much ready for use, and it was dug out, wheeled over to whichever part of the garden needed it most and spread around on the soil. Then the second bin was forked into the third space, the first into the second and there we were, ready to go again.

This system gave us a good amount of compost pretty regularly throughout the year, more in the summer than the winter, of course, and was the least labour intensive. All kinds of stuff went onto the heap. We made nettle and comfrey tea, fermenting the leaves in a large tub full of water. This was used to water plants, and the gunge at the bottom was thrown onto the heap too. Ash from our wood burning stoves went on, all the stuff from brewing beer and making wine, sawdust from the wood pile — in short, anything organic that was produced from our life.

Kibbutz Ketura, Israel:
desert agriculture

Date founded — 1973
Approximate number of residents — *ca.* 225
Location — southern Arava Valley
Spiritual or ideological affiliation — Reform Jewish
Visited — several times throughout the 1990s

In a forbidding climate where rainfall is so rare that some years it doesn't rain at all, the only way that Ketura can exist is to pump water up from deep aquifers or import it by pipeline from elsewhere. Despite the ecological drawbacks to this, there are other, over-riding, geo-political and social justifications for locating communities in this area of the Arava Valley. Ketura took on these environmental challenges and turned them into advantages.

A long-term experimental desert farm was set up, testing new varieties of drought-resistant crops. These might take a decade or more to develop, and were in turn dependant upon other technology and marketing of the resulting fruits as juices or jams. This is long-term investment, but in a world threatened by global warming, is exactly what is needed.

The clean desert environment, virtually free of agricultural or industrial pollution, was the ideal place to grow medicinal plants, which were exported to Switzerland where they were processed into natural medicines for a global market. This is a classic example of turning special conditions into an advantage by exploiting a niche market that few other places could develop.

The combination of environmental awareness, and an appreciation that the unstable political situation of the Middle East required co-operation between the countries and peoples involved, led to the setting up of a university department of ecology. Together with Tel Aviv University, a degree standard ecology course was created, inviting students from Israel, Egypt, Jordan and the Palestinian Authority to learn and work together. The idea was that many of these graduates would eventually become professionals within their own countries and would have an informal 'old boys' network which would encourage co-operation at an international level.

ABOVE. The forbidding desert landscape surrounding the Kibbutz.

RIGHT. Ecovillage training group in 1998 in the experimental arid forestry orchards.

RIGHT. Students from Egypt and Jordan at the Arava Institute, Ketura, in 1998.

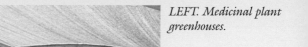

LEFT. Medicinal plant greenhouses.

BELOW. The Arava Valley, one of the driest places in the world.

After making compost for a few years it became a matter of feeling for it, of intuitively knowing what was right and what was wrong. In many ways making compost for the garden is not unlike making food for the family, in fact this analogy goes much further. One of the fundamental principles of organic cultivation is that you take care of the soil, feeding it the right nutrients in order to build up a healthy humus. This then takes care of the plants, in turn producing healthy growth. The same is true of human beings: give them good food, plenty of exercise, fresh air and they will generally be pretty healthy. But just as in cooking food, when making compost you first need to follow some fundamental rules before you can make it just from the feel of things. Have a look at the table for the active ingredients in different kinds of compost ingredients (p. 255). I never felt inclined to learn any of these, but found it useful to compare things when they became available to us, in order to get a feel for how much we might use and whether I should look actively for other ingredients to balance things out. When you make compost regularly, you will also get a feel for how different heaps work out differently for the garden and can then apply them in the places most needed. In short, time spent thinking about your compost is never wasted.

Plants and their spirits

Plants have senses. According to an article in the *New Scientist*, September 1998, they can detect and react to light, sounds, chemicals, vibrations, touch, water, gravity and temperature. By July 2002 the same magazine went as far as reporting that Tony Trewavas of the University of Edinburgh was finding good evidence that plants had also developed reactions that could only be described as showing intelligence: 'A plant's computational capacity can probably match that of many animals.' The plant learns by trial and error and modifies its strategy.

In the *Secret Life of Plants,* Peter Tompkins and Christopher Bird found that plants did all kinds of amazing things, like sensing moods and feelings in people around them and having responses to situations which were not merely physical. At a plant workshop I attended here in Norway in 2002, plant biologist Dan Winter wired up a tree to his computer and we watched the response of the tree as we alternately projected love and hate onto it. There was a clear response in the electromagnetic field associated with the tree.

Try it yourself! A simple experiment goes like this: set up a number of sprouting trays with the same variety of seed from the same source. Take simple tap water. Water a third of the trays straight from the tap, ordinary tap water with no treatment. Take the same tap water, put it in a jar and meditate on the jar of water, showering it with love and security. You might feel silly, but you don't need to tell anyone about it. You will know if you are doing this with genuine feelings or not. Clearly it will only work if you are honest with yourself. Use that water to sprout another third. Take the same tap water, fill a jar half full and shake it rhythmically for five, yes, time yourself, five minutes and then use that for the last third. Note how the sprouting differs in the three sets of trays.

How we describe this phenomenon is not entirely clear to me. The *New Scientist* people maintain that plants have intelligence, others (*Secret Life of Plants*) maintain they have feelings, yet others again (biodynamic farmers) that they have spirit. Maybe it's not that important how we define this, or which words we use. What is important is that we work with plants holistically, that we use our intelligence, our feelings and our spirit. That plants do have spirit seems not to be in doubt for shamans and for practitioners of biodynamic agriculture. It might be just those of us in the middle, neither shamans nor biodynamic farmers, who have problems accepting this. Perhaps here we have a confluence of one of the oldest spiritual systems with one of the more recent. Whatever we believe, though, it is clearly important what we do, so let's get down to real gardening and farming.

Mulch gardening

In a natural forest, unless the trees are very dense, the space under and around the tree gives an opportunity for other plants, many of them annuals, which grow and die in one season. In addition to being pretty and giving shelter and sustenance to a vast number of insects and other creatures, these plants have a function in soil improvement. As they die and rot down, they provide a cover which creates soil as it decays. This is called a natural mulch. In some ways this was the Permaculture breakthrough, something which Wes Jackson and Masanobu Fukuoka also perceived: that generally speaking, in nature the soil is not turned over and exposed to sun, rain and wind (ploughing) but is added to from the top by a continuously decaying layer of organic matter (mulch).

We have a number of different strategies for keeping our garden area free of other plants, whatever they are, let us call them weeds. We can just clear them away, but they will come back after a few weeks, from sprouting seeds or re-growth of roots. We can spray them with a poison, which will get rid of them for a good long time, even a residual poison which will linger in the soil and inhibit growth for several seasons. Even though the limited use of some poisons might be tolerated, (you purists might just ignore that statement) it should be our aim to do without them altogether.

What we can do is clear the weeds away and put down a mulch composed of various things which will eventually break down in a natural process. On top of the clear soil we can put a layer of wet kitchen waste, such as vegetable peelings and leftover food. This will start things off by going into decay mode pretty instantly. On top of that I have got the best results by using thick cardboard or layers of newspaper. Some people react to the possibility of chemicals in the newsprint, but I have never found anything in the literature indicating that this is a problem. The fact is though that brown cardboard is easier to put down, very easy to get hold of — there seems to be mountains of it accumulating outside even the smallest shop — and it contains very little other than recycled cellulose. Just remember to strip off the tape, if there is any.

On top of the cardboard, you can put a thick layer (at least 10 cm and even 20 cm is fine) of old straw or grass clippings. Anything organic that will break down, but does not contain too many seeds will do. For this reason, hay is not recommended, it could contain really a lot of weed seeds. One of the best results I ever got was using spoiled silage from a dairy farm. A thick layer of that totally inhibited weed growth, began decaying straight away, warmed up the soil, and produced a great crop of clean and tasty potatoes in record time.

The secret of this system is the mulch soil interface, the place of action. Here there is a continuous activity at the micro level. It's a bit like having a very thin and active compost heap happening right across the garden. Soil is a living thing, it thrives on stacks of microbial activity. This system of breaking down the soil components continuously releases nutrients for plant growth. Adding mulch from time to time makes sure there is a supply, and at the same time inhibits weed growth. Any weeds that do get going in these upper layers either wither from lack of moisture once a drying wind springs up, or can be pulled and left to die and decay on the surface. No more back-breaking weeding and carting off of weeds! The deeper layers of cardboard retain moisture and keep it dark and wet. In the gardens that I established in the Middle East, we could get by with minimal watering throughout the summer with this system. Down below the thick layers of cardboard the soil retained most of its moisture for a long time.

Small scale vegetable planning

I must confess to being quite impressed by the total anarchic just-scatter-a-load-of seeds-about model, but have never had much success with it. It may be that it is best suited to a tropical climate where seasonality is less important, and the vegetables just come and come regardless of the time of year.

For those who want to try it, however, it really is just that. Prepare some ground, mulch it to cover the weeds, make a mix of your favourite vegetable seeds and throw them about as evenly as possible, water them well in and put a very light mulch over them to protect against birds and drying out. Wait and harvest!

It is always worth experimenting with these things. There are really two things to be harvested in gardening, one is the produce itself, the vegetables, the other harvest is experience and knowledge. You can only eat so much, sure you can give away your surplus or trade it, but knowledge and experience you can never get enough of.

Here's one little number that we found really good to clear new ground in a temperate cool climate. It worked well for us in Lincolnshire in the east of England. We hoed the ground roughly (this was before I got into mulch gardening, today I would just mulch it over thickly, even less work!) and put in new potatoes over the whole patch except for one little corner where we prepared the soil more thoroughly and sowed leek seeds. New potatoes come through fast and you harvest them small, so we were enjoying the first of them after just a couple of months. As they grew to maturity we cleared the lot, kept what we wanted for ourselves (including seed potatoes), and gave away or traded the rest. After harvesting potatoes the ground is pretty well worked over and the weeds are either gone or dug in; then we just levelled the ground and planted out the leeks we had in that little corner. By this time they were just the right size. Now leeks grow slowly and can stand right through a winter even with spells of freezing. We ate them over a long period of time, during the worst of the weather I was prising them out of the frozen soil with a crowbar! Next spring the ground was perfect for gardening: we could put some chickens on to do a last little clean up, throw some compost on and were ready to grow anything we wanted.

From my experience in vegetable gardening, I have found that planning pays off. During the years that Ruth and I had a little smallholding in Lincolnshire we supplied ourselves with most of our vegetable needs from our own garden and developed a good model for organizing our garden, which worked well for us. This being over twenty years ago, my memory plays tricks on me when it comes to all the details, but I do remember feeling overwhelmed by the amount of work we were faced with during that first year and trying to find some way for it not to be so chaotic. What we ended up doing was taking enormous sheets of paper, writing down every variety of vegetable as a list down the left hand side and dividing up the paper into twelve columns along the top, for the months of the year. Then we wrote down the task associated with each vegetable for each month. Somehow it seemed much easier for us to have a list of specific tasks rather than a general feeling that we need to do lots of weeding, lots of planting out and lots of sowing all in one go. As we did tasks we ticked them off, noting the date, and in this way adjusted according to timing and seasonality for the following year. By doing this the lists became more and more specific to our location each year.

Different varieties of vegetables take different nutrients out of the ground, and have a variety of pests and other problems associated with them. For this reason we found it best to organize our vegetables into groups and rotate these round the garden. The garden we divided up into four main plots and gradually fenced them in with netting, so that by opening gates we could let the chickens into one plot for a length of time. In this way we could let the chickens finish off the last few things that were in there, scratch around for any insects or pests and they would give a good manure or top dressing while they were there. The groups were rotated around the plots year by year; all the years we lived there we enjoyed a good supply of vegetables and had a good surplus to give away and to trade. We had no fridge and no freezer, we pickled, preserved and dried our crops and in the dry and cool climate of east Lincolnshire we managed to have something fresh off the garden in every month of the year.

6. Water and Sewage

Hooking into the water cycle without messing it up

The planet water

How we came to call our planet earth or *terra* I really don't know. Had we been South Sea islanders or sailors on the high seas, we would surely have been aware that most of our planet is covered in water. When we saw the first pictures of our planet from space, this was one of the most striking observations.

Our planet is water. Water covers about sixty-six percent of its surface and, funnily enough, that's about the percentage of water in our bodies. Ponder that for a while! You really think it's a coincidence?

The ecological water cycle keeps this substance moving continuously from place to place and from state to state. I mean from liquid, to ice, to vapour (not from Tennessee to Michigan). On its way round the planet, water picks up other substances, either by total integration, called solution, or by literally picking it up, in suspension. In this way DDT found its way from the gardens and farms of America to the penguins of Antarctica in only a few years. Today, the artificial substances that we release into nature are guaranteed to be around the world in 80 months or thereabouts!

There are about 326 cubic miles of water, of which 0.02 percent is available as fresh water to which we have access. That's it! There isn't any more, it's not a substance that just creates itself or is unlimited. It's really important to understand that fact. We don't live in an unlimited water universe. When we pour chemical pollutants into this 0.02 percent we manage to pollute all the rest. That's not very smart for the future of our world. Luckily there are natural systems in place which can deal with a certain amount of pollution over time and dilute it. But when we overload the system, release life-changing substances or genetically changed organisms, we are creating new situations which our planet is not designed to cope with.

Water is essentially a mysterious and magical substance which behaves in surprising ways. It expands when frozen, most other materials contract. It is a fluid with no shape, yet carves shapes in the substances it passes across which are instantly recognizable as 'water carved.' It is so soft that we can hardly hold it in our hands, yet it wears down rock, the hardest substance we have. In its

Terre d'Enaille, Belgium:
sewage solutions

Date founded — 1992
Approximate number of residents — 15
Location — southern Belgium
Spiritual or ideological affiliation — environmental
Visited — three days in the summer of 1998

This community was very small, with so few residents it's hard to define it as a village. But it did have a much larger and wider group of active supporters. They owned extensive forests which had been set aside as protected areas for wildlife, and formed the basis of research areas and were open to the wider membership just once a year.

What impressed me most of all at Terre d'Enaille was their sewage treatment. Their housing was at the top of a small hill, and the wastewater was collected together and ran into ponds and wetlands strung in a series below the houses. Gravity led the water from one into the next, each one with an ecology which treated the water, taking out various pollutants. At the bottom the water was clean enough to support fish, and could be used as irrigation on the vegetable gardens which lay on the flat land below, or it could be diverted into local streams.

The biomass growing in the wetlands and around the ponds was regularly harvested and used as food for the adjoining worm farm, where it was turned into worm castings which in turn were used as compost and soil enricher in the gardens.

This system, small as it was, displayed a wonderful cycle of use and re-use. The live fish provided a monitor of water cleanliness. The breakdown of the waste products, separated out by growing plants and transformed by the digestive action of the worms, provided enough biological breaks to ensure that pathogenic materials were effectively filtered out of the cycle.

Terre d'Enaille later had a dispute with the Global Ecovillage Network over attitudes to capital, and formally ended any association with them.

LEFT. The worm farm stretching down the hill.

LEFT. Vegetable gardens manured and irrigated from the wastewater treatment plant.

ABOVE. Looking up at the wastewater treatment plant.

RIGHT. The final pool in the wastewater treatment plant.

BELOW. The buildings of the village at the top of the slight rise.

liquid form, it is the basis of life. Without water, we die within a few days.

The water supply is essentially a village concern and here the Ecovillage is clearly the most effective agency. To let each single household arrange for its own independent water supply seems to me unnecessarily anarchistic. There are only a few sources of water: rain (we might include condensation from fog here, but that's a really localized and rare possibility), surface water, shallow wells and deep-bore drilling.

Collecting rain water seems pretty sensible. Unless you live in an area with serious air pollution, this will be clean, easily collected from the roofs of buildings and its supply dictated by the rainfall regime which is usually fairly easy to determine from the meteorological records. Most houses built today have a system for leading roof water away from the house, to divert this into barrels or tanks is so simple; just put the barrel or the tank where the gutter downpipes are! There doesn't seem to me to be any excuse not to do this. Collecting condensation is more complicated. I have read about systems in South America, where nets are hung up across the prevailing winds coming in off the Pacific, which collect enough moisture to trickle down and create the possibility for plants to grow. Plants in desert areas may collect dew on their leaves and by mulching with large rounded stones, this may also help collect a few precious drops. These are all strategies that should be considered, but I don't see that they will make a significant difference to the water supply that is needed today by people. One figure I saw was 22 litres per day per person, for drinking, cooking and washing. For a family of five, that's a lot of water every day! To supply water for a whole village, you need to get serious.

Surface water may be contaminated; indeed, in most populated areas, it seems certain that it will be. If you have farmland around you, you will find the run-off contains all kinds of fertilizers and chemicals, unless it is an area that is predominantly organic (pretty rare!). If you live in an industrial area, it could be even worse. Roads also contaminate with oil and rubber residues being washed off into surrounding streams and ponds. Test the water regularly; it might be OK for flushing toilets and watering the garden, but you will probably need another source for drinking (rain water, maybe).

Shallow wells, which we've used for many years, suffer from the same problems as surface water. However, filtering through several metres of soil could well clean up most of the contaminants; again, regular testing will be required to monitor the quality. In most countries, drilling for water, whether shallow or deep, is subject to local controls and co-ordination with other bore holes; you need to check with your local authority. This will also give you a chance to find out about the quality and the regularity of supply. In these days of overpumping and falling water levels, you need to be aware of your local situation.

Deep bores pose a different set of problems. By pumping from deep down, you will be tapping into water supplies that have built up over centuries and often millennia. If you can determine what the replenishment rate might be, you will have some idea of how much you can pump. If you take out more than is being replaced, you will deplete the supply; you can work out by very simple mathematics how long it will take you to pump the water supply dry. It might even be worse: in coastal Israel the fear is that the local aquifer will be reduced to such low pressure that salt sea water will be sucked in and contaminate the existing water — forever! Clearly, if sustainability is one of our aims, it's really important to get our water supply worked out. Another problem with deep water is that it usually has high mineral content. It's been sitting around down there for a long time, giving the minerals time to dissolve into it. When this is used for watering the soil, the minerals or salts will slowly build up, causing soil salinity. Better to concentrate on using rain water for the plants, you might want to use the deep water for drinking and other domestic uses.

There are a few principles we might want to keep in mind as we plan for water:

— Use water as many times as possible as it passes through your system.
— Slow down the water flow across your property.
— Use gravity to move water around as much as you can.
— Solve the problem of contaminated water as close to the source of contamination as possible.
— Ensure that water leaving your property is clean.

You might want to refer back to these principles periodically in your water planning. Looking at the landscape planning, the best general solution you can come up with is to plant trees and rip up the soil. Creating deep cracks without turning the soil over is a very effective way to help deep penetration of runoff. Planting trees will further help this. Here again, starting high up, keeping the water at a higher level, and letting it gradually percolate downhill into cultivated areas and eventually to ponds and streams is the best strategy. The Permaculture idea of multifunctionalism is very clear here. Trees can give yields of fruit and timber as well as retaining water and sheltering a great variety of other organisms and creatures.

To slow down run-off and further encourage penetration into the soil, swales can be constructed wherever possible. These are the very opposite of drainage ditches, being shallow ditches dug along the contour lines to stop the water running away, often very effective when combined with roads and other places where you do need the water to be led away. They also create two different micro-ecologies which is always useful: a slightly wetter condition at the bottom of the swale and a slightly drier on the top of the bank thrown up downslope. You might want to accentuate this by judicious planting, or just let nature take its course. By choosing perennials, you might get an extra little crop from these swales. In the same vein, if you have wet places on your property, consider planting them with appropriate plants rather than draining them.

It's amazing how effective this approach to water management can be. In an interview with Rajendra Singh in the *New Scientist*, September 2002, he described his work in rejuvenating rivers in Rajasthan in India. This area had suffered severe deforestation in the 1970s; the soil had dried out and the rivers no longer ran. Village after village was being deserted, as people no longer had a basis for their farming livelihoods. In the mid 1980s, Rajendra moved to a small village and began constructing johad's, ponds that collected water from tiny rivulets and streams. He and his helpers encouraged farmers to plant crops that needed a low water input. They built check dams on rivers, they plugged rain wash gullies and built swales. The water that was previously being lost in flash floods began to accumulate underground, the groundwater rose, wells and springs began to flow and today the rivers are back in action.

Small, well thought-out modifications can work wonders. The principle is simple: keep the water on your land! Use it as many times as possible.

Our crimes against water

If we look at the way water is treated on most farms and indeed in rural planning generally, it seems as if water is a nuisance which should be got rid of as quickly and as invisibly as possible. Streams and rivers are straightened, put underground into pipes, ditches collect rainwater and it's all shunted off downhill. Now we know better, having checked out Permaculture, and found that the most dynamic ecologies are where land and water meet. So we would prefer to retain as much of our water as we can, creating little dams and ponds where possible, and making sure our streams meander leisurely across the landscape. As a rule of thumb, it's no bad thing if you can achieve about 15 percent of the surface of the farm under water. You might lose some land, but it will be made up in increased productivity and climate modification.

To regard water as a nuisance instead of the life-giving gift that it really is, seems to me the height of insults, and a certain indication of ignorance and stupidity. Unless we live in an area of extremely high and regular rainfall, with waterlogged clay soils, we should be aiming to keep as much water as possible on and in our land. Swales instead of drainage ditches, ponds instead of pipes.

Constructing dams and creating streams are jobs that require skills in landscape understanding, often a complex permission procedure and large machinery making drastic incursions into the landscape. It would be beyond the scope of this book to give you those skills, but it would be worth looking at some of the factors and creating an awareness. The seriousness of such intervention must not be underestimated. Major, or even minor landscape modification will create changes that last for many generations. In the Negev Desert I have slept in the shade of trees that are there by virtue of the water catchment systems that the Nabateans built over two thousand years ago!

There are a number of considerations when planning dams and water systems:

— It's better to have a few smaller dams rather than one big one.
— Dams should be situated in places which can catch water from as large an area as possible.
— Swales can be constructed to lead water to a dam.
— A smaller dam immediately upstream from a larger dam will collect silt and prevent the larger dam silting up.
— Dams can be multi-purpose, creating microclimates by reflecting the low winter sun.
— Dam walls can be used as road foundations and wildlife areas.
— Damage from earthworking should be repaired as soon as possible.
— Soil can be removed and used elsewhere.
— Always think whole site planning, a dam is not just a dam, it's a part of the whole drainage and landscape picture.
— Construct windbreaks to reduce evaporation from dams and ponds.
— Site ponds and dams uphill from areas that you need to irrigate, then use gravity to move the water.
— You can seal a dam or pond with clay, if you have some on site.
— When irrigating, use drip methods, they are the most efficient.

Having established bodies of standing water on our farm, we need to make the most efficient use of them and that means multi-use for us Permaculture designers. Not only is the water a source of irrigation, an insurance in case of fire and a climate modifier, but it also creates a new ecosystem, breeding plants, organisms and fish.

Aquaculture can be defined as complex water environments yielding plant and animal products. Fish farming has got a bad name from being carried out as a monoculture with high energy inputs and low-quality products, suffering from weaknesses and illnesses. However, creating a watery environment which will produce a surplus of fish has many benefits:

— It can be one of the most efficient methods of getting high-quality animal protein.
— Fish are cold-blooded and their weight is borne by the water; they use most of their energy to create meat.
— They can be fed on waste products from other activities, such as food processing.
— Dams can be located on marginal land, making it more productive.

Think complex! A number of different types of fish, animals, plants and organisms can be combined. A farm in England had a pond that experienced an explosion of tadpoles every spring. At that time they let the chickens in to the banks of the pond, which was fringed with tadpoles. The chickens ate the tadpoles, turning them into eggs and meat. The same pond grew willows for basket making, provided water for irrigation and had a couple of varieties of fish which fed off various nutrients run into the pond from the farm. Pond weeds were harvested regularly and fed to the pigs. When considering varieties of fish, pond weeds and edge plants, check out the local area and determine what grows naturally. Establish local species as far as possible, they will grow better, often have a guild type relationship and will attract other species without you having to do very much; but remember all this takes time. It may be as much as a few years before a pond is stabilized with a wide selection of interacting species. You will be able to harvest a range of surpluses.

Another crime against water is often the way we waste it in irrigation systems. Now, it's a fine Permaculture principle to observe how nature creates rain which waters the land, mimicking that by setting up overhead sprinklers. However, this does lead to a lot of evaporation, which in nature is never lost, as it just goes back into the water-cycle. But in the case where we have worked hard to store the water, worked hard to transport the water to the garden and then built a system for spreading it out again, every drop is actually costing us. It seems a shame to do all that just to let much of the water evaporate back into the natural cycle.

When I first started gardening, before I had heard of Permaculture and drip irrigation, we constructed a drip system from really simple things. We had a barrel collecting water from the roof and from our bath, this barrel was on some wooden blocks slightly above the level of the kitchen garden. A hose led to the vegetables and was connected to a piece of old hose the same length as the rows in the garden. This hose was drilled every few inches and had a twig jammed into the end. Whenever we watered, the hose was moved down a couple of rows every now and then, and this functioned just fine. Later, living in Israel, I found systems that were really enormous and very sophisticated, with pressure gauges, timers, computer controlled amounts and so on. For larger systems it's certainly worth checking out well made systems that have a certain amount of automation, but of course you run straight into much higher initial costs. For smaller gardens, especially if you have some time to spend on it, rigging up something improvised from what might be lying around is perfectly adequate.

A combination of drip irrigation, good mulching and watering in the evening is probably about as good as you'll get. The water will percolate down through the mulch in the cool of the night with minimum evaporation and might even attract a little condensation from the cooler night air.

Biological sewage systems

We usually think of sewage treatment systems as nasty, smelly things which should be hidden from the public eye. Wrong! We need a new way of thinking.

Current waste and wastewater treatment technologies are often end of the line solutions where recycling is difficult or was not considered when planning the systems. By separate treatment of blackwater (toilets) and greywater (kitchen sinks and showers), reclamation and recycling to agriculture of about 90 percent of the nutrients in domestic wastewater can be obtained. This requires a change in sewage system infrastructure and the use of highly water efficient toilets, or composting toilets. If we could have simultaneous treatment of toilet and food waste, potable water consumption can be reduced by 20–30 percent.

Decentralized treatment of greywater in urban areas can be performed by simple mechanical and biological methods. Local greywater treatment using sandfilters, indoor treatment in greenhouses and outdoors in constructed wetlands and ponds and aerated with Flowforms (for more information on Flowforms see later in this chapter, p. 171) are all tried and tested strategies within Permaculture design. Flowforms offer an aesthetically pleasing and interesting option for this treatment. A pond Flowform system can easily be incorporated into parks and provide the possibility of decentralized greywater treatment in urban areas.

Greywater can either be treated, (see below for a couple of different systems which are tried and tested) or it can be used directly, depending upon how concentrated the pollutants are. Piping it straight out into non-food plantations is probably the most effective for the least work. Growing timber, fuel plants or just plain old biomass is ideal. If there is any danger of bacteria going through the system, there is at least no chance of the humans being affected by them. If you do need to use the greywater on food crops, consider which types. Fruit orchards can be watered during the non-fruiting times pretty much by anything. The same is true of berries. Try to avoid using contaminated water on such things as salads, for obvious reasons. In any case, if you can effectively separate grey from excreta, the treatments described here can be much simpler, probably just a filter bed and a pond will get your greywater up to vegetable garden watering standards.

A slightly different challenge is treating what we might call agricultural and also industrial wastewater. Dairying and initial food processing involves a lot of washing, with the water coming off high in soil and organic substances. These are not pollutants in the sense of being dangerous bacteria or chemicals, they are just excreta and dirt in high concentrations, and this water can be used to irrigate orchards and reed beds very effectively. You might consider a system of ponds which yield fish or other high protein organisms. The crossover to industrial type pollution is a little hazy. The more you process food the closer you get to this. If you are brewing beer for instance, you can get some fairly heavy stuff coming out when you want to sterilize equipment. Machine workshops such as tractor garages can give quantities of industrial oils or lubricants containing heavy metals that you might not want going into your soil. Here you need to get into the treatments described below.

Natural water treatment technology utilizes existing physical, biological and chemical responses in the environment to provide the necessary processes required for the cleansing of wastewaters. Let's look at two different systems in more detail.

In a temperate climate. Uwe Burka developed treatment systems at Oaklands Park Camphill Village in England and wrote this up in some detail (see Book List, p. 267). This was a real Ecovillage strategy and is required reading for anyone attempting to do something similar. The figures quoted below are for a system which was designed to treat wastewater from a community of about 100 people, incorporating a biodynamic farm and other food processing facilities servicing the village itself. The system was constructed with village labour and began effective treatment in 1988, monitored by the local water authority. It was based on an existing septic tank with a capacity of about 12 cubic metres and a retention time of 2 to 3 days. To this was added a new settlement tank of about 5 cubic metres. After desludging in these tanks, the sewage was moved to a series of open beds. The primary stage beds were planted with *Phragmites* reeds. After that the water was moved to secondary beds planted with *Scirpus lacustris*, *Iris pseudacorus* as well as *Phragmites* and subsequently to the tertiary beds where *Sparganum*, *Acorus calamus* and *Carexelata* were added. Aeration throughout the system was by using

Flowforms. The increasing complexity of the plant ecology reflects the gradual removal of various contaminants from the water. The final pond was fringed with a variety of plants, and contained carp, goldfish, bream and rudd. The total area used was about 100 square metres, about 1 square metre per person. The estimated cost of constructing the system was estimated to come to a per capita price of about £325, as compared to a mechanical (conventional) system cost of about £400. Most of the work was carried out by village residents, reducing the real cost to about a quarter of that quoted. Since then aquatic sewage treatment incorporating Flowforms have established in many if not most Camphill villages throughout the world and have contributed significantly to the acceptance of these systems by local authorities.

In a hot, dry climate. In the *Permaculture Drylands Journal*, Michael Ogden describes a system he set up in New Mexico in the United States — a very different climate from that of temperate England. The wastewater to be treated was seen to be of two different kinds: the polluted water itself and the thick liquid from the bottom of the septic tanks, called septage. This latter presented a significant challenge, composed of ammonia, grease, oil, hair and hydrogen sulphide gas.

The first treatment was in a pond, where aeration and mixing were done mechanically, and a greenhouse controlled the temperature and contained the smell. From this pond the wastewater was led outside to a reed bed planted with our old favourite, *Phragmites communis*. Here the water was periodically pumped up, flooding the bed and then allowed to trickle down through the gravel. This is a mechanical way to mimic the periodic flooding that takes place in natural river deltas, and it builds up a very different set of micro-organisms. From the outside reed bed the wastewater made its way back into the greenhouse to a lagoon dominated by water hyacinths. Here most of the remaining pollutants were digested by the rich, largely anaerobic micro-organisms. The water hyacinths were periodically harvested to be composted. Still in the greenhouse was a gravel bed, where the wastewater was further cleaned, to be drained outside into a further gravel bed before draining away into a meadow planted with native arid land species.

There are three principles being demonstrated here:

— More ecologies are better. Alternating pond, marsh and meadow gives a greater variety.

— Alternating aerobic and anaerobic environments is highly efficient.

— A breadth of varieties of species will treat the pollutants most effectively.

Few people in modern societies are aware of the ultimate destination of their wastes and this detachment is a significant factor in the levels of environmental pollution which are now widely understood to threaten the future of life on the planet.

The philosophy of liquid waste collection and treatment adopted by sewage authorities in the developed world over the last decade has been based on centralization and mechanization. The arguments behind this are ones of ease and economy of maintenance, reduced land costs and chemical neutralization through mixing processes in the sewers. All these arguments have a foundation of truth but have led to a detachment of responsibility on a wide scale. Numerous cases are reported of industries having disregarded given standards. If sewage treatment were practiced more locally, the effects of misuse of the system would be locally felt and environmental awareness raised accordingly.

By careful planning and the separation of blackwater from greywater, institutions and local neighbourhoods would benefit from the siting of reedbeds and pond systems which could treat the greywater, turning it into water for irrigation of parks, small vegetable plots or public swimming pools. Thus we could incorporate small wildlife areas into urban settings for the benefit of schoolchildren and other residents.

Living Machines

John Todd together with a group of associates at the New Alchemy Institute in Massachusetts, pioneered the use of living ecologies to perform useful work. These grow foods, treat sewage, detoxify harmful chemicals, regulate climates in buildings, transform wastes and generate fuels.

Physically, Living Machines consists of a series of tanks through which the waterborne material flows, a kind of designed river. Each tank contains an ecosystem built up from materials gathered in the wild, or from other Living Machines. These ecosystems include microbes, invertebrates, plankton, fish, flowers, molluscs and shrubs. They are first selected by the designer, but the machine itself organizes and develops its own ecosystem, often rejecting some organisms in preference to others. This self-organization is typical of ecosystems in the wild. The gathering of species by the designer and self-organization of the ecosystem is a unique example of co-operation between human being and the natural world.

Living Machines take a period of trial and error to be set up with the designer gathering organisms from a variety of environments in order to carry out the task that is required. Treating mild sewage might involve selecting from ponds or lakes, where nature treats its own waste. Transforming more concentrated wastes from food processing factories might find the designer looking at pig wallows, other polluted ponds or even into the internal stomach ecologies of the carp or other living creatures. Organisms basically 'live off' the pollutants, organizing themselves downstream, with the primary material getting 'cleaner' and less 'nutritious' as it passes from tank to tank. At the bottom end of the system the water is quite clean and there are finer organisms 'scrubbing' the water to give it its final quality, to a standard where it can be released into the natural environment with no danger, fit for swimming in or even drinking water.

Over the last couple of decades Living Machines have been designed to carry out many tasks throughout the world, and can be found in communities, factories and polluted rivers. They are perfectly suited to Ecovillages, being a village sized technology based on working with the natural world. They are 'contained ecosystems powered by sunlight.' In colder climates they can be enclosed within greenhouses to maintain a temperature that ensures the efficient working of the organisms all year round.

Thomas Crapper's terrible legacy

Poor old Thomas! He invented something which made an enormous improvement to life in his London in the nineteenth century. That was a time of extreme water pollution; many if not most Londoners were literally drinking sewage! There was no sewage collection or treatment, and the wastewater ran straight into the ground, mixed with the ground water, which was pumped up and used for drinking. During the middle years of the century a vast sewage collection system was designed and built, and the flushing toilet was designed to move the excreta from the houses to the sewage pipes.

Thomas Crapper was the designer of this toilet; he gave his name to a ceramic bowl attached to a pipe, connected to a water tank which could be emptied out into the bowl, flushing away the excreta with it. This led to a number of great expressions in the English language. 'Pulling the chain' really gets rid of things. The invention of the slot machine to get you into the public toilet cubicles gave rise to 'spending a penny' and Thomas gave his family name to the activity we all engage in while sitting on the bowl. Eventually his name came to mean the substance we might otherwise call shit and in general all that 'crap!'

I really think a terrible insult has been given to Thomas. In his day he did a tremendous service to London in particular and to city life in general. Even I consider polluted water far more desirable than regular epidemics of cholera. The trick is to live without incurring either! As you might realize from having read this chapter, this is entirely possible. I mentioned earlier the principle of separating greywater from excreta. I must emphasize that the treatment of greywater is most effectively done as a neighbourhood, community or Ecovillage joint design. But what to do with the other stuff, old Thomas's legacy? Here we might consider household solutions. The main reason for this is transport. If we want to move excreta from place to place, the easiest way is by water. This is Thomas's idea and is still true today. The problem lies at the other end, separating the water from the excreta. The ease of removal is far outweighed by the complications of subsequent separation. If we don't want to move it, we have to treat it on the spot. Enter the latest solution, the composting toilet!

Here the Scandinavians led the way. Already in the 1970s rumours were reaching us in England of a toilet called the Clivus, developed in Sweden to treat excreta for the Swedes who had holiday cabins in remote places on the Baltic coast. Soon a whole range of composting toilets were being developed. Even we of the East Midlands Alternative Technology Group set up a prototype which I used for several months before coming to the conclusion that piss running across the floor was not desirable!

Today there are so many designs for composting toilets that you can get really confused. But we can distinguish some different categories. I guess the first question is whether you want to build your own or want to buy one off the shelf. There are those that compost on the spot and others that need emptying every once in a while onto another composting pile. In any case, the finished compost is recommended for non-edible tree manuring rather than the salad end of the garden. We are still trying to break any kind of bacteria loop that could build up. One of the more imaginative solutions I have come across is a desiccation system developed for hot, sunny countries. Here the excreta is separated from the urine and left to bake under glass in a ventilated chamber exposed to the full glare of the sun. The excreta turns into a white powder which can be strewn onto compost heaps or straight on the mulch round trees. Again avoiding the food trees and crops. I've never tried it, but I have observed dog shit turning into a white powder in a few days when left out in the Middle Eastern summer sunshine.

If you are taking over old buildings, you will be inheriting old systems and will have to make do or modify what you have. It can be really expensive to put in completely new and different systems. Depending upon what you have, you might consider building toilets outside, or attached to the outside wall of your house. Clearly, unless the climate is really pleasant all the time, you don't want to have to go too far when you need to go to the toilet! If you are building from scratch, then there is little excuse not to go for separation of as much as possible. Separate your greywater from human waste, and separate excreta from urine. Treat them all differently, and you will reduce problems and costs to a minimum. Greywater we have covered in some detail. Urine is not such a problem; basically it's sterile when fresh, it just smells bad after a while, with all that ammonia. In India there's a therapy consisting of drinking your own urine called Shivamba Kalpa. Yes really! Very widespread too, but it might not be too popular in western cultures, and in any case you can't drink it all, so some of it needs treating. It's actually a very good fertilizer and can be treated more or less in the same way as greywater. Build a series of ponds and root-zones and use it for irrigation. You can just pour it fresh straight onto your compost heaps: really good for keeping them moist and builds up their nitrogen content nicely.

With the excreta I would suggest either bucketing it out onto a compost heap that is used in an orchard, or else building a real composting toilet. The easiest option is to buy a good composting toilet, there are lots of them on the market.

In a village context it really is important to have a planning session on this subject. If every house is going to come up with its own individual solution, you run into the danger that some individuals may not get it right, and generate unwanted smells or health hazards for others. The other point is that to build a good self-composting toilet might cost some money and take a couple of weeks work. Multiply that by the number of households and you will get some idea of the total costs involved. Can you design a better common system for less work and a lower price? Worth talking about for a little while.

If you are going to build it yourself, which is probably the cheapest option, given that you have time, the best thing is to scour the literature to give yourself an idea of what needs doing. The principle is to have a toilet room, more or less normal size, situated above a compost chamber, which should not be much smaller, but has a slope of about 25 degrees towards an opening where you can easily come in and out when you need to empty the compost. Unless you are in quite a steadily warm climate, it would be worthwhile having heating cables built in and a drainage pipe. A fan for venting out is also required, this needs a kind of chimney to bring any unwanted smells above the rooftop and off into the wind! Insulation is necessary and if you can run to a thermostat you should regulate the temperature to around 25 degrees Celsius. Set up three switches in the toilet: one for the heating cables, one for the fan and the last for a light. Throw in a few bucketfuls of starter, earth or compost, and some hay, bark, peat or sawdust. You are ready to crap!

The top is pretty much a normal loo, you don't need to make a big deal, but it would be worthwhile to separate as much of the urine as you can by installing a separate system which takes the urine straight out to a compost heap in some way. Once or twice a week you can throw in some lime and a few handfuls of earth, compost or sawdust, perhaps a bucket of earth if there is an extra run on the place because of guests or visitors. For normal family use you probably need to empty this once every year or two, leaving the last couple of months additions. Put on good protection, gloves and so on, and wheelbarrow the stuff out to a separate compost heap for another years good processing. Then you get really nice, rich compost you can use around trees and other biomass production.

A slightly simpler system I saw on a film from a Permaculture farm in England involved basically the same, but instead of the system doing most of the composting in the chamber below the loo, the excrement went straight into large wheeled bins which could be switched out every half year or so, to a set of separate compost piles, just as the system I described above. Make an estimation of your use and buy or make bins to the required size. This system is much simpler, you can dispense with the slope and the heating cables, but you need to empty more often. The extractor fan is still important.

Some people might react negatively to this amount of thinking and planning devoted to the waste products of our body, but it's really important to take responsibility here. Learn from what happened in London in the mid nineteenth century, when literally thousands of people died of cholera from the unhygienic conditions. Whether you choose to solve this by each house finding and building its own solution or you decide to construct communal loos is not in itself the issue. The principle here is that you as a community need to address the issue. Mistakes made by individuals will affect everyone.

Flowforms

Flowforms were first produced by John Wilkes, whose research led him to consider their application in the treatment of sewage. Coming from a background in sculpture, Wilkes worked with Theodor Schwenk, director of the Institute for Flow Sciences and author of *Sensitive Chaos*. Schwenk had studied with George Adams — all three had a background in Goethean science, developed further by their study of anthroposophy.

Water is a precious commodity, it is there to support life. Water is a mediator between the environment and the organism. It takes in every influence and spreads everywhere. In a meandering stream, a falling raindrop, a curling wave, a tumbling cascade or a swirling vortex, water exhibits a restlessness and potential to adopt a host of rhythmical forms. In all living things, rhythms are present. The pulse of blood through the arteries and veins, the alternating expansion and contraction of lungs, the peristaltic movements of an earthworm, the pulsating body of a swimming jellyfish all give expression to specific rhythms. In the body fluids of living organisms order and rhythm predominate. As the main constituent of sap, blood, lymph and other bodily fluids, water circulates incessantly in distinct rhythms. Somewhere hidden in this phenomenon of rhythmical movement is the secret of water's quality.

Rhythm is generated by means of resistance, it assumes a 'breathing' regularity. The rhythmic meandering riverbed is formed by the resistance of surface and gradient to flow. The organs of the body are also created in a similar way. They then proceed to regulate the flow of blood and other bodily fluids, just as the river regulates the flow of water.

Flowforms generate rhythms in a comparable way by means of very specific proportions. The apertures or shapes through which the water flows are designed to resist the flow to such a degree that it hesitates. The flow momentarily loses its linearity or in other words its subjection to gravity. This unstable situation creates an oscillation which is then maintained by the shape of the Flowform.

By building a variety of bowls across which the water would flow under gravity, it is encouraged to swirl in definite, lemniscatory (figure of eight) paths, based on patterns observed under natural, healthy conditions. Rhythms within and between the bowls can be attuned and harmonized to create a veritable symphony of movement. These were the bowls that came to be known as Flowforms. Preliminary investigations found that water passing across Flowforms became highly oxygenated and thus showed promise for wastewater treatment. The animated, rhythmical motions of water passing through Flowforms also produced a more ecologically vital condition. John Wilkes asked himself if such motions could enhance water's life supporting capacity. If so, what combinations of rhythms would best meet the requirements of wastewater treatment? Would different ones be more appropriate for irrigation? What about storage and drinking water?

The use of Flowforms was first really applied in Camphill communities where wastewater treatment systems based on this research were installed in several countries in Western Europe, particularly the British Isles and Scandinavia. We looked at this earlier in the section on biological sewage systems. They show highly positive results, especially in the context of isolated rural communities.

The use of such systems in health clinics and hospitals has also been tried and found to be of tremendous benefit in the recovery of patients undergoing treatment. In the home, the office, the workplace and in enclosed public spaces, Flowforms have the capacity to humidify the atmosphere and load it with health-giving negative ions, in addition to the aesthetic appeal of the sight and sound of falling water.

The treatment of sewage should be seen not just as a problem to be overcome, but as a unique opportunity to demonstrate nature's remarkable qualities. Flowform cascades, ponds and created wetlands can be constructed with the aim of being quality amenities for the benefit of local residents. Rather than being placed out of sight and mind, consciousness raising is possible, deriving pleasure as well as an educationally rewarding experience. Some care and guidance needs to be exercised, though. I heard the story about one such installation in England where one of the workers tending the plants there was found to be washing his hands in the tumbling stream of the cascades before eating his sandwiches! Which just goes to show how attractive these water parks can become.

Water as intelligence

According to John Wilkes the water cycle is a sevenfold process. Most of us are familiar with the basic idea of this ecological cycle. Water evaporates from the sea, falls as rain on the land, and flows back to the sea via rivers and streams. Wilkes analysed this process further, and found a rhythm of contraction and expansion hidden within. If we begin with the diffuse water vapour in the atmosphere, this contracts, thickens, until it becomes visible in clouds. There is additional contraction until rain drops large enough to fall are formed and these drops coalesce into streams and rivers.

Cloud	1st contraction
Precipitation	2nd contraction
Spring	3rd contraction
River	
Delta	1st expansion
Ocean	2nd expansion
Evaporation	3rd expansion

As rivers reach the sea, they begin to expand and this can be seen really well in the delta. Look at any map of deltas and you'll see how they expand across the coast as they reach the ocean. The river loses itself into the vastness of the ocean and from the surface evaporation takes place. We are back at the beginning and can now discern a kind of breathing rhythm, with two polarities, one the diffuse, invisible water vapour in our atmosphere, the other the river itself.

Life seems to appear in the harmonic, rhythmical, middle part of the water process. Just look at the river in our history back to its mythical origins. The so-called great civilizations started on the banks of the rivers, the Nile, the Euphrates and the Tigris, the Indus and the great rivers of China. My own Christian and Jewish traditions sing songs about the rivers of Babylon and crossing the Jordan. Most of the largest cities of the world are situated around rivers. To come closer to home and nearer to personal experience, I know that when I'm off hiking in the wilderness, my dream campsite is always under some trees overlooking a bubbling stream or rushing river.

In our own Permaculture design, we've looked at the principle of bringing the streams up to the surface if they have been buried in pipes, or creating increased flow by slowing down the run off rate. We try to lengthen the streams and rivers by looping them around as much as possible, and this whole strategy is based on creating additional edge by the river bank. We know that this is the interface where life is most prolific. It is here, in a mature stream or river, that water exhibits its most rhythmical patterns. It's here that water shows it has a memory.

How can we give water information connected to the living world and thereby help it to support living organisms? When we learnt things at school, dominated as we were then by a materialistic and even simplistic scientific view of the world, water was just another substance, formed of 2 molecules of hydrogen combined with 1 of oxygen. Not very exciting, how can such a 'thing' have memory? I can see myself now being trashed by the teacher trying to introduce such an idea in 'O' level physics! But Wilkes and his colleagues have done a tremendous service by delving deeply into the way that water behaves.

When water is in movement it generates within its volume manifold whirling movements. It is these which respond in their veil-like structures to events of the cosmos. These surfaces also form the 'organs' that carry information with which the water can be imbued. Surface and rhythm are two basic ingredients of all life forms. Water is filled with surfaces when in movement. All nature is dominated with surface and at the same time all life forms depend upon water.

These researchers found that fluids, when left to flow by themselves, tended to create asymmetrical patterns, whereas living organisms had a tendency towards symmetry. Lawrence Edwards, a pupil of George Adams, investigated the shape of organs such as seeds, cones, buds, eggs and the heart. A great majority of these shapes are found to be of a special mathematical order called 'path-curve' surfaces. In some mysterious way, water retains a tendency to behave in these curves. In this mystery lies the idea that water has a form of memory. Changes in the curved patterns can occur if different substances are introduced into the water, even if they are reduced to tiny, insignificant proportions. This seems to be the principle behind homeopathic medicines, which really only give the water a memory of a substance. When analyzed chemically, the substances are hardly found to be there, reduced to some parts of several millions.

Adams had the idea to bring water into closer relationship with living processes by allowing it to caress such 'path-curve' surfaces thus imbuing it with information related to the organisms it would support. This was the challenge that Wilkes took up, and he found that it was just such surfaces that can be built into the Flowform. By looking at water in all its aspects, not just the purely material ones, we have found that water really has a memory and a tendency in nature to stimulate life, to help create organs and organisms.

Working with these tendencies is what Permaculture is all about. Co-operation with nature. Understanding how we can work together, water and us!

If water has its own form of intelligence, we might attempt to honour it by exercising our own intelligence when designing with water. We might try to bear in mind our most basic principle. That we should try to use the water as many times and in as many ways as possible. A good group activity when starting the planning process might be to have a brainstorming session and note how many things water can be used for. Don't spend too long, don't be critical and try to get as long a list as possible. You can use this list as a check list when you get to specific planning on a map.

I'll start you off: irrigation, drinking, fish farming, climate modification, transport of nutrients from one place to another, reflection of sunlight, fire fighting, beauty, wildlife attraction ... now you continue.

7. Energy Sources and Alternative Technology

Designing for power — Harnessing nature to do work for us —
Hooking into natural energy cycles

Wasting our fossil fuel reserves

This is a book about planning, giving positive ideas to solve our problems, big and small. My assumption is that most of you are already aware that there are problems out there and that you don't need to be told so much what they are and why they need solving, but rather how to go about it.

It has been said so many times before that I feel it could be wasting our time to repeat it here, but just for the record: we are wasting our capital by following the present course of burning up the fossil fuels we have inherited from the rotting swamps of the carboniferous period. There is no doubt that oil is a precious commodity, given to us to be used, but not to be wasted. The oil molecule is so complex, the result of such long and unique development, that it's a real shame just to burn it up! Probably the best use we can make of it is in the realm of recyclable plastics, with the by-products used in other ways.

There are so many renewable sources of energy that we really shouldn't need to use fossil fuels, or at least only sparingly, or as an equalizer. The problem with some of the renewables is that they are not reliable. The wind blows only intermittently, the sun goes down every evening, or is hidden behind clouds, the waves calm between storms and even falling water can fail us in a dry spell. The best is to make systems of storage, but I can see the sense of burning biomass or oil in order to keep the supply of energy constant.

The use of electricity as a way of moving energy around seems to be here to stay and is pretty efficient too. It's fine to have a water mill grind your corn direct, or a wind turbine to pump water from a well. Really a good idea if the conditions are right, but this requires a locality which lends itself to it. Not always the case, but fine if you have it. The widespread availability of electrical appliances, tools and equipment means that you will have to develop a pretty special lifestyle if you don't want to use electricity.

Some societies manage fine, the Amish spring to mind and that's an option that an Ecovillage should at least consider, even if only for the few minutes it takes to decide no. With their refusal to make use of modern technology, the Amish have developed an agriculture which behaves in a really interesting way compared to our modern one. It seems that it withstands the vicissitudes of the economic system by staying strong in times of agricultural demise.

Many communities make a conscious decision to embrace or eschew certain technologies that others take for granted. Good for them! At least I hope in most circumstances it's the result of debate and thought. Better that than just a blind woolly acceptance of things 'as they are.' When I lived on Kibbutz, our community accepted TV in private houses only in the late 1980s and even then only after literally several years of debate. Even today, there are many people within the Camphill movement who are deeply doubtful over the use of computers and mobile phones. The choices of technology should be considered very early on, it makes a real difference to your practical planning if you decide positively or negatively about electricity, the internal combustion engine, whether to generate only your own power or hook into national networks. This point will come up when I consider different technologies and what some of your options might be.

The nuclear waste legacy

I can't really see an Ecovillage developing a nuclear power station. The investment is ridiculously high, the skills required difficult to get hold of and the national security considerations so complex I doubt you'd get permission. Not to mention that it's morally reprehensible to throw garbage around for others to pick up! Nuclear waste, however carefully we store it, is going to be around and be dangerous for many thousands of years. Not the gift I would be proud of to give on to future generations.

However, we do, most of us, subscribe to nuclear power when we switch on the light, if we live in a country which generates electricity by producing war-grade plutonium! There are ways around this. Not using electricity from the grid is the easiest to decide and the hardest to implement. Refusing to pay a percentage of your bill equivalent to the nuclear energy generated is easier to do, but occasionally lands people in jail. This became an organized movement in England some years ago. Campaigning against nuclear power is yet another strategy, as is generating a certain amount of your own power.

The bottom line is awareness. There are many things in the world we can't do so much about, but we can be aware of them and come up with creative strategies. Awareness doesn't mean we feel powerless and depressed, just that we know what's going on. Stay clear of depression, it really puts a kink into your creativity!

Kibbutz Samar, Israel: solar power station

Date founded — 1977
Approximate number of residents — *ca.* 180
Location — southern Arava Valley
Spiritual or ideological affiliation — collective and environmental
Visited — several times during the 1990s

Kibbutz Samar, together with Lotan and Ketura, form a group of communities which have a high environmental awareness, but are located in an extremely challenging locality. Samar's response to this was to look at the energy side of their location, and it didn't take them long to realize that they were in an area where solar power was highly relevant. Checking data from the meteorological office, they found the Southern Arava to have the best solar conditions in Israel, and decided to go ahead building their own solar power station.

They negotiated a deal with the national electricity board, which enabled them to hook up to the national grid, using that as their battery. When they produce less power than they need themselves, the national grid makes up the shortfall, when their panels are producing more than consumption they sell the surplus to the grid. Because of the special conditions obtainable on a Kibbutz, they can make a number of savings which leads them to claim some of the lowest establishment and operating costs anywhere in the world. They are located in a barren, uninhabited desert, so the actual site is free. It is inside the Kibbutz fence, and is part of the guarded living and working area. Security does not cost a penny extra. The site is next to the welding shop, which means making and erecting the frames for the panels is a minimum outlay. There is no need for access roads, and the connecting line to the Kibbutz substation is short and entails minimum line loss.

By adding on panel by panel, as their economy allows, gives them a relatively debt free approach to the whole project, ultimately to become one of the largest in Israel. It's amazing to me that the government energy authorities don't give them more support. This is so clearly the way of the future.

ABOVE. Ecovillage training group in a discussion circle on the shade covered lawns of Samar.

LEFT. Close-up showing the solar panel installation, as simple and cheap as possible!

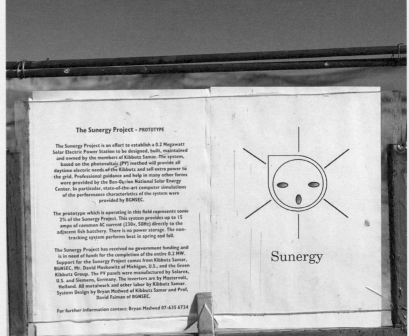

The Sunergy Project - PROTOTYPE

The Sunergy Project is an effort to establish a 0.2 Megawatt Solar Electric Power Station to be designed, built, maintained and owned by the members of Kibbutz Samar. The system, based on the photovoltaic (PV) method will provide all daytime electric needs of the Kibbutz and sell extra power to the grid. Professional guidance and help in many other forms were provided by the Ben-Gurion National Solar Energy Center. In particular, state-of-the-art computer simulations of the performance characteristics of the system were provided by BGNSEC.

The prototype which is operating in this field represents some 2% of the Sunergy Project. This system provides up to 15 amps of common AC current (230v, 50Hz) directly to the adjacent fish hatchery. There is no power storage. The non-tracking system performs best in spring and fall.

The Sunergy Project has received no government funding and is in need of funds for the completion of the entire 0.2 MW. Support for the Sunergy Project comes from Kibbutz Samar, BGNSEC, Mr. David Moskowitz of Michigan, U.S., and the Green Kibbutz Group. The PV panels were manufactured by Solarex, U.S. and Siemens, Germany. The inverters are by Mastervolt, Holland. All metalwork and other labor by Kibbutz Samar. System Design by Bryan Medwed of Kibbutz Samar and Prof. David Faiman of BGNSEC.

For further information contact: Bryan Medwed 07-635 6734

Sunergy

ABOVE. Experimental mud and palm leaf addition to existing housing stock.

LEFT ABOVE. Experimental solar turbine focuser.

LEFT. Sunergy, the solar project of Kibbutz Samar.

FAR LEFT. On the left the late Brian Medved, tragically killed in a car accident, founder of the solar project and member of Samar, in conversation with the author.

On the other hand, don't be fooled by smooth-talking technocrats in suits or white coats either. Nuclear power is dangerous, unnecessary and mostly a lie! It's ridiculously expensive, makes waste that we don't know how to handle properly and its main product is weapons-grade plutonium. Even if we stop today, future generations will curse us for leaving them the enormous amounts of dangerous waste we have already generated.

We don't need it and we are now going to check out the other options we have.

Falling water

Growing up in England when I did, I thought of hydro-electricity as one of the best options around. Clean, quiet, non-polluting, renewable and capable of producing enormous amounts of electricity. Even possible to regulate and store by using any excess to pump water back up to reservoirs where it can sit as a lake until needed. Then I came back to Norway to live for a bit in the seventies and eighties and found that there was a tremendous anti hydro-power lobby among environmentalists. So there is a catch!

In order to have a supply of water, you need to dam up rivers, creating lakes that can be piped down to the actual turbines. Some places are pretty natural and require very little modification. They got tapped first. But of course demand for power has risen enormously and the hydro-folks have been out there looking for more sources. Amazing how clever they are! Lakes are created in wilderness areas, rivers are diverted, sometimes through mountains and across watersheds. Some valleys lost their rivers, other valleys were lost to lakes. Farms had to be moved or abandoned and wildlife disturbed. In Norway it culminated in the Alta River issue, which mobilized thousands of protesters, shiploads of police, numerous court cases, bombing of bridges, diversion of ancient reindeer migration routes and in the end was shown to be a disappointment for the local community. The dam was built and the power station produced electricity. Local people got a few cleaning jobs, but the technicians came mostly from other places and most of the power was exported to surrounding countries.

Hydro-electric power is often regarded as one of the most ecologically friendly sources of our power, until we come to Norway! Here some of the bitterest conflicts between 'greens' and the authorities have taken place over the water issue. The damming up of large reservoirs, the regulation of river systems and the diversion of water from spectacular waterfalls to pipes has caused friction for decades.

Today it's hard to find a river or lake in Norway or Sweden that hasn't been dammed or regulated. You might say that for the few wilderness freaks who like to canoe (like me!) that's not so important, but incursions into our fast disappearing wilderness areas has to be considered carefully today. Like so many other things, the issue might be regarded as a conflict between the large and the small. Nearly all the protests arise when large power corporations decide to build large dams, creating incursions into the natural water systems. One way around this, which is much more appropriate for us also, is to create microsystems. This means building very small power plants and using water from relatively small streams without altering the natural drainage more than just putting a falling stream into a pipe to create a strong jet at the bottom.

The contribution of micro power stations is enormous, estimated in Norway to be 10 percent of the total needs. By a combination of easing regulations and having technology that will allow energy to be fed into the grid, this production can be stimulated, to be driven largely by private initiatives and investment. The payoff comes in local production and the dispersion of technology to the local level. Ecovillages can be highly instrumental in forging ahead in this way, and may even be able to create a niche market for themselves at the local level in building and maintaining microsystems.

The amount of energy you can get from a small water source depends upon the combination of two factors: the amount of water running through the system and how far it falls. Basically you get the same energy output from 100 litres per minute falling 10 metres as from 10 litres per minute falling 100 metres. From the point of view of which kind of machinery you need, the less water the better, larger amounts require large machines, regardless of how far it falls. From this rule of thumb, it might be clear that the less water you have falling further makes for smaller, lighter hardware. So if you're really into this technology and have a choice of sites, go for the mountainous places, where lots of little streams flow fast down steep slopes.

There's quite a bit of technical stuff you need to get through to make use of this technology, but it's all pretty basic. Research on the ground involves finding out as accurately as possible the vertical fall and the rate of flow. Measuring the fall is pretty easy, just get out there with a tape and a friend! Remember it's vertical height we are looking for, not just distance, that comes later. You need to devise a process with sticks and a level that you can sight across. Rate of flow demands more complex stuff. The best is to block the stream, direct the water into a pipe and start filling measured buckets. Calculate how many seconds it takes to fill the bucket. Do this several times, as accurately as you can, to get an average. What you are looking for is how many litres per minute, so remember to divide by 60 to get from seconds to minutes! You might need to do this lots of times in different seasons. We have a stream beside our house where I live now that has no ponds, lakes or even bogs above it. The response to rain is really fast. Because we don't have a lot of rainfall, the stream is pretty much dry most of the time. Once it rains and the ground has soaked up the first bit, the stream builds up quickly and can be very full and picturesque. Great to look at but not really a very good hydro-power option.

This is just another example of how accurate site knowledge is essential for your planning. It's no good just visiting once or twice and making your observation from this the basis of your planning. Ideally you want to check things out over several years. Failing that, talk to locals who have lived there a long time. This is true not just of stream flow, but of many, many factors: climate, frost dates, soils and so on. I hope that this is becoming a refrain that we come back to again and again. There really is no substitute for knowing the site in as great a detail as you possibly can!

Once you have the fall and the rate, you need to measure distance, pipe size and the location of the actual turbine, the batteries that you want to charge (if you decide to store the electricity yourself), and how far the whole thing is from where you want to use the actual power. Putting the turbine and the battery as close together as possible makes sense, because the turbine works best when producing direct current (DC) power, which charges batteries really well, but loses a lot if transmitted over distances longer than a couple of hundred metres. You can always turn it over to alternating current (AC) with an inverter afterwards.

If you have lots of fall, you can use the water several times. Build a whole series of turbines going down the hill if you want, the pipe going from one to the next. Just bear in mind the distance from turbine to battery.

In several countries you can hook into the national grid and supply power from your own system, using the grid as a battery. This is probably the best option and the way of the future. At a village level, it makes a lot of sense: we have real, up-and-running systems at Kibbutz Samar (see pp. 178–181) which has a solar system; in our own Camphill Vallersund here in Norway there is a large wind turbine. At this point we head into heavy technical stuff, national regulations and people with degrees in engineering. The best is to have an electrical engineer in your Ecovillage group! If you don't have one, get one or hire one!

There are many ways of getting the machinery required to harness this power. Off the peg systems can be used; in the United States Harris Turbines produce a variety that can be tailor-fitted to your requirements, and the rest is just water piping and standard electrical equipment. If you want to build your own stuff, it will be less efficient, require a variety of tools — welders, metal cutting and bending stuff — and some inventiveness when it comes to coupling pipes to homemade turbines. For efficient, hard wearing installations that will last a long time with minimum maintenance you will probably find that it's best to buy. For electrical components you might look into using car or lorry parts from wreckers yards. A lot of large vehicles use 24 volt set ups and you can get this pretty cheap second-hand. Very few vehicles are scrapped because their electrical equipment stops working! If you decide to go for 24 volt all round, you can get lights, radios, cassette players and more to fix up your whole place. It's a good option, but will require that you store your own power, needing banks of batteries with all that this entails. The other drawback is that these systems don't really give enough power to run heavy equipment such as power tools, or washing machines. They are best suited to single homesteads which require just some minimal lighting and a music system.

Once you step up to a village scale things begin to look a lot different. First of all the scale changes considerably. Even a cluster of ten homes (which is a pretty small village), requires ten times the amount of whatever you need (that was pretty obvious!). You will naturally begin to specialize, with one or two people agreeing to look after the power supplies while others care for the gardens, for instance. At this point it becomes a serious option to go for more complex stuff, hook into the grid and tackle all the bureaucracy that will be required. Obviously, storage of all the electricity needed for a village would need an enormous bank of batteries.

Water power can effectively be used for mechanical power, and here it can be as local and as small scale as you want. For obvious reasons, location is the key concept. Mechanical power doesn't really transport over any distance. A mill for grinding corn, or running a small saw mill has to be built where the power is. The skills needed for this kind of construction can only be hinted at in this book, but they are considerable! We lived in the Norwegian Arctic many years ago. I got to know a retired carpenter there who told me how he had helped his father build a sawmill where the only steel component was the actual saw blade! Everything else was made of wood, even the bearings and the gears. The skills that he and his father had were built up over generations of working with wood, and these skills are few and far between these days. Lucky you if you have someone like that in your group!

Don't be discouraged! You can get lots of components from your local vehicle wreckers; every Ecovillage needs a metal workshop with a welder, cutter and drill anyway. You can build all kinds of Mickey Mouse constructions that can utilize falling water and put it to good use. Be creative and think how you can get it to grind your corn, turn your potter's wheel, or running tumbler grinders for making polished stones for beauty and for sale.

We, who grew up in the last half of the twentieth century, have experienced concentration at many levels: concentration of power, of populations in cities, of technologies, of money and wealth. The exodus from rural areas to the swelling cities is experienced as a law of nature, that's what people do. We coined the term megacity and thought that this would continue more or less indefinitely. According to a new analysis of UN census statistics published in the autumn of 2002, this may not be the case. Cities are growing more slowly than expected, more people are leaving cities than moving in. The slower, but continued growth is largely a factor of birth rates.

This would indicate that more people are staying in rural areas and perhaps some people actually moving in. An indication of dispersion. When this trend becomes appreciated, the idea of dispersing sources of power might also become more widespread and the technologies that we are discussing here, that are being developed in Ecovillages, will be more appropriate.

From a short article in the *New Scientist* in June 2003, Fred Pearce quotes Karl Yeager, president of the US Electric Power Research Institute: 'Power grids will become more like the Internet — networks for sharing electricity among millions of independent domestic and community generators.'

Dispersion is in fact a really ecological concept. As Permaculture designers we should look for the ways energy flows in, and instead of damming them up to create concentrations of power and wealth, we should hook into the flow as it goes by. Energy is available at all times, in all places, from a variety of sources. If we can latch onto it and create networks which make it available to us and others — where and when we need it — we will be creating a truly ecological energy system. Perhaps Karl Yeager is painting a picture of future energy networks that is really Permacultural!

Wind generators

In the early seventies, wind power was radical and undeveloped. All kinds of rumours and legends were circulating. One company, Jacobs of Vermont, had developed a wind generator for use in Antarctic monitoring stations before the Second World War and these generators were reputed to be the best in the world. The company had gone out of business, but long-haired techno freaks were scouring the world for surviving models. Another company, the North Wind Power Company, specialized in reconditioning these wind generators. A small group of alternative technology types up in the north of England landed an amazing contract with the Mongolian government to bring electricity to outlying and nomadic yurt people. Wind generators were developed by them to satisfy this highly specialized market, the company became a huge success and the envy of us all. People came back from Crete with drawings and photographs of the sail windmills traditional there, and they swept through Britain like a fashion craze. We even built one out of junk and displayed it in the main square in Nottingham in 1976.

The main trouble with wind power is its unevenness, the wind seldom blows at a completely steady rate, so the power output is like that, unsteady. Sometimes there is no wind at all! But if the power can be stored and then used as required, you have a really excellent source of non-polluting, reusable energy. The other option is to use it when there is wind, that's how windmills ground corn in the old days. When it was calm, the miller took a day off! Another way to get round this uneven supply is to use it solely for heating, which has a number of advantages. Just run the generated electricity straight into heating cables in an insulated water tank. Any heat that is generated will be taken up by the water, it really doesn't matter if there are surges when the wind velocity goes up or down, whereas a battery can get damaged if you don't have a control box attached. The heat can be stored until needed, then pumped round your house for heating. An alternative is to get some old-fashioned storage heaters — they used to be all the rage in England back in the 1970s — and hook them up directly to the generator. Again, any heat would be taken up by the thermal mass of the storage heater and leaked slowly into the surrounding room or house.

Wind is the result of differential temperatures, the warming of the sun and the cooling in the shade. Day and night, winter and summer, north and south, wind is the attempt to restore equilibrium after the effects of duality. Solar energy one step down the line. You can have a wind generator and follow it with another one a few hundred metres downwind, with no loss of power. I cannot envisage overkill of wind generation to the extent that winds get slowed down and we suffer from global calming! There is some opposition to extensive forests of large wind generators and, though I can understand it, I don't hear the same opposition to enormous pylons carrying electricity all over the place. In any case I'm biased and totally non-objective, having gone through that period in the 1970s when windmill generators became one of the symbols of the alternative technology movement. The sight of the propellers turning was like an anarchist flag flying in the wind!

Despite the mainstream power people still being so besotted with fossil fuels and nuclear power, wind is becoming more accepted. World wind generating capacity climbed from 17,800 megawatts (MW) in 2000 to 23,300 MW in 2001. That was a one-year gain of 31 percent! From 1995 until 2001 the wind generating capacity was increased by 487 percent! Forward projections are more dramatic still. According to the European Wind Energy Association, Europe alone is expected to be generating 60,000 MW by 2010. The countries which are spearheading this development are Canada, China, Italy, the Netherlands, Sweden, the United Kingdom, Greece, Ireland, Portugal, France and Japan. These facts and figures are taken from an article by Lester Brown, president of the Earth Policy Institute, in the December 2002 edition of *Resurgence* magazine.

Again, the first thing you need to do is to check your site. This is much easier to do than for water. All you need is to put up a recording anemometer and read off the results. Either there is wind or there isn't. It will vary according to time of day and season, and you need to build up a picture. Again, you should do this for a year, things can vary a lot. However, don't be discouraged, you can crib the figures from other people!

Weather measurements have been recorded properly for decades or more now. All you need to do is to get in touch with the national meteorological service and you'll get something from near you. Get it as detailed as possible. Kibbutz Samar crunched their way through *hourly* sunshine recordings for *several decades* before going solar. You can probably get just as detailed a wind history by going to the right place. Don't rely completely on these figures unless the wind recorder is actually on your site. Wind varies a lot with topography. A hill, a wood or any other obstruction can completely change the picture. If you can take wind measurements on your actual site, do it for a few weeks and compare it with recordings taken by the national service. You might be able to see a correlation and can extrapolate from that.

You will also want to know from which direction winds are blowing and this is usually displayed as a wind rose, showing graphically how much wind from which point of the compass. Bear in mind that really high winds, or violent turbulence, can destroy equipment very easily. Talk to locals and if your location is prone to storms, make sure you build systems that fold up or turn off when wind velocities get up to certain levels.

Armed with these facts, you are in a position to consider your options. They end up very similar to the things we thought about connected with water power. Do you want electricity or mechanical power? If electric, are you going to store it yourself or hook into the grid. One option with wind is to use the excess to pump water into a storage dam. Then you have a considerable steady supply, given that your dam is large, and you can draw the water off into a turbine which gives steady power all the time. It's really just like nature! The more complex your systems, the more sustainability you create.

Solar power

Solar power already does most of our heating. Absolute zero, at minus 273°C is what happens in far outer space where the sun does not shine. Most of our planet is already up to an ambient and relatively comfortable temperature in the zero to 30°C range. All done by the sun! What we need to do is to adjust the final temperature by a few degrees, occasionally down, but mostly up. It seems a pity to use valuable coal, oil or work demanding things like biomass in order to do this when in most places on the planet there is abundant free stuff coming in at us from the sun. Thirty years ago we thought we were the first to think of this, but in fact, global visions of solar energy use have been around for some time.

Frank Schuman started experimenting with solar power in America in 1906. A boom in ideas and technologies drew him and his partners in The Sun Power Company to Florida, Arizona, and then to North Africa. A 1,200 square metre solar collector was built outside Cairo and so impressed Lord Kitchener in the years immediately before the First World War that he offered Schuman a 120 square kilometre site in the Sudan to develop the technology.

In 1914, Schuman wrote in the *Scientific American*:

> I have taken as a basis the figure of 270 million horse power continuously throughout the year being equal to all the coal and oil mined during the year 1909 throughout the world ... Taking the actual work of our plant as a basis, it would only be necessary to cover 20,250 square miles of ground in the Sahara Desert with our sun heat absorber unit ... Surely from this showing, the human race can see that solar power can take care of them for all time to come.

What a vision! Nearly a hundred years ago. And such a crime that it all got pushed under the carpet in the years of the First World War and that afterwards the money-grubbing oil industry took over.

Still, never too late to save the world! For our purposes, planning for our Ecovillage, we can range the options from the simple to the complex. The deciding factors will be what level of skills and competence you have in your group, and what kind of budget you can set aside for power production generally and solar power specifically.

The simplest approach is to design your buildings for passive heating, planning the size and orientation of windows and overhangs to allow winter sun to enter and excluding the summer sun. This we looked at in the building section. The next step might be as simple as coiling a black water hose on the roof on its way to the shower and you'll have hot water for washing in whenever the sun shines. Next step up in sophistication might be to make the collector a little more efficient by enclosing it in a glass fronted, insulated box with a black background and bringing the heated water up into an insulated tank for storage. Thermosyphoning it by utilizing the water's natural propensity for rising when heated by placing the tank above the collector. Warm water rises up into the tank and stays there till you need it. Install a pump, expand the size of the collector, and you might circulate the hot water round your building through some radiators — or even under the floor — and hey presto, you have a solar-heated home!

By this time you are working with a plumber, making sure the connections are tight, and that the pump fits the work, and that you don't get undesirable side-effects, like the whole thing working in reverse at night, when the collector will cool down below the temperature of the house. Either you will have to turn the pump on and off yourself, or install some thermostats to do it for you. None of this is terribly complex, but there is often a need for a card-carrying plumber and electrician for the purposes of building regulations, insurance and official approval. Unless you are planning a cluster of unregulated yurts, tipis or caves, you will need these qualified people anyway, so make sure you have some in your group or get someone to qualify.

Clearly, solar energy is coming in as heat, so it makes most sense to use it just like that, to heat our buildings and water. But it can be turned into electricity by installing a variety of different collectors. As we saw earlier, electricity is a fine way to have energy transported, utilized in a wide variety of ways to do work and it can even be stored in batteries. Combine wind, water and solar, and you've got really a great system with some good backups. It would be quite a complex system, needing good engineering and sound maintenance, but at a village level it might supply all your needs, with storage being the water in a high level dam and the water turbine giving regular even electricity day and night, winter and summer.

Upgrade this idea to the global level, factor in large wave generators stationed off the coast, a few tidal generators where the geography allows it and couple the whole show together in super grids. Now we have a science fiction type vision where all our energy is nice, clean, sustainable and available all over the planet. The technology for this is all here, except for the last link up of the super grids. Had we put the money that we have wasted on nuclear power into developing this, we could be enjoying it today! But let's not get discouraged, Ecovillage examples can still show people that these things work and a working system speaks louder than a thousand protest demonstrations. If the lab people in the white coats and the technocrats in dark suits can't supply the vision, then we can.

The easiest way to make electricity from the sun is a photo voltaic (PV) collector. Just buy it (you can't make it in your cellar at home!) set it up facing the sun and plug in. Of course the supply varies with the amount of sunlight, so you'll have to run it through batteries or some other storage. There are some problems with PV collectors. The industry which produces them uses a lot of energy and has some dubious pollutants. They are relatively expensive, but on the other hand seem to last a long time. They don't seem to wear out or be destroyed easily. A friend of mine from Samar took a panel out into the desert and used it as a target for machine gun practice. Even after it was seriously shot up, it was still delivering at 80 percent efficiency. There are many models on the market now and the technology is not yet old enough to be able to give an appraisal of how long the panels will last. The place I know which have been 'racing' (comparing) different panels the longest is the Solar Energy Centre at Sde Boker in the Negev. They've also been trying out a wide variety of other solar energy collectors and have built up some serious experience. David Feiman, the director, is one of the planet's most knowledgeable experts in this field.

Making use of solar power is not just another technology. It reminds us that we are connected with the cosmos, it brings an awareness of the rhythms of life, the daily cycle of day and night, the slow swing of the seasons. It brings home the weather, cloudy days and still clear days.

Bio energy

Coal, oil and natural gas are the mineralized products of ancient forests and swamps. It took geology a long time and many complicated processes to produce these materials. We can by-pass this process by growing the stuff ourselves. We won't get exactly the same complex molecular structures, but we can get oil, fuel and energy from various crops.

Trees are the most obvious. In our community we have a large forest on the slopes behind us. We can use timber from this forest to build some of our houses and to run our heating systems. We have two wood fired central boilers in our two building clusters, piping hot water round to heat our homes. To boost the heating during cold spells and to brighten up our living rooms, we have wood burning stoves and open fireplaces. The latter, by the way, have doors so we can close them down and get a much more efficient fire that last longer and is much safer. Open fires are traditionally pretty wasteful in their operation, often known as 'heating for the birds.' Build on some cast iron doors, close fitting, and you can enjoy the sight and sound of the open fire when you snug around the hearth on a cold winter's night, but you can still fill up with fuel, close the doors and leave it, knowing it won't shower the room with sparks and burn your house down. It can keep burning for hours, giving lots of gentle heat through the night.

Harder and heavier woods give more heat than lighter per cubic metre. Below is a list of the most usual kinds of fuelwoods with kW values per loose cubic metre of material.

Rowan	1,606
Beech	1,528
Oak	1,469
Ash	1,469
Maple	1,417
Birch	1,339
Pine	1,177
Black alder	1,177
Sallow, goat willow	1,151
Asp	1,014
Spruce	1,014
Grey alder	962

It's worth getting to know different woods. Birch has a smell that is really an incense. It always reminds me of fires out in the woods. It doesn't spit and burns with a slow, gentle flame. Spruce has a sharper, more spicy smell, and spits and crackles in a really cheerful way. It's great to start the fire, like fireworks, but watch those sparks, either put a tight mesh cover or sit by the fire and watch, ready to sweep up those flying sparks lest they set fire to your furniture! Oak, which we rarely get here in Norway, has a heavy serious smell and burns for hours.

Wood warms you many times. When we lived in England, there was always a need to get wood. When friends used to turn up at weekends, we would get good and warm going for walks collecting waste wood out of the hedges and copses around where we lived. We would get warm again when we cut, chopped and stacked it. By the time we got to actually burning it in the stove, we had really got our value from it. And none of that actually cost us money!

The best way to get wood is just to collect it from the woods, fallen trees, thinnings and dead branches. If you have old waste timber from buildings that need renovation or just are falling down, that's also fine. You need to check for impregnations, though. Some building timber, in fact a lot, is impregnated to stop rot. The stuff they use is mostly a poison based on arsenic and the timber should be treated as dangerous waste. If you just bury it, the poison seeps into the ground water and if you burn it, you get poisonous gases given off. Stay clear of impregnated timber!

Coppicing is the traditional way to set up a sustainable supply of timber. It's tried and tested, been going in England for at least a thousand years. The idea is that the tree will establish a root system and all you need to do is to cut off the tops, and the stock will shoot out new growth very quickly. If you allow ten years for regrowth, you need to take out just a tenth of your coppice every year. Establish a good mix of trees, deciduous are the best, and plan to take out a selected few from various parts of the coppice. That way you keep the character of the wood intact. In ten years you get a good growth, poles as thick as your arm, at least. They can be used for all kinds of things as well as firewood. Fencing, pole construction, funky furniture.

Methane from manures and sewage seems to be a good way to get the most from this material, but it does require quite a large amount to make it worth while. There seem to be various points of view on this. In India the Go Bar Gas system became very widespread, a real alternative technology, using old oil barrels for the digester and old tractor inner tubes for the gas containers, with bits of piping connecting the thing together. In China similar digesters were constructed out of concrete, but based on the same idea. Small scale and relatively easy to construct and run, they supplied gas for cooking or heating on a domestic level. They converted animal and human manure into a slurry that could be used on the land, and took out the methane which in any case would be given off in a less controlled form. In New Zealand, a country with many more farm animals than human beings, this became very widespread and the agricultural department encouraged it by sending advisors round to help farmers set up and run.

Instead of converting vegetable residues (biomass) into methane in a digester, the material can be heated in a controlled atmosphere and will produce a gas not unlike propane. This was used during the Second World War to run cars; it was pretty inefficient but worked nonetheless and with today's improved technology, could be improved on a lot. A really good use for waste bits of wood from a timbering business. Conversion ratios of 70 percent to 80 percent are possible and very little modification needs to be done to an ordinary petrol engine. It never seems to have been taken up in any widespread way since the Second World War and there are widely opposing views on the feasibility of this. My guess is that it requires someone who is really committed to making it work. As always, my approach to creativity is to be encouraging and non-critical, and let people loose on making it work. And let people know how you did. We can all learn from each other!

Vegetable oil seeds can be grown, pressed and used as fuel. It does not differ much from diesel in terms of burning characteristics and it's not a big technical adjustment to switch your motor from one to the other. Growing crops for oil such as oil seed rape or sunflowers is only possible in certain climates. Up here in Norway I don't hold out much hope. Pressing can be done using all kinds of other technologies: both wind and water offer themselves as possibilities. Adding value to your own crops is always a good idea and the waste from pressing oil can be used as animal food, or even fuel. Either way it can find its way back into the soil, as manure or as ash, or if neither of those two seem to be appropriate, just compost the stuff direct.

Alcohol can also be produced. Any sugar heavy crop can be used, it doesn't have to be grapes! Sugar beets are probably the most efficient and grow in cool climates. When we lived in Lincolnshire I spent one autumn and winter harvesting sugar beets in pretty miserably cold weather. There are plenty of other crops which yield sugar for fermentation. Barley springs to mind as the classic for beer and whisky, though it does require quite carefully controlled sprouting and drying. Whatever you grow needs to be put through a process of fermentation and distillation. Again you will end up with waste products which are organic and can be used as animal feed, fuel or direct compost. In the case of alcohol production, there will be other considerations of cleanliness and sterility which might involve chemicals or processes which could be problematical. You can sterilize with heat, steam for example, which is nice and clean, but demands quite high energy. Or you can use chemicals, but their disposal can be problematic.

In both of these cases, oil or alcohol, you will soon realize how much work is required to get the internal combustion engine ticking over and delivering work for you. This realization is perhaps the most valuable result of all this. It's so easy with cheap oil: just fill up your tank and drive away. You don't actually pay for the long geological process of forming mineral oil underground from the swamps of the carboniferous period and you don't pay for the pollution of the oil spills and the refineries, or the wars over oil resources. All that is hidden and passed on to you in taxes, deaths, ill health and the prospect of running out of oil some time in the near or distant future. Growing and processing your own fuel will bring home to you how much work all this is, and will hopefully put the price per kilometre travelled up to a high and realistic level. Of course the temptation is to go back to good old Esso and Shell, and many of us do this.

However, don't think that I am dismissing the idea of these home-grown vegetable fuels. They can be stored and used as required, a really important feature. You might want to use a generator to power washing machines or power tools for occasional use. This would be ideal. The oil can be used for cooking, and fuel you direct. And the alcohol can be used for drinking, in moderate quantities, of course!

A word of warning about growing these things if you intend to use machinery on your farm. An energy analysis might be in order here. If you can factor in the cost of transport of materials needed and the amount of fuel you will use to run your tractors or whatever you are using, you will find out how much energy is required to grow your crop. Now compare that to the expected yield of oil. Clearly, if you are heavily mechanized, you might find yourself using more oil than you are harvesting! Not much point really, is there?

Unconventional sources

Human body heat is generally not included in energy source lists. But in fact it can contribute seriously to domestic heating. In Sweden, not noted for its balmy winters, there are houses without conventional heating systems: no open fires or wood burning stoves, no boilers, radiators or radiant heaters — just a solar panel to give a boost now and then, and a heat exchanger to extract the warmth from the air coming in from the used air leaving the house. And super insulation in walls, ceiling, floors and especially round windows and doors. In this way heating costs can be cut to a third, yes, from 15,000 kWh to 5,000 kWh annually! The human body heat is boosted by the use of ordinary appliances for such things as cooking and a Scandinavian tradition of lighting candles during meals, and again, often in the evenings when folks are hanging out together in the living room. Super insulation really works and that's where the strawbale house has a lot to contribute.

Animal heat. Animals on the ground floor, humans above. This is a classic design strategy. Some European cultures have traditionally used this, the Swiss and the Breton spring to mind straight away. Others, such as my own Scandinavian, don't seem to take it into account at all, when you might expect them to because of the harsh winters. Here the tradition is a house for every use, farms consisting of clusters of large and small buildings around a yard. Animals need a minimum amount of heat, mostly generated by themselves, though some of it can come from the manure composting below them if there is a cellar to shovel it into, together with the bedding straw. Good insulation around the animal quarters will retain enough heat to keep it comfortable, just remember they need ventilation too. Perhaps a heat exchanging ventilator can be installed! If you construct the living quarters for the humans on the next floor above, you have a floor that is, well, not exactly heated, but at least not cold. Given that you insulate the rest of the house well, walls and roof, you will retain most of that heat, and take the chill off the building, making subsequent heating less critical.

Some people might object to the noise and the smell. The latter you should be able to deal with by building the correct ventilation systems. Stale air can be vented away up through the roof, or out into the downwind side of the building. The noise is something you might get to enjoy! Could be quite romantic and bucolic to hear the lowing of the cattle calling you to milking, the bleating of the lambs in the spring, or the cock crowing to wake you up in the morning.

Hay Box Cooking. This is also known as Retained Heat Cooking. A much more accurate term, as you don't really need a box full of hay to practice this. Hay Box Cooking can reduce your energy use on the kitchen stove by up to 80 percent and easily 50 percent. It is also a method which makes timing less critical and burning food virtually impossible. The easiest is to bring the food to be cooked up to the boil, simmer for a few minutes while you get an insulated container prepared. This can be a box filled with hay, but it could be anything else. We use a large basket with a couple of old blankets which we wrap around the saucepan. The principle here is that it should be insulating and wrap as closely to the pan as possible. Cooking time is of course much longer than on the flame and timing is less critical. Great for such things as soups and stews, especially if you have to go out and want to come back to a ready meal. This isn't strictly speaking a source of energy, but after all, 'a kilowatt saved is a kilowatt earned.'

Geological thermal heat. Here we have two sources: hot springs and the earth itself. Unless you live in Iceland, Japan, New Zealand or some such place that has hot springs, forget about tapping into the first source. If you do and have natural hot water bubbling up from down below, you're really lucky, or at least blessed by the gods; all you need to do is build a set of radiators connected with water pipes and send the water round the house, boosting with a small circulation pump if necessary. If the water is really hot and coming out as steam, you are doubly blessed. Put a turbine on it, run a generator, let the steam cool down to water, then send that round your house, greenhouse or village, and let the generator power the pump.

Even if you don't have hot water laid on by geology, the ground itself can be a source of heat. Here in Scandinavia, even when the outside temperature drops to minus 30 centigrade or below, the ground will only freeze to a metre or two deep at most. Below this the ground is then 30° warmer than the air. So bore a deep hole, put in a heat extractor and concentrator, and you have a source of heat for your building or your water. As long as the system is modest, you have a free source of heat that is sustainable, non-polluting and inexhaustible. If you go overboard and install massive systems, beware! You could end up with your house sitting on a super cooled ice block! These systems have relatively high capital investment costs, but are really cheap to run. Definitely worth considering.

Trees shaking in the wind. I can't really see this as practical, but I felt I had to include this for its creativity factor. When it comes to technical solutions to the things that challenge us, we need to release creativity and come up with innovative solutions. The best catalyst for creativity is enthusiasm and fun. Maybe you could throw an invention party. The worst downer is criticism, this will turn off your creativity tap in seconds flat. So who am I to gainsay trees shaking in the wind?

The idea is to tie three or four long ropes as high up the tree as possible, then lead them down to the ground around the tree and through blocks and pulleys to rotate a flywheel on a ratchet. As each rope tightens, it pulls the wheel round in turn, giving you a rotating wheel. Connect that up to a generator or a pump or whatever you need, maybe gear it up a bit on the way, and hey presto you have power!

Bicycle power. Pedal power has been claimed to be the most efficient way of generating energy yet invented. Phil Brachi worked out in *The Bike Book* (quoted in *Radical Technology*, see Resources section) that a bike takes about 250 kWh to produce and that a biker does the equivalent of about 1,500 miles to the gallon. This was in the early seventies, when *really efficient* cars were doing about 45 miles to the gallon! No doubt things have changed since then, but the principle is clear, bikes are in a league of their own as far as energy expended relates to work done. Certainly it's a great way to get around and generally uses a technology that's pretty accessible to most people. A small welder for the tricky bits and the rest is just simple hand tools, with an electric drill if you need to make additional holes. Throw in a big pile of broken bikes and you can make a really wide assortment of stuff, from composite bikes to rickshaws to stationary power units. Again, creativity can come up with some great ideas.

The people at Rodale in the United States, a research place dedicated to organic growing, experimented extensively with pedal powered ploughs and other field tools. Basically you set up a winch at one end of the field, have some pedalling with the right gearing and a steel cable pulls the field tool of your choice across the field towards you. Set up two winches, one at each end and you get pretty much the system that was pioneered over a hundred years ago with stationary steam engine ploughing. Another application is to generate electricity, hooking the bike up to a small generator, get one for free out of a trashed car. Take the same stationary bike and hook it up to a hand mill for grinding corn, or any other job that needs doing for mechanically reducing things, a compost chopper for example.

These ideas have been around for a couple of decades or more, but never really caught on. One reason for this might be the low cost of energy, even generated from conventional power stations. Admittedly the cost is artificially low, as it does not factor in oil depletion, spillage in transit and pollution, but still, it's what we pay out of our pockets. One contributor to *CoEvolution Quarterly* in 1978 calculated that pedalling was saving 3c an hour, not a very high saving! Transport, with a good bike on a good road, is one thing, but stationary power devices need to be checked out well if you are going to rely on them seriously.

There is no doubt in my mind that every Ecovillage needs a bike freak, a large heap of old bikes and a few simple tools. Bikes for everyone to get around on, free bikes for visitors, a bike fixing service, a bike club for the youngsters and now you come up with more ideas. The bike was one of the great inventions of the mechanical age: it's fun, it makes you feel good and it's low impact.

Hydrogen, water. Here's one for the more scientifically minded. Hydrogen technology is not something you're going to be at the forefront of developing in your Ecovillage, but you might keep your ears to the ground. The idea of endless amounts of virtually free power by splitting hydrogen molecules found in sea water has been a prize dream of many scientists and we're getting closer all the time. There are now some cars and buses running on this, it's still pretty experimental, but it's coming our way. If you want to be really up-market, find out who is working on this near you and offer to use it experimentally. Ten years ago Lebensgarten Community in Germany had an electric car running off a solar panel, which was really a good showpiece to illustrate the principle.

With lots of visitors coming through on courses, it was good publicity for the company producing this technology. Companies developing new technologies of this kind need motivated people who are prepared to document and monitor usage, at the same time giving positive publicity.

When we hook into energy sources other than just connecting to the grid and accepting that somewhere, someone is either burning coal or oil, or firing up a nuclear power station, we also create an awareness inside ourselves of other parts of our world. Alternative energy sources are not just sustainable and non-polluting, they give us the opportunity to grow as human beings, to appreciate our connections to the rest of creation. Some people say grace before meals, an excellent tradition. Maybe we should introduce a grace before switching on the light too! Thanking creation for providing us with energy.

8. Alternative Economics

Money — Income creation — Business

What is money and what is it for?

One way to understand money is to look again at the development of consciousness. As we have seen already, there has been a tendency towards individualization and freedom over the last 200 years. The human being has become more and more aware of him- or herself as an individual and social forces have tended to disintegrate. At the same time as close contact between people has disappeared we have also distanced ourselves from the natural world. We shove things away. We abstract ourselves from reality. In the economic sphere mathematical laws have come between individuals.

Rudolf Steiner envisaged a spectrum between nature and capital, between the concrete and the abstract. This can also be seen as a developmental model of economic development:

1. The subsistence economy (closest to nature) was the current one in Scandinavia not so very long ago. Today, self-sufficiency is practically invisible in the public economy.
2. Handicrafts begin to specialize.
3. Industry grows out of specialized handicrafts.
4. Distribution of products grows out of industry and handicrafts.
5. In the financial economy (based on non-productive capital) money becomes the main issue and the actual products can disappear. This economy becomes invisible and also abstract.

Just like in the rainbow, when light is split, each end of the spectrum shades off into the invisible, infrared and ultraviolet. Self-sufficiency, or subsistence, is not often measured, or indeed measurable (1). Like women's work in the home, it doesn't exist officially. With peasants and artisans, the farm or the product is the most important aspect, profitability and economics are merely means to keep the continuity. Economics as such has not yet begun in its own right (2). As we move towards the finance economy, the motive for carrying on the activity changes from the product or the service being the central issue to the money transaction becoming all-encompassing (3). Just like in the game of Monopoly hotels are no longer places where people stay and enjoy themselves, but merely plastic or wooden counters that are placed on a board and traded between players (4). The finance economy is also invisible in the sense that it does not deal any longer with concrete products, but with the abstract fantasies of money (5).

In the real economy money is a tool which can create. It is the measure of energy which circulates within the economy. Money is the unit, economy is the process. Economics consists of distribution, products, values and relationships. We feed ourselves from the world, we fetch products up from the ground, we use them, share them and dispose of them. The economy is like a natural cycle; as the natural ecology creates biomass, the economy creates value.

Surplus money can be put in the bank, this can grow and finance other cycles which spring forth from the natural economic cycle. Culture, research, state administration, aid and care for people must all be carried by the value that is created. In the old days, corn stores often functioned as savings banks. This was a visible form of insurance, to be stored in times of plenty and used in times of need. This is a process of metamorphosis, a breathing in and a breathing out.

Money creates effects in society. If too much heaps up in one place, there will be a corresponding lack somewhere else. When that happens in the economy we all know what human consequences the unequal distribution of wealth, capital and income can result in.

Today the finance economy is several hundred times larger than the natural economy and has torn itself away from nature. It has grown to many times the size that the natural economic cycle can bear. This creates illusionary values, as short-term profits become the priority in pension funds, in insurance companies and in capital investments. Today there is a tendency for successful companies that are highly productive to close down their production facilities in order to concentrate solely on finance. In purely abstract economic terms they can become highly successful, but they have moved from concrete realities into a fantasy world, the invisible world of the finance economy. Awareness of aims in a company is very important. If the aim is to create as much profit as possible, the enterprise will go in a certain direction. If it is the quality of the product or service which is the highest aim, it will develop differently.

The money in my pocket all looks the same and my first reaction is to think that it's also the same as the money in the bank. If we look a bit closer we find that we can give money different qualities.

Consumption money can cover daily use. Here there is a dynamic between thrift and profligacy. Thrift will create a surplus which will become:

Savings. These lie in a dynamic between greediness, where we try and get as much we can out of our investment, whatever we invest in, and indifference, where we don't concern ourselves with what the money is used for or how much it gains in interest. Here we think in a longer time scale than we do when we consume, when we are really concerned with gratifying needs. Maybe we can invest in long-term interests. If we have even more surplus money maybe we can create:

Gift money. Banks and foundations can manage these sums. How far are we willing to give this money full freedom? Can we give it away as a grant? A new idea first needs gift money to be developed. This we call risk capital. Completely free money is necessary for development, both for human beings and for enterprises. A loan might be necessary to develop the concrete idea, and trust and hope have to be created in order to raise this. The loan must be paid back when the enterprise gets going, when it enters the consumption economy.

This might all sound a bit abstract, but can be applied to real life situations.

I go into town, I need a new pair of socks, I fancy a cup of coffee and my eye is caught by a new book. I buy all three and use the cash I have in my pocket. Literally pocket money. When I go shopping for food, or pay the electricity bill, I pay with the same kind of money, the cash we need for everyday life, running costs, living expenses.

If we live thriftily, we will save some of our income. This we don't need for everyday living expenses and can be put aside. Right now our village is about to open a shop in our local town, and we are using our collective savings to buy shelves and paint and extra stock. Thinking about this shop has been a long creative process in our community, and this 'investment' is now another kind of money, a means to create something. This is the second kind of money, creative investment.

We try not to use all our surplus in investment, but keep some aside for gifts. What do we believe in that we want to support? Who needs our help? What chance factors (are there such things?) bring us into contact with people or projects that are dependant upon goodwill in order to develop? This money has been raised up into the spiritual sphere of gift money. This is the third kind of money, a spiritual gift.

Personally I find it helpful to think of money in these three terms: everyday living expenses, creative investment and spiritual gifts. Without a balance between these three, life would be a lot poorer!

Money is a tool which we have created. It's powerful, it makes or breaks people and nations. We can use it for good or bad. In our Ecovillage planning, it's important that we understand what this tool is and how we can use it. We might begin with a study session discussing the following questions:

— How can we create stable money systems as one of the fundamental pre-conditions for a sustainable economy?
— What is to be learnt from the countries where different models exist?
— Do we need more crises before the necessary changes can be made? Or is it possible to carry out experiments in a less stressful and dangerous political situation?
— What are the necessary ingredients for a sustainable money system in terms of governance, decision-making, technical solutions, funding and awareness?

Money is an agreement within a community to use something as a medium of exchange. It resides in the same space as all social contracts, such as marriage, rental agreements and political parties.

One problem with money is that it has been used to measure the wrong things, giving us false values. Our time and the ability to work are assets which we have been freely given, and measuring these in monetary terms stifles them and makes us mechanical beings. When Ruth and I grew our own vegetables for home consumption, I worked part-time on local farms in order to earn the cash we needed. I worked for hourly rates and if I had measured the value of our vegetables at the same rate not only would we not have been able to afford them, they would have been some of the most expensive vegetables in the world! Patently absurd! My time was my own, it didn't cost me anything, it was a pleasure to be out in the garden, it kept me healthy and the joy of eating our own produce was never diminished.

Most communities I know of don't want to take the leap from an economy where work is measured in money. It's radical and frightening for us brought up in the western world, where the norm is to earn money by work. For those communities which do make that leap, something happens which totally transforms them in terms of social glue. Money becomes a tool which you can use to get to know each other better. Work becomes something which you give and receive freely. Instead of personal money making you *im*mune to others, sharing money makes you *com*mune with them. From my experience of Kibbutz and Camphill, there is a tendency over time to slowly privatize and regularize, but many old-timers will talk nostalgically of the old times when cash was kept in a bowl in a public place for people to take as needed.

It's worth considering a shared economy when planning the Ecovillage. It may be that it's a system which might be limited to the pioneering phase, it might be limited to an inner core of dedicated radicals, or it might be limited to certain aspects of the economy. The basic element is not clever book keeping or a good sense for business. The base is trust, without which it is probably the worst system you can have. By having a shared economy you can attain a new sense of community that cannot be attained by any other means I can think of. You don't 'get what you pay for.' You get what you *don't* pay for!

World economics, the gold standard and porridge oats

Richard Douthwaite in his excellent and highly recommended book *Short Circuit* identifies a number of events which destabilized the global economic climate. For many centuries money was based on real things. I already mentioned that in some places corn had been used as a form of savings, but during more recent times money has been based on gold, the value of a national currency corresponding to the amount of gold reserves held by that nation. In August 1971 Richard Nixon took the American dollar off the gold standard. Because of the international importance of the dollar, this had effects upon virtually every other currency. Money was no longer linked to something tangible and currencies could float freely, at the whim of the trust and beliefs of the world's stock exchanges.

When we started a wholefood co-operative nearly a decade later in England, we were only dimly aware of the effects of the global economy, but we were aware enough to worry about inflation eroding the value of our business. We didn't have any gold, in fact we had very little capital at all, but we did have organic wholemeal porridge oats. We regarded it as a pretty staple food and something which was easily grown in England. We linked our wages to the price of oats!

Douthwaite goes on to list a number of other events: Britain joining the Common Market in 1973, the Tokyo GATT treaty of 1979 and the abolition of exchange controls in the same year by Margaret Thatcher. Other countries went through similar processes, and the combined effect was to create an economic climate where interest and exchange rates fluctuated wildly, making it very hard for small businesses to get started and stay in the game.

This structural instability has in turn created a renewed interest in alternative forms of financing, and may be one contributory factor behind the growth of barter systems, LETS and CSAs. The inability of the conventional system to deliver has led to people finding alternatives. Not a bad thing after all!

Shareholder protectionism and instability

Most enterprises are owned by someone, often by shareholders creating a company. The stock exchange buys and sells the shares, and the money generated can be used to create capital for new enterprises or the expansion of existing ones. There are also share funds, collections of shares which you can buy, and which help spread the risk. These things are invented in order to create profits, but they break the relationship between the investor and the company. Here it pops up again, this tendency towards fragmentation and individualization.

Now in any business venture there are a number of groups involved. If we take an average production business, making, for instance, furniture, employing a few hundred people and located in a small town, let's take a look at who these might be. First of all, there are the actual workers and then the people who own the shares (given that it's a shareholding company). Both these groups expect to make a living or a reasonable return on their investment. Next we have the families of these people, who are also dependant upon the business. These people in turn make use of a wide range of services in the town, shops, entertainment and so on, which again employ people. Everyone pays taxes of different kinds which help to provide municipal services like schools, health services, libraries, etc. The economy is like nature, we are in the end all connected to everyone else. We now see that we can define a number of interest groups:

— Workers
— Shareholders/owners
— Surrounding community
— Municipality

In a truly democratic or community controlled situation each one of these groups has a right to say something about the business. No wonder ordinary people get upset when distant shareholders decide to relocate production in countries where the labour cost is lower. Why in the world would we want to protect just one group and rely on some abstract notion like 'free market forces?' Surely we would want to protect everyone involved against instability and insecurity.

Global economics is complex stuff. Most people don't really understand what's going on and are being misled by a lot of the popular media. Some people tell us that somehow it's best when something called 'market forces' are allowed to control the economy by having a 'free market economy' run unhindered. These same people are generally associated with the Transnational

Corporations (TNCs) where the aim seems to be the opposite of what is stated. The so-called 'market forces' are actually the profit motives of the said TNCs and the 'free market economy' really means the total freedom of the owners of the TNCs to do what they want. These owners are of course the shareholders. Now in the early days of capitalism it was theoretically the case that lots of people could buy shares and control companies through a democratic shareholder association. Today that isn't the case any longer. Shares are traded in blocks on the stock exchanges and owned and controlled by these same people again! Ross Jackson in his book *And We Are Doing It* called this system 'shareholder protectionism' and showed how it was touted as freedom for everyone, but that this was a Great Lie and really meant freedom for a tiny proportion to make enormous profits at the cost of everyone else and the environment.

By making rules for trade, we create specific conditions. It's our choice what we do, there is in fact no natural law or objective 'market force' out there forcing us to do anything. In the old days in India, before the British invaded, there was a tax system imposed upon the movement of goods throughout the land. Around every city and along all the roads, there were tax gates. As you brought things past the gate, you had to pay a tax. The faster you travelled the higher the tax. People carrying things on their backs paid very little, carts and carriages paid more. The further you travelled, the more tax gates you had to pass and so the total tax paid became higher. The effect of this was to keep resources within regions and encourage the trading of items which had low weight and high value, like gold or spices. Locally produced goods were nearly always the cheapest, local production was encouraged. This sounds like the sort of alternative economy many of us have been envisaging for some time!

In the village where I live someone asked recently whether we run our economy or does the economy run us? In your Ecovillage you might want to consider starting up with other models of ownership and control of businesses. This is an ideal way to connect with local people and demonstrate that other models are practical and worthwhile. Classic Permaculture again, let us make a business that educates people while thriving!

Indicators of sustainable economic welfare

An article in the *New Scientist* in the summer of 2002 drew attention to the fact that Italian women were having fewer babies. Now it may not be a bad thing for the population to fall — and, short of war and catastrophe, having less babies is a sure way of getting that to happen. Normal stable replacement level would be maintained if women have 2.1 children as an average. It seems that

European countries have a birth rate far below this. Italy is weighing in at 1.2 babies per woman, with Spain, Greece, the Czech Republic, Russia and Armenia showing similar figures. In fact over 60 countries around the world have birth rates below replacement level. The implications for the future are tremendous. Europe would be a very different place, with an ageing population, labour in short supply and countries competing for younger immigrants to come and do the hard work.

At the beginning of 2004, Kofi Annan, the Secretary of the United Nations, recognized this in a speech he gave in Sweden, where he pointed out that soon the European countries will be inviting immigrants from other parts of the world to do their work for them as their indigenous populations gradually aged.

The number of people and their ages, the country's demographic structure, are fairly easy to chart. You have just have to count them. They give an indication of something that is going on, a hard fact. Finding out about the quality of their lives is a bit harder. One measure of economic welfare used to be based on counting up the total value of goods and services produced in a country and dividing by the number of people involved. This would then give you the Gross National Product. This is still used today and we can compare a relatively high GNP from one of the western countries with a really low one from some poor place in Africa and feel sorry for them. If the government can somehow get the GNP to rise they pat themselves on the back and use it for their next election campaign. It seems very nice, but it doesn't really tell you how well people are doing. If a company is busy producing something and paying lots of wages to their employees, that will register as a rise. If one of the results of their activities is lots of pollution, that doesn't show. But as soon as health personnel get employed trying to cure those who get ill from that pollution and government financed clean-up operations get underway, that also counts as a rise in GNP, as long as everyone gets paid. The government can continue to pat itself on the back!

The economists who rely on this simplistic notion have not yet learnt basic maths. It's just not enough only to add up, sometimes you have to subtract!

Simon Kuznets, who invented this way of measuring economic activity, never intended it to be an overall indicator of human well-being, but due to the popularization of economics and possibly the laziness of economists, this is what it has become.

As a reaction to this there arose in the 1960s and 1970s a range of new indicators. The 'Measure of Economic Welfare' (MEW) by James Tobin and William Nordhaus, Japan's 'Net National Welfare' (NNW), The Society for International Development created the 'Physical Quality of Life Indicator' (PQLI) and the United Nations Environment Program developed the 'Basic Human Needs' indicator (BHN).

Lebensgarten, Germany:
conflict resolution as a business

Date founded — 1985
Approximate number of residents — *ca.* 100
Location — northern Germany
Spiritual or ideological affiliation — cultural and
ecological innovations
Visited — 1996, 1998, 2000

The buildings at Lebensgarten were constructed during the 1930s as a residence and munitions factory by the Nazis. The process of turning them into an Ecovillage community dedicated to conflict resolution is given a concrete shape by the very fact of taking this tragic beginning and turning it into something positive. Even though I was aware of this past, and tried to imagine the slave labour that the Nazis had used, I had only good feelings there, feelings that were reinforced by starting each morning with sacred chanting, culled from all the world's sacred traditions, followed by circle dancing in the village square. That certainly gave me a good appetite for breakfast and a positive attitude for the day!

Someone told me there that because they have had so much conflict within the community, and managed to survive it, that they have become pretty good at conflict management and resolution. So much so that it has become a business, they act as conflict consultants to a wide range of businesses, local government and other groups. I always consider the acquisition of skills necessary for the group to develop, and then the marketing of these skills as a very good example of how Ecovillages can utilize the lifestyle they create.

In addition to that, the sorry state of the building mass, having been a British Army base after the war, and then lain derelict for close to a decade, gave the founders of Lebensgarten the impetus and the need to do some serious renovation. This they did by retrofitting with all kinds of environmentally sound energy systems. Solar heating, insulation, landscaping and the reconstruction of the central area as a community focus all have been done thoroughly and it is now a showcase of examples.

LEFT. Circle dancing in the village square to greet the day.

LEFT. Solar greenhouse on the south side of Declan Kennedy's house.

RIGHT. *Members of the European Ecovillage Network meet in 1998.*

RIGHT. *When the weather is good, the communal dining room spills out onto the terrace. On the roof at the back can be seen the massive greenhouse windows which heat the building.*

What these have in common is a focus on wider phenomena than just money transactions. A two column approach was introduced, not just seeing everything as an asset, but deducting unwanted or negative effects such as pollution and war.

What we are seeing today, with the benefit of distance and hindsight, is that both GNP and indicators such as the one developed by the New Economics Foundation in London, the 'Indicator of Sustainable Economic Welfare' (ISEW) continued to rise in a similar way until the 1970s. Since then the alternative indicators have tended to fall, while the GNP has continued rising. There's more money sloshing around, but freed from such realities as gold, its value has become an abstract thing that has no meaning in the real world. In the meantime, consumerism, resource depletion, pollution and human misery caused by wars and conflicts are increasing.

One way of noticing this downward trend was mentioned by Bill Bryson in his book *Made in America*. He quotes from Juliet B. Schor, *The Overworked American*, that the amount of leisure time has fallen by almost 40 percent since 1973: 'Almost uniquely among the developed nations, America took none of its productivity gains in additional leisure. It bought consumer items instead.' It seems that, as we get richer, we are working longer hours. Instead of translating our new wealth into fun and leisure, we are just buying more consumer goods. Who is ruling: us or the economy?

The quality has gone, the human spirit has been neglected. In our transactions, we have lost the art of human beings meeting each other and meeting each other's needs. We need to get out of this spiral of greed and negativity. Ecovillages are not a sure panacea, but they do represent a real opportunity to bring the spiritual and human aspect back into economics.

LETS and other self-generated systems

LETS stands for Local Exchange Trading System, or Local Energy Transfer System. Sometimes known as Green Dollar Systems, they are generally attributed to a scheme started by Michael Linton in Canada in 1983. In fact, it's nothing new, it's just a group of people who agree to trade amongst themselves, creating a new form of money. Margrit Kennedy, in her book *Interest and Inflation Free Money*, gives a number of examples of similar systems which were set up and often subsequently suppressed. In the 1980s, LETS seemed to capture people's imagination and the idea flourished. It's pretty simple:

New Bassaisa, Egypt:
self-help into the future

Date founded — 1993
Approximate number of residents — temporary work group
at time of visit
Location — just east of Suez City
Spiritual or ideological affiliation — ecological
Visited — one day in 1996

New Bassaisa was established by young people from Old Bassaisa in the Nile Delta to help ease the pressure on land they were experiencing there. When we visited there was a membership group of over 90 families, with a group of younger people working to build the infrastructure. Trees had been planted for windbreaks, with olives for oil. Animal waste was composted and was helping to create soil in the sand between the windbreaks. Human waste was being processed for bio-gas and used as manure for the orchards.

We found two types of methane generators and solar panels. The buildings were constructed of local materials, their design inspired by the 'father' of modern mud architecture, Hassan Fathy, using mud brick arches and traditional Arab design forms.

The example of New Bassaisa lay in its combination of a social economic form with an all-embracing ecological planning. By forming a co-operative and pooling resources and labour, they had managed to create facts on the ground. Everything they were building had a deliberate environmental component, and was expressed in a way that reflected their traditional Arab cultural background.

ABOVE. Mural depicting the move from Old Bassaisa to New Bassaisa.

BELOW. Planting windbreaks and olive trees in the desert.

ABOVE. Partially completed storage building based on design by Hassan Fathy, using free standing Nubian arch technique.

LEFT. Methane digester, the slurry will be used for soil building.

BELOW. Solar panels on the roof of the first completed building.

A number of people, it could be your Ecovillage group, make a list of goods and services that you can trade with each other. You agree on a common currency, which can be linked to the national currency or not, that's up to you. If you give it a snappy name it helps generate interest from others and gives you a sense of identity. That's one of the reasons why the term Green Dollars was so successful. When we started in Israel we called them Beads. With some friends in Lincolnshire many years ago I traded in Schumacher Pounds (we all shared an admiration for *Small Is Beautiful*). Having done this you elect a committee to write a directory of goods and services and who is offering them, and to keep track of transactions. Now you can start trading.

Trading is easy. I look in the directory for what I need, maybe a good massage after all the stress of building the Ecovillage! I find who is giving massage, ask them how much (how many Beads), I enjoy the massage and we send off a note to the bookkeeper telling him or her that I used, let's say 5 Beads, putting me 5 Beads in debit, and the masseur 5 Beads in credit. At the end of the month a newsletter to all the members includes a list of everyone, showing their balance. Some will be in credit, others in debit. The more debits and credits there are, the busier you have been and that's a measure of success! You might consider putting a ceiling on how far you can go into either credit or debit, in order to protect yourselves against individuals accumulating too much either way. That's the old principle of keeping monetary pollution down. As the system grows it might be worthwhile considering giving those who keep the books and issue the newsletter a few beads for their work.

That's the theory. Now let's look at a couple of examples.

A decade ago **Avalon LETS** in the West Country in England combined the trading scheme with meetings in cafes and a number of other social gatherings. They had a list of rules which members had to agree to abide by, essentially ensuring that no one could cheat by getting lots of services without giving any. By combining social togetherness, this created another safeguard in that members got to know each other, making cheating yet more difficult. Here is yet another example of getting economics to generate social wellbeing. Not only could individuals join, but they encouraged businesses and other groups to take part. Transactions could be either wholly in Gebos (their currency units) or a mixture of Gebos and cash. Only Gebos were registered in the scheme.

Years before Michael Linton created Green Dollars, I was part of a very informal group in Lincolnshire where Ruth and I lived. In order to share tools and labour, each one of us kept a little dog-eared notebook where we recorded favours done, agreeing beforehand how many **Schumacher Pounds** each one was worth. In this way we kept an awareness of our transactions and attempted to keep them equal. Had we stayed in the area, it might well have developed into another LETS type scheme.

I was sent the following report a few weeks ago and it was exciting to see that the idea is still current and expanding:

In Chiemgau, in Bavaria, six young women, all in their late teens and students at the Steiner school, started an enterprise in 2003. It had a built-in mechanism that made it possible to support good causes such as the local Steiner school system.

Those wishing to participate in **the Chiemgauer** purchased 100 Chiemgauer for 100 Euros. This local currency was used to pay goods and services in participating stores. Of this 95 percent remained with the business, three percent going to the charity and the two percent remaining to the Chiemgauer administration to cover overheads. The Chiemgauer was time-stamped and there was a 'parking charge' for not circulating the money. This gave an incentive to the user to spend the local currency, rather than hoard or save it. This feature ensured that the currency was kept in circulation, which in turn was good for business in particular and for the region in general.

The biggest start-up effort was to convince the businesses to participate. In the early days some speculated that no one would. After two months of conversations and follow-up phone calls about 35 companies were willing to take part. The system was officially launched in January 2003. After 100 days the 'Chiemgauer club' had 100 members. After a few months all the members reported that by using their Chiemgauers they have a stronger feeling of belonging to the local community and of contributing to its socio–economic well-being!

The idea of 'aging money' or time-stamped money is in fact thousands of years old. There were several periods throughout history — including Dynastic Egypt and the Central Middle Ages in Northern Europe — where demurrage (negative interest money) was used.

There is a wide variety of social purposes with such systems: from resolving local unemployment to elderly care, from mentoring kids to resolving environmental problems. What they all have in common is to be able to operate in parallel with the conventional money system, matching otherwise unmet needs with unused resources.

Local capital, business and income creation

In many countries there is no conventional explanation of how people can live. In the early 1990s official food production figures in Russia were so low that economists and newspapers around the world were announcing that people were starving in Russia, that there was not enough food to go round and food aid started being sent by the trainload from the US and Germany. Teodor Shanin, professor of economics at the University of Manchester and now rector of the Moscow School of Social and Economic Sciences, had been studying peasant economics for years and was then carrying out studies in rural Russia. He found that people there had a highly developed informal sector, that food and services were being produced, and that barter and other forms of exchange were flourishing. Times might have been hard, but no one was suffering serious hardship. He coined the term 'peasantology' and maintains that the worst thing you can do to a naturally developing economy is to wade in with multinational loans, food aid and other interventions from the World Bank and the International Monetary Fund.

If we look at what nature does in regeneration, in the colonization of new or disturbed areas by pioneer plants, maybe we can apply similar methods in economics. What might pioneer businesses be?

Low input levels characterize worn out land and shattered economies. Sunlight comes in but is dispersed in nature, money is around, but thinly spread in the economy. Nature regenerates land by establishing waves of different plants that accumulate energy and organic matter, each wave contributing something to the overall organic richness and helping the next wave to establish itself. We call it succession in the natural cycle. Pioneer plants produce large amounts of highly mobile seed. It's this which makes it capable of establishing itself quickly on worn out or disturbed land. High light requirement is important in areas where there is no shade and often implies that the pioneer plants can give shade to succeeding waves of plants which grow slower.

Similarly, we might imagine how we can use this model in order to regenerate a local economy. Home-centred enterprises lead the way. Self-sufficiency would be the pioneer economic wave. We can have great diversity; trade, barter or other forms of exchanging goods and services would spring up as people got to know one another — their needs and their capabilities. This would be the second wave of our natural economic regeneration. Farmers' markets might be the third wave, as the new economy 'goes public' and begins to draw in more people. Farmers' markets are now showing a rising popularity, they often include crafts, but everything has to be locally produced products, they have to come from a certain radius to enhance the local market. A successful farmers' market encourages people to come to town to buy.

Harman Centre, Turkey:
traditional Anatolian agriculture

Date founded — mid 1990s
Approximate number of residents — 3–4
Location — Anatolian plateau, a few hours drive east of Ankara
Spiritual or ideological affiliation — ecological
Visited — short visit in the mid 1990s, twice in 2000,
teaching and visiting

In the summer of 2000 I was invited to teach a three day course 'Introduction to Permaculture' by the Harman Centre (The Anatolian Centre for Ecological and Holistic Living) in Turkey. They were a continuation of the Hocamkoy Turkish Ecovillage Movement, and there had been contact between them, the Global Ecovillage Network, and the Green Kibbutz Movement for some years. The seminar was held in the Anatolian village of Hasandede, where the Harman Centre was producing organically grown food, and initiating a number of other projects, including the building of a nearly completed strawbale community centre. The relationship between Harman, the local authorities and the village residents was extremely positive.

Beginning with running a shop in Ankara, selling organically grown foods, the Harman Centre moved to Hasandede to have greater control of the production and processing of this food. During the seminar I was there the preparation and drying of zucchinis and apricots were in full swing. The domestic garden produced some of this, but mostly it was commissioned from local farmers and gardeners. The organic certification was organized and controlled by the Harman Centre, ensuring a uniform high standard. This had brought them into contact with local growers, and was having some influence on local practices. One producer that we talked to admitted that he would not use chemicals on his own family's food, but implied that he had used chemicals freely on commercial crops previously. With access to organic consumers, and the higher prices commanded by organic produce, this attitude was undergoing change.

The educational part of the Harman Centre, involving courses with participants coming from all parts of Turkey, also provided some part-time employment for local people (the food was really good!). Their work brought them into contact with local artisans who still kept alive the old Anatolian country crafts in building, gardening, and food preparation.

I have recently learned (January 2005) that the Harman Centre subsequently closed down. This does not diminish its value as an example of a positive ecological model, inspired and informed by the Ecovillage idea.

LEFT. Sun-drying apricots on the roof.

BELOW. Traditional irrigation technique being practised by the peasants of Hasandede village.

LEFT. Preparing fruit for drying in the court-yard of the Institute.

BELOW. Crops being irrigated plot by plot by shifting earth across the water courses.

How can we encourage this type of economic development? Here are some questions which can serve as starting points in your planning:

— What types of products and services can be supplied?
— What is the optimum size for pioneer enterprises?
— Do we need new business regulations?
— Pioneer business zones?
— Pioneer trading zones, markets?
— A Pioneer Enterprise Festival to stimulate ideas and innovations?
— A Pioneer Enterprise Council might link local government, entrepreneurs and local business people.
— Is it possible to predict how enterprises will fade away to allow stronger businesses to take over?

The Ecovillage can be a really powerful catalyst in this sector. By developing self-help, LETS systems, CSA groups and generally stimulating local dependency, it can have a tremendous force for change at the local level.

Community Supported Agriculture

Today, in the West, there are very few people involved in food production. In the UK less than 3 percent. In the United States there are so few that farmers no longer constitute an official statistical group! But we have no choice whether to farm or not if we want to eat, so we either have to support farms where other people do the work for us, or we have to do the farming ourselves. Farming also helps to create our culture, our food is a great part of our everyday life (or should be!). Just think of fish'n'chips in England, or Bratwurst and Bier in Germany.

In the global economy it is difficult for farmers to make a living. Will the idea of cooperation and mutual support be able to give new inspiration to agriculture? There is a desperate need for a new set of economic relationships, a new social community development.

The idea of a new relationship between the grower and the consumer arose in the 1980s as a reaction to the growing food miles and the increasing role of the supermarket forcing its way in between the farm and the kitchen. By 1990 there were estimated to be about 60 CSA schemes operating in the United States. By 1997 this figure had topped the 1,000 and it was estimated that over 100,000 households were involved. This could mean at least a quarter of a million people (the population of Iceland!). Though the schemes were very varied and different, there was enough of them to distinguish certain common features:

— A dedication to quality (organic or biodynamic)
— Diverse, with crops and livestock
— Labour intensive
— Multi dimensional, producing, processing, delivering
— Educational and cultural dimensions
— A dedication to environmental improvement

A CSA (see p. 222) can be defined as a system of farming where the producer and the consumer share the risks and the benefits. It ranges in the level of involvement:

Farmers' market	Lesser Involvement
Box scheme	↑
Subscription schemes	↓
Whole farm CSA	Greater Involvement

The Soil Association in Britain has been actively involved in promoting CSAs. It has found that there are many benefits. For consumers — that's most of us who like to eat — get fresh food from a known source while improving understanding about food production and the real costs involved. We improve our knowledge of new and traditional varieties and become familiar with the produce of different seasons. By having access to a farm as a resource for education, work and leisure, we improve our health through better diet, physical work and socializing. This in turn gives us a sense of belonging to a community. In a wider sense we help to influence the local landscape and help farmers to use more sustainable methods.

Farmers benefit by receiving a more secure income and a higher and fairer return for products by cutting out the middle man. They can raise working capital and financial support from local communities and become more involved in the local community. A CSA responds directly to consumer needs, and encourages communication and cooperation with other farmers.

Society as a whole can benefit by having fewer 'food miles,' less packaging and more ecologically sensitive farming with improved animal welfare. Care for local land is encouraged and local economies are enhanced. CSAs improve social networks and social responsibility, and improve the sense of community and trust in an area.

Whole farm CSAs

These are most advanced in the US and there are a few in Europe. There will be a circle of consumers, in association with the farmers. This circle undertakes to carry the budget of the farm. An annual meeting will review the previous year and set a budget for the next. Shares can be allocated and each consumer pledges to support the scheme. Payment should be made by monthly standing orders. Then everything that is produced is freely available to all the members. self-employed partnerships are to be preferred to employing people, as this better preserves the free individual initiative.

We can define the principles of this type of enterprise:

— Supporting organic and biodynamic farming
— A new economic model, based on mutual support
— Practical involvement at all levels
— To be transparent in all affairs and strive for consensus
— Opportunities for learning and therapy
— Networking with other CSAs
— To use the farm for social and cultural activities
— To develop an inclusive sense of community
— To work with other organizations

Stroud Community Agriculture

In November 2001 a public meeting drew 80 people, linking a biodynamic farm to the local community in Stroud, Gloucestershire, England. Working groups were set up to look into payment systems, vegetable distribution, communications, coordination, and it was expected of those involved that they had a commitment to regular meetings.

The scheme was launched in July 2002 with 20 members and a celebration. There was a £10 membership fee and £20 shares were issued, with quantities of produce linked to the shares. The 90 acre farm had an annual turnover of *ca*. £120,000 which included reasonable salaries for the farmer and the workers. Approximately 180 people were needed for the scheme, each contributing about £60 per month, as an ideal. By January 2003 the scheme had about 200 supporters with 70 paying members at £10 per month and 40 paying for vegetables at £20 per month. The monthly income was about £1,100 per month.

Tablehouse Farm Cooperative

This enterprise began in 1995 to rescue two biodynamic farms which were running with heavy losses. They were linked to Emerson College in Sussex, England, and with a surrounding community fully sympathetic to the principles of biodynamic farming. Membership was based on £100 shares, which did not give a return to begin with. They were a measure of support by the local community. This provided capital, while the land was owned by a trust. The produce, beef, fruit, vegetables and milk, was sold in local farm shops and elsewhere.

How to start a CSA

Talk over the idea of setting up a community supported garden with a small group of interested people. When the ideas are clear and you have some support, call for an open meeting, contacting as many people in the area as possible. This is especially easy for an Ecovillage: you already have a core group and possibly the right place. Otherwise use a school, a kindergarten, a gardener's club, a church or an environmental centre as a meeting place. It's often better known to the local people and you already have a potential interest group.

Put forward a number of concrete ideas that you have already worked out. If there is interest and you can generate enthusiasm, get a list of those who would like to involve themselves, and their telephone numbers. A small, informal collection of money might be worthwhile at this stage, to cover initial costs of telephone calls, letters and paper. It also creates a sense of commitment.

Form a core action group and delegate tasks. Define the vision, the aims, a practical plan and a rough budget. Check back in the chapter on the Social Aspect (p. 59) for tools to do this effectively.

Create democratic processes based on consensus right from the start. Make sure your meetings are tidy, well run and fun! Don't forget to take notes and keep a running account of what you decide. Be systematic and delegate as much as possible. Get people involved and try to avoid a 'one man show.'

When it comes to labour, it has been found to be more effective to have several part-time gardeners rather than fewer full timers. Be definite in the distinction between paid labour and volunteers. You might ask each member to put in an hour or two every week of free labour as part of their membership commitment. This has a social benefit to people who are not living in an Ecovillage, and could create a strong point of contact between the Ecovillage and the surrounding locality.

Make sure to plan the garden well. You can begin with a list of vegetables that are wanted; then check out the Garden Plan and Schedule (see Appendix, pp. 251–53). When setting the contribution that each member of the scheme should pay, it has been found that a certain built-in flexibility is worthwhile. Half and full contributions, 5, 10 and 20 kg boxes each demand a slightly different weekly commitment financially. For those who have little money but lots of time, consider a half price membership combined with a certain contribution of hours per week.

Get a newsletter going as soon as possible. It doesn't have to be glossy or even that nice, just get it out, making sure it has good relevant information. It's the one thing that glues people together and creates a common bond. It's also good to have recipes, especially if there are unusual varieties of vegetables being offered.

Have lots of patience! Most CSAs take three to five years to get established and to settle into a pattern. They can be a real asset to a budding Ecovillage by supplying life filled, health giving food, by improving the natural environment and by creating educational and cultural experiences.

3

Putting it all together

9. Design Hands-On

Group dynamics — Project presentation

Creativity

Fundamental human needs are defined as food, clothes, shelter and work. These only refer to physical needs and are not specific for humans, but can be applied to animals, plants and machines. That which defines humans is identity, a mature personality set in a unique cultural and social context. Identity gives a starting point for everything else: for the ability for self-realization, for local democracy, for sustainable development and for creativity. Creativity is the ultimate expression of individual identity and when exercised in a group, gives expression to the group identity. We freely create a higher order of being, the co-creative group.

Creativity is the realization of ideas. It is the activity when we come closest to God the Creator. Ideas rise up in our thoughts, in the non-material world. Some of these ideas we can realize in the material world as objects or actions. The path from idea to object is design and that process is fuelled by creativity. Permaculture is one of the tools to make that creative design process function more smoothly.

Identifying patterns can be of great use as a catalyst for creativity. Patterns can be linear or non-linear and they can be found throughout nature. As we saw in Chapter 2 identifying patterns in nature is an essential part of Permaculture design and can be of tremendous help in releasing creativity. This book is written as a linear pattern, the words wouldn't make much sense if we jumbled them up, or read them in a different order. Maps and diagrams, however, present all the information at once, in a non-linear way; it is up to the reader in which order to follow them. Patterns emerge more clearly and are easier to memorize.

The patterns of the stars in the sky have since earliest times been used as starting points for myths and legends, as well as navigational aids. The Australian Aborigines use landscape features as cues for telling their myths and legends: each rock, stream or hill is the starting point for another story and the landscape as a whole creates a mythology.

Maps are our best tools for design; just as you learnt to read books, you will need to learn to read maps. It does take time and effort, but is actually much easier than learning to read the ABC. Most maps have a key to symbols. Good topographical maps give a wealth of information about scale and grid referencing somewhere beside, below or above the actual map itself. Learn contour lines, scales, map symbols, directions, grid references, cross sections, high points and low points, streams, rivers and roads. I was lucky enough to have this forced down my throat at school and have been grateful ever since. Maps are great! You can read one like a book when you get into it. Start with maps of places you are familiar with and begin by tracing routes that you know. Your way to work, your favourite walk, where your friends live. Each time you come across some symbol that you don't know, check it out in the key.

A very good way to learn map reading is to make maps. You don't need to create detailed topographical maps with contour lines and spot heights. It's enough to start with simple sketches, showing a few important elements and how they fit together. Just as ecology is about relationships, so are maps. The individual symbol for house, road, stream or forest has no value other than in the context of its relationship to the other symbols. Without the idea of presenting and digesting information in a non-linear way such as a map or a diagram, you cannot really get into pattern hunting and design.

With using maps comes the compass, where you can find direction and relate the map to the ground. This is where the abstract notion of the map connects with the physical reality of the world. The compass always gives the correct direction. You have to trust it. If you are into wilderness travel and faced with the stark reality of fog, whiteout or darkness, you will learn to love your compass! Like God the creator, the energy flow of Chi, the innate goodness of the Human Being or any other universal value. Maps, on the other had, are like Holy Scripture. They are human-made and need to be read, and this requires learning and interpretation. The compass is inscrutable, mysterious and dependable. It only gives you direction, but really, that's what we need most in life.

Even maps can become overly familiar. As an exercise in recognizing new patterns, try taking a map of the world, your country, or the region with which you are familiar. Turn it upside down and check it out. First of all it will look completely different! It becomes a new world. You can pretend that you are on a new unexplored continent or on another earth-like planet. Check how things hang together, how they are connected, how they are separated. Another exercise can be to hang the map on the wall and step backwards until the details are out of focus. Then get an idea of the general shape of things. Just let your eye flow across the map without any order, open up, let the ideas and patterns emerge, be receptive. You can slowly move closer and let the details come back into focus. Try doing this with a small group of two or three and you'll be amazed at how many things emerge. Don't be critical of each other and jot down any thoughts that come up.

I got very excited a few years ago when I came across an idea called Mind Mapping. Tony Buzan has registered this term as a trademark, so I won't use it any more. If you want to explore further you need to buy his books. However, the practice of writing down key words on a sheet of paper and connecting them up with arrows, is free; anyone can do it and benefit from it. Arrange the words in any order you want, connect them up with lines where you find connections and then redraw the thing clustering ideas together in groups. Create more complex diagrams by relating several key ideas together on one sheet. This is a tool, like Patrick Geddes' thinking machines. Put it in your tool box and try it out when you get to putting things together in your design.

Creativity is about thinking differently, thinking outside the usual framework, making new and surprising connections between things that were not previously connected. Turn problems into solutions. Turn effects into causes. Turn the world on its head and make ridiculous statements. Be prepared to be foolish and to be wild. Create that sense of trust in your group that you can brainstorm and come up with the weirdest ideas. You can always evaluate them out later.

Group dynamics

I used up most of my material on group dynamics in Chapter 3. The central question here is how to create a group spirit, how to set up ways of working together. When I first conceived the idea for this book, I was thinking of writing for a group which wanted to create an Ecovillage, going through a process of learning together. Designing the Ecovillage as a group process could be the first and most valuable step towards creating a group identity that is the most important foundation and premise for success.

Just like in natural ecologies, diversity is fundamental. A wide range of skills, experience and ideas amongst the designers will make the design holistic and realizable. In today's technical world, there is no way of getting round specialization. In many cases you will need qualified people in various things. Some local authorities only allow qualified agriculturalists to run farms. Insurance companies won't insure buildings that haven't had their wiring done by authorized electricians. If you haven't got the right license, you can't drive a truck.

This is where the group dynamic can really help. There is a tension between the need for specialized skills and the ideal of holistic planning. The individual

La Paix-Dieu, Belgium: Permaculture housing development

Date founded — 1997
Approximate number of residents — at the time of
visit: two houses
Location — Jehay, central Belgium
Spiritual or ideological affiliation — environmental,
Permaculture planning
Visited — for a couple of hours in 1998

My immediate reaction upon seeing this site was that finally Permaculture is going mainstream. This was no bunch of hippies chanting or wafting sage incense about with eagle feathers. This was a housing development created largely by and for middle-class commuters, who wanted to live more ecologically, with a sense of community, honouring the place they lived with its embedded history written into its landscape. At that time it was still largely a greenfield site, but we looked at the plans, and saw here a serious process of planning and working together with the local authorities in order to create something that would work. And all this had been done with a consciousness and methodology anchored in the Permaculture tradition.

It is inevitable in our modern world that we build more and more housing. Too much of this consists of financially driven projects that set houses down in lines and groups that have no relationship to the context of the area. At La Paix-Dieu they had successfully combined a Permaculture process lasting a couple of years with creating a large housing development that would appeal to ordinary middle-class commuters. It is important that the idea of environmental planning gets across to more and more people, even if it may get watered down in the process.

ABOVE. View of the greenfield site to be developed.

LEFT. Looking at the plans of the proposed ecological development.

BELOW. Looking across the site from one of the first completed houses.

can supply the skill, while the group can supply the overall thinking. Just as the body is composed of legs that are great for walking, but pretty useless for banging in nails, so your group is be composed of specialized limbs. Now all you have to do is to train and get good at banging in nails while running! Your agreement needs to be based upon the vision and the aims, while your specialization needs to appear in the skills that are required for each area.

Design process, step by step

You can go at design with a blank of sheet of paper, and just scribble and sketch until you have hammered something out. You need to be a pretty special person to be able to come up with something credible from such a process. But don't knock it, some of the most amazing ideas and designs have been created by foolish scribbling by highly gifted people. For most of the rest of us, especially if we are working as a team, we need a process, a clear design path.

Design is about using patterns and patterns will reveal designs to you. If you asked me to define Permaculture in one word, I would answer 'design.' Design is about understanding the relationships between components and ordering them in such a way that their interactions enhance their performance. This in turn creates synergy and the multiplier effect. By creating dynamic relationships, we raise components into a higher order of existence, the ecology takes on a life of its own. I experience this as a step up the spiritual ladder. Relationships are abstractions, unseen ideas that exist in our consciousness, but that have real concrete effects in the physical world. No wonder that so many religions go on about love, perhaps the ultimate relationship. It is totally abstract, existing in the sphere of our feelings, sometimes affected by our will (or lack of it), but what an effect in the physical world! Children are the first things that springs to mind. War and peace the next two things.

Very briefly, the process could be followed like this: information, description, analysis and finally design. It's really hard for me, an ordinary mortal, to think of things in any other order. How can I possibly make a design if I don't have the information I need about the place and the aims of the group that's wanting a plan?

An acronym that was introduced by Graham Bell at his first Permaculture design course in Israel has stuck with me ever since: BREDIM. I have used it in all the courses I have taught.

Boundaries. This sets the parameters of the design. Physically it's no bad thing to actually walk around the perimeter of the site. You get a good perspective into what you are about to deal with. There is also very often a wealth of material that gets shoved off towards the edges, material that can be regarded as resources. The idea of boundaries also includes such things as limits and questions, the actual design brief.

Resources. You can both brainstorm a list and walk the site making a list. Be as inclusive and as wide as you can. Include both human resources such as friendship and goodwill, and of course the physical resources such as timber, good soil and water.

Evaluation. When we come to the evaluation of the resources available, we need to set aside a lot of time and energy. Here we can take each element in turn and subject it to a rigorous assessment. Needs and yields are two good categories to do this with. From Mollison's *Design Manual* the example of the chicken has become a standard example in Permaculture literature and we may as well continue this fine tradition. The exercise consists of putting two headings on the board/flipchart and then brainstorming for a few minutes to get a list under each heading.

Needs (inputs) of a chicken:	*Yields (outputs) of a chicken:*
Shelter	Eggs
Food	Manure
Warmth	Feathers
Water	Meat
Earth to scratch	Clearing weeds/insects
...	

This is a fun group exercise and can be done for any element within the design. Try tree and pond, try compost heap and access road. When you have a number of elements, cross reference them by matching the yields from one to the needs of another. This exercise will create design by itself. As the various elements link together in a functional web, patterns will arise and the first outline of your design will emerge. This is Permaculture design! You are now deep into what this book is all about.

Design. You're halfway there if you carried out the evaluation really thoroughly. What you need to do now is to put all this together, make a design plan, or better still, many design plans. Split them up into different functions, use plastic overlays or several maps and diagrams.

Implementation. A design is great, but you need a way of getting there, it's impossible to do everything at once and often things need to be done in the right order. If you are planning to produce great quantities of organic vegetables for sale, you need to make sure your distribution and sales are already in place when the first boxes of delicious lettuces have been harvested. They can't stand around for days and weeks while you scour the surrounding locality for a shop or a farmers' market to sell them in. In the same way, many things, most things, will need some kind of capital investment, and you need to be clear how and when that will be available to you. This is part of your design.

Maintenance. Assuming you're into an Ecovillage as a long-term proposition, you need to be clear how you will keep it running. Roads will need repairs, the gutters on your houses will need to be checked for dead leaves and other rubbish every year. Even the best Permaculture food forest will need some maintenance. Getting things the way you want them is only part of your design, keeping them that way is just as important. The fact that you include maintenance will also create a favourable impression upon outside support. People like to see that you have thought through all the aspects of what you want to.

Design is fun, especially as a group exercise. By nurturing creativity we generate enthusiasm, motivation and energy. We have all experienced these arising spontaneously, what I am trying to do here is to give you some suggestions for generating this creativity and maintaining it.

Another very good exercise to clarify your thinking as a group is to use what we call six hat thinking. My memory associates this with Edward de Bono, but I have not been able to find the exact reference. I have included a couple of his books in the resource section because I find him one of the most stimulating thinkers around. One exercise we did on one of the Permaculture design courses was to make six coloured hats and put on the appropriate one to indicate what kind of thinking was going on. It's a really good exercise in self-awareness.

Blue — thinking about thinking. This is a kind of introspective exercise, as well as considering the process itself.

White — information. Here the aim might be objectivity, as far as that is possible.

Green — creativity and brainstorming. It's important here to be totally non-critical, though encouragement is always useful. Enthusiasm always helps creativity.

Red — feelings. It's always good to share feelings, but it's important to protect privacy by making sure it's voluntary and free. Those that don't want to say anything should feel OK about that.

Yellow — positive assessment. When evaluating, make a list of all the good things.

Black — risk assessment, negative. Make sure to spend a little time playing the devil's advocate and list all the things that could go wrong with any given idea. Murphy's law can strike anytime, even in Ecovillages!

Site assessment

Before you start on this, you might check back to Chapter 4 and make sure you have read about zoning (p. 99). This is basic to the process of site assessment and gives a foundation upon which to hang the information. A quick recap:

Zone 1 — Homes and food (security) gardens.
Zone 2 — Close Spaces and Orchards.
Zone 3 — Larger open spaces and gardens.
Zone 4 — Reserves, fuel forests, windbreaks, etc.
Zone 5 — Wildlife corridors, native plant sanctuaries.

These zones are in theory concentric circles, but need modifying with two more factors:

Sectors are parts of these circles having specific attributes, such as the sunshine generally coming from a southern direction in the northern hemisphere, the prevailing wind direction and fire risk areas adjacent to the site.

Vectors further modify the pattern by creating dynamic flows cutting through the site, such as water courses, existing or planned roads and tracks, wildlife corridors and the hills and slopes.

Maps, plans, lists and lots of paper for making notes on are also essential. Most of all, an open mind, an observant eye and a good dose of creative searching for patterns. Again, it always helps to do this with others, insights arise easier when bounced off other insights. It might be good at this point to collect in groups with a variety of skills in each one. Earth skills such as geology, geomorphology, botany and biology are all useful, but don't get stuck only in the material world. Remember you are also looking for the spirit of the place, the genius loci. One exercise that we have often used is to sit quietly in silence and ask the spiritual forces present what they want of us, how can we help them to realize the full potential of this particular place? Some people find this easy, others are embarrassed by the ridiculous idea of having angels at the bottom of their garden.

Try looking at it another way. In the natural succession that all ecologists find in nature, the plants and animals work together to create a series of guilds, one building upon the next, enriching nature in order to give the next guild someplace to start. There is clearly an intelligence at work, an order which we can understand. It's slightly different in each locality, depending upon geology, rainfall and so on. This you could call the spirit of that place. You can appreciate it

Camphill Botton, England:
working with people with special needs

Date founded — 1955
Approximate number of residents — 350
Location — north Yorkshire
Spiritual or ideological affiliation — anthroposophic
Visited — 1980, 1995

Botton village was the first Camphill Village Community for adults. When Karl König and his group of largely Jewish refugees from Nazi Europe founded the first Camphill School in Scotland in 1939, they concentrated on working with children with special needs. By the 1950s it became clear to them, and to the parents of the children, that children grow up and become adults! At that time there was nowhere for them to go. So Botton Village was created, and set a new direction for the Camphill movement.

My first visit to Botton was a real eye-opener. Here was a whole valley, four good sized farms, clusters of houses, a real alternative community. It was then the first large community I had experienced apart from Kibbutz, and I didn't realize at the time what a significance it would have on my life. In many ways, Botton is the flagship of the Camphill Village movement, and has established a cultural tradition which subsequently has stretched around the world, still inspiring the creation of new villages every year.

The combination of spiritual community building with physical work has created a community tradition that has real force into the future, an alternative culture that speaks directly to our needs today.

RIGHT TOP. View across the valley with one of the farms in the foreground.

RIGHT BOTTOM. Rock House, one of the large family houses where co-workers live together with those with special needs.

ABOVE. Community gardens with cold frames.

LEFT. Sign in the middle of the village, showing some of the workplaces.

BELOW. The chapel.

as an abstract notion, or you can personalize it by giving it a name and a shape in your imagination. You don't need to believe in it, but you can be open to the idea that this gives positive results in the real world. As an electrical engineer you might understand the exact workings of electrons as they pass charge along a cable. To someone who doesn't really understand this it doesn't matter so much. I press the switch, the light comes on. In the same way I might not really be into having fairies at the bottom of the garden, but I am usually impressed by getting good fresh vegetables from it. If the gardener believes in fairies, what do I care? Being respectful of both the engineer's electrons and the gardener's fairies is what this kind of group dynamic is all about.

However you approach site analysis, the aim is to assess what the situation is in a particular place and how you can help to fulfill its potential. Zone, sector and vector planning are tools to help you on your way, and so are water and energy audits. You can't have too much information, this could be overwhelming, so you might like to take this list as a starting point:

— **Location**: Set your site in its broadest context. Continent, country, surrounding area, distance to towns, cities, etc. Overall bio-region. What kind of access is there?
— **The physical**: Geology, soils and landforms. Slopes, aspect, drainage, streams, rivers, lakes, any other water features. Climate, weather, incidence of extremes, storms, hurricanes, flooding.
— **Flora**: Detailed descriptions of the different types of plants, especially trees, by species, mapped out. Are there crops growing? If so, what kinds? Native and introduced plants? Is there a history?
— **Fauna**: Animals found at your site. Signs of wild animals, domestic animals. Birds. Are there seasonal variations?
— **Human**: Has there been previous settlement on this site? Give details, what kind, how long ago and for how long? Existing buildings, structures, landscape changes. If there are people still living on the site, or nearby, talk to them, ask them what they know of the history of the place. Are there legal constraints? What kind of local services are there?
— **Spiritual**: What kind of feelings does this site arouse in you? Are there sacred sites? Can you check out subtle energies by dowsing, or by swinging crystals? Are there churches, graveyards, standing stones, or any other indications of past spiritual activity?
— **The brief**: Here you need to go back to your own vision and aims. How many people are you planning for? 10? 100? 1,000? What kind of Ecovillage do you have in mind? Self-sufficient? Self-supporting? Commuter? Seminar centre?

Woodcrest Bruderhof, New York, USA: a Christian Collective

Date founded — 1950s
Approximate number of residents — 300–400 people
Location — New York State
Spiritual or ideological affiliation — Anabaptist Christians
Visited — a day in the summer of 2004

The history of the Bruderhof is a legend among contemporary collectives, an adventure story full of action, excitement, tragedy and success. They were born out of the youth movements which swept the German world in the 1920s. After contact with the old Hutterite communities in the USA, this particular group, which had focused around Eberhard Arnold, decided to adopt the traditions of these Anabaptists, who traced their history back several hundred years to the Moravian Brethren of Bohemia. With the rise of Nazism, the Bruderhof were forced to leave Germany, moved to England, and with the outbreak of the Second World War, were forced to flee again, this time to Paraguay. They lasted there for over a decade, enduring hardships including a really high child mortality. In the 1950s they relocated to the USA, and are now established in six communities on the eastern seaboard, two more in England, and one in each of Germany and Australia.

The Bruderhof are a collective based on simple Christian faith and pietism. They have only minimal pocket money, virtually no private possessions, large families, and a very high rate of children returning to the community to live after having tasted the modern world. They are not at all inspired by the Permaculture and Ecovillage movements, but are socially active, pacifists and peaceworkers. In the twenty years I have had contact with them, they have been in a constant growth.

What was interesting to me on our visit was that their youth group had built a strawbale house, clearly sensing that there is something going on in alternative circles which was filtering through to them also. One of their questions to me was how they could learn more, and who to connect to. They might have things to learn from the alternative ecology movement, but I don't think many realize how much they have to teach about community organization and conflict resolution. In these fields they are masters. Their industrial organization is also very modern, and extremely effective. They make toys and equipment for physically handicapped people, and each community makes different components, the finished products being assembled as the orders come in.

LEFT. Strawbale house built as a youth project, with some of the participants. In front of the building is a totem pole also made by them.

BELOW. Mural in the Dining Hall, depicting people who have inspired or played an important role in the development of the Bruderhof Communities. Do you recognize any of these people? If you recognize all of them, maybe you should consider getting in touch with them!

ABOVE. Detail of the verandah railing of the strawbale house. This was made of local materials, handmade by members of the youth group.

BELOW LEFT. A band setting up for a rehearsal. As in most tightly knit collectives, there is a rich cultural life with constant preparation for a forthcoming event.

BELOW RIGHT. The dining hall. Here all the 400 or so members of Woodcrest eat their meals together. This is real community!

ABOVE. View across the rolling forested hills of the Hudson Valley in New York State, from one of the hills in the centre of the community.

LEFT. The kitchen crew. Women still wear conservative clothes, based on mid-European traditional styles, mixed in with American pioneer fashion.

I find it hard to imagine having too much information. Obviously you don't want to spend decades gathering facts, but you should get as much as you can within a reasonable time. In order to be really efficient you might sit down as a group beforehand and brainstorm into what kind of facts you want to gather, list them according to the categories above and create a questionnaire. This is probably the best preparation for the exercise, as a group you begin to get a feel for what you are looking for, you get a shopping list. If you spend some time doing this and some time writing the list out properly you will emerge with a very useful tool. Make lots of copies.

Each person ought to have a copy, with plenty of room for writing on, preferably on a clip board. Take with you measuring equipment. Compass, thermometer, long tape measure, jars or bags for soil samples, a hammer, a trowel, a knife or a clipper. Take cameras and make sure you get lots of pictures, the artistic can draw sketches of the place. Get pictures from the same place at different hours or in different seasons. Do site walks at different times of day and in varying conditions. Take a walk during heavy rain and look at how the water runs. Check out the site at night, at sunrise, at sunset, at midday, full moon, no moon. Note facts, but listen to your feelings also and share those that you want to with the others. Are there places which you find spark off special feelings? Can you identify any sacred sites? Sit quietly with your eyes shut and listen. Are there different smells in different places? Feel textures, taste leaves and plants (be careful, don't chew on poisonous stuff!). Use all your senses.

As much as you can, write everything down. Lists and maps. A useful tool is to take a map of the site and photocopy it lots of times, then you can note a different set of facts on each one. Even better are clear plastic overlays, the superimposition of varying data can give rise to yet more insights.

Report writing

This is where you combine the site analysis, which should be factual, with the vision that you have created together. Here is where your dreams begin to attain reality.

Get everything written down. Make sure you keep minutes of all your meetings, it's enough to make a note of just what you decided. If you have someone in your group who likes to fiddle with bits of paper and can keep things in order, you're in luck! The process is as important as the final result. Making sure you keep the process good and remembering the highlights, will be reflected in the final product.

Split up into working groups and give separate people the responsibility to write different bits. Get the builder to write out your building proposals. If the builder isn't a writing person, create groups of two or three where these skills can be balanced out. Use diagrams and maps as much as you can. Pictures are really important and a few well timed jokes or funny cartoons do a lot to create a good feeling for those reading it. Try to avoid 'officialese' and turgid report style. Write it as it is.

With today's computer technology, it's best to write one long, everything-in-it, report. Scan in all the graphics, so you can print it out as it is. Then you can pull out what you want for any specific application, editing out the bits that are not appropriate.

A good idea is to get someone not directly connected with the project to read it through and ask them if the thing makes sense. It often happens that when you get totally immersed in something, things appear obvious to you, because you know all about it. But someone who is not familiar with every detail and every aspect will need to be filled in. It's also good to proofread and get out all those annoying little typos.

Project presentation

At some point you are going to have to show other people what you want to do. Each presentation will have to be tailor-made. You will probably need to present your proposal slightly differently depending upon who you are talking to and what your aims are. You might have to raise a loan, attract more members, negotiate planning regulations or change a legal status. Each of these requires a slightly different emphasis. You will certainly have to set up a legal entity. The aim of a presentation is to create trust and forge partnerships. At every stage you, as a group, will have to work together with outside agencies. Make these your friends. However critical you might be of 'straight' society, however much you might believe that you are creating a viable alternative, however much you think you are better than everyone else, it does not help to assume a holier-than-thou attitude. Humility is still a virtue, and is often recognized and appreciated.

Teaching, caring for people less fortunate, job creation and environmental protection are all seen as worthwhile projects. Most people in finance, planning or regulation, would probably be happy to be associated with a successful project which does a worthwhile job. It can rub off on them too and they can bask in the glow of your success. Who cares! Let them bask, it doesn't hurt you, and their co-operation and support can make all the difference. Let them take the credit!

Speak the language of whoever you are presenting to. If you move to Spain (lots of empty sites there!) you will need to learn Spanish.

If you are negotiating with a local authority or with planning regulators, they may not be too sympathetic to a 'radical alternative commune dedicated to exploring astrality and communing with elemental beings in plants and rocks.' Even if that's what you're about. You might try describing yourself as a group that wants to help worthwhile social causes and combine practical with spiritual work. This is not about lying, it's about presenting yourself in a language that makes sense to your listener and creates sympathy for your project.

To some agencies, a snappy PowerPoint presentation will give a favourable impression. To other people, a more personal, straightforward description is the best approach. It's up to you to do some homework and find out a little about the people you are about to meet. An Ecovillage project is highly diverse and manifold, so you can present the aspects which you think would be of interest to the agency you are meeting.

Looking to the future

Permaculture design and Ecovillage projects are impulses of our time, a response to the past and a direction into the future. There are no rigid constraints, you and I are creating as we go along. There is no hidden group in a closed room directing us, no conspiracy theory here. Most of what we have been talking about is common sense. Really the only reason for using these terms, Permaculture and Ecovillages, is to team up with like-minded people doing similar things. That has a real value in terms of learning from each other and for keeping up the momentum.

In the 1960s I hitch-hiked throughout Europe, criss-crossing the continent nearly every summer. There was a feeling of community amongst us as we met at cross roads and petrol stations. We swapped stories, gave each other tips, shared food and felt good, but we had nowhere to go except the next junction or some attraction. Today there is a heavy sprinkle of communities; we have created a new international nation, a culture which looks to the future, which is building a positive way of life, and which is largely inclusive and welcoming. There is tremendous variety: large, small, spiritual, non-spiritual, urban and rural. About the only thing we share is a positive impulse to build a better way for us to live together with ourselves as people and with our planet.

Appendices

This is the reference part of the book. It seems to be a part of our fast-moving modern world that things go out of date, they become superseded, information goes stale, people move on to new things. The periodicals and the organizations will inevitably change over time. My hope is that some of the other lists here will have a more enduring life. The books, at least the best of them, should be able to withstand the ravages of time.

Happy hunting and good luck with your project!

Garden Plan

To achieve rotation, we divided our crops into four groups. The division was based on a mixture of theory and experience and was neither strict nor always orthodox. Radishes, for instance, were theoretically confined to the root patch, but in practice we found a short row sowed every week through the summer gave us a steady supply of fresh radishes and could be located pretty much anywhere between other things. There is also a factor we call companion planting. This has to do with two considerations, one is that certain vegetables like to grow with certain others, the second consideration is that certain crops deter specific pests which are prone to damage some vegetables. Garlic and marigolds were also worth putting in anywhere, as they both were effective pest control plants, deterring all kinds of insects. Garlic we could eat any amount of and marigolds just look pretty.

Group 1	Group 2	Group 3	Group 4
Potatoes	Legumes	Brassicas	Roots
Potatoes	Peas for drying	Cabbages	Onions
Peas	French Beans	Broccoli	Carrots
Broad Beans	Haricot Beans	Cauliflowers	Salsify
	Fresh Peas	Brussels Sprouts	Beetroots
		Outdoor toma-	Kohl Rabi
		toes	Lettuces
		Lettuces	Parsnips
		Radishes	Pumpkins
		Turnips	Radishes
		Swedes	

Our garden was long and thin, our house and shed were at the northern end, and with a long chicken run running down the middle. This was really determined by an established group of apple and pear trees, which gave the chickens shade and which we had no desire to dig up. At the furthest end of the garden we established compost heaps and bees.

So we had four plots, arranged after these principles and they rotated round the chicken run. The fences around the chickens were cunningly planned so that we could open up any area by simply shutting and opening gates. In this way we could let the chickens into one area for a length of time, and this would help to clean up weeds and pests, which the chickens love to eat, and put a little 'top dressing' of chicken manure on the soil. All we needed to do was to let our feathered friends have a good go at it, rake it over afterwards and we had a well prepared seed bed for the next round of vegetables.

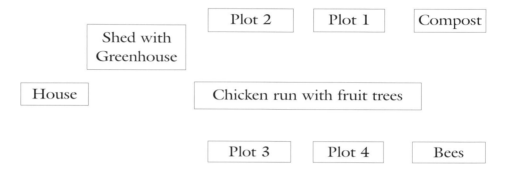

We found that self-sufficient gardening is a completely different game than maximum cropping. Our aim was to keep a modest and even flow of food coming in off the garden to our kitchen.

This rotation was worked out for a few years and worked really well for a situation where we had to think carefully about storing some vegetables for the winter. Some really hardy ones kept going through the snow and frost, and gave us a glut of many varieties in their own time. We had neither fridge nor freezer, we dried, stored, pickled and preserved what we could during the summer, and enjoyed fresh vegetables throughout the year. By having regular gluts we found that we would really be looking forward to a certain variety and by the time it was finished, we were quite glad to have to wait most of another year for another taste of it. Our year revolved around the season's vegetable.

Opposite you can find a GARDEN SCHEDULE, adjusted for temperate climate (Lincolnshire Wolds, England, *ca.* 130 m above sea level, 500–600 mm, annual precipitation, 53° N).

	March	April	May	June	July	August	September	October	November	December
Early Pots	Chit	Plant	Earth Up		Dig up when flowers open		Dig up			
Main Pots	Chit	Plant	Earth Up		Earth Up		Dig Up	Dig Up		
Broad Beans	Sow 1	Sow 2	Pinch tops		Pick 1	Pick 2				
Leeks		Sow seeds			Plant into early pot space				Earth up	Pick
Early Peas	Sow 1	Sow 2	Sow 3		Pick					
Fresh Peas		Sow 1	Sow 2	Sow 3	Sow 4	Pick onwards				
Dried Peas		Sow			Harvest when pods split					
French Beans		Sow 1	Sow 1	Sow 2	Sow 3	Pick often				
Swiss Chard		Sow 1	Sow 2	Pick	Sow 3	Sow 4				
Courgettes		Sow indoors		Plant out		Pick often				
Runner Beans				Sow		Pick often				
Kale		Sow	Thin out					Pick onwards		
White & Red Cabb		Sow	Thin out		Pick to thin		Pick onwards			
Savoy		Sow	Thin out					Pick onwards		
Late Broccoli				Sow		Plant out			Pick onwards	
Cauliflower & Sprouts		Sow	Thin out						Pick onwards	
Chin Cabb					Sow	Thin out				
Turnips		Sow 1	Sow 2	Sow 3	Pick 1	Pick 2	Pick 3			
Tomatoes	Sow indoors		Plant out	Stake	Mulch		Pick			
Early Broccoli			Sow		Plant out					
Onion Sets & Shallots	Set	Set			Loosen roots	Dig up	Dry in sun			
Carrots & Beets		Sow 1	Sow 2	Sow 3	Pick onwards					
Swedes & Parsnips		Sow	Hoe and thin				Harvest		Harvest	
Radishes		Sow and pick all the time								
Lettuces			Sow and pick all the time							
Garlic	Set						Harvest			
Flowers	Sow whenever									

Compost Ingredients

Material	Percent content		
	Nitrogen	Phosphorous	Potash
Farmyard manure	2.5	1.0 – 0.1	1.5 – 3.0
Fresh poultry manure	1.5	1.0	0.5
Old poultry manure	1.2	2.0	0.9
Sheep manure	0.5	0.3	trace
Pig manure	0.5	0.2	0.5
Horse manure	1.5 – 0.5	0.2	1.0 – 0.4
Cereal straw	0.4	0.2	1.0
Peat moss	0.7	0.1	0.2
Bracken	1.5	0.2	0.8
Alfalfa hay	2.5	0.5	2.0
Saw dust	0.1	0.1	0.1
Fish scraps	8.0	13.0	4.0
Hoofmeal and horndust	12.5	1.5	trace
Dried blood	7.0 – 14.0	trace	trace
Wool and silk shoddies	5.0 – 14.0	trace	trace
Seaweed	1.5	1.0	5.0
Wood ash	trace	1.5	8.0
Spent hops	3.0 – 4.0	1.0 – 2.0	trace
Human faeces	1.1	1.3	0.3
Human urine	6.9	3.2	3.4
Activated sewage sludge	6.0	4.0	0.6
Finished compost	2.0 – 2.5	1.0 – 0.5	2.0 – 0.5

These are often approximate values, different sources will give some variations. There are so many variables in waste products! The amount of dry matter and moisture will also vary; just a shower of rain before you gather up the manure from your chicken run will have an effect! However, the comparisons are worth making a note of and the whole thing will give you some idea of how to balance things.

It's really important to keep in mind that these three ingredients, nitrogen, phosphorous and potassium, are just three indicators of the material ingredients. There are in addition many trace elements and lots of other factors. If the material is formed into hard clumps, it needs to be broken up, if it is very wet, spread out so the moisture can distribute itself around the heap. If it is very dry, it needs watering and so on.

In addition to the chemical constituents, there are other, physical characteristics which you need to be aware of. A great deal of the texture of compost has to do with its water and air retaining qualities. Porosity and physical bulk, the roughage of the matter, are aspects which are really critical in creating a soil which lets the air get down into it, which drains well and which retains moisture over time, even if the weather is dry. We gardened in eastern England and the rainfall was not much more than in the Galilee in Israel. There were often long periods without rain and it was essential that the soil stayed moist.

Making compost is like cooking food. In fact it is food for the soil and ultimately the plant. Make it in good cheer, think positive thoughts, be glad! It might sound like hogwash to some of you, but there are spiritual forces at work out there in the garden and your spirituality makes a difference. Each plant, each tree, groups of plants and even the compost heap itself has a spirit or angel, if you like, and you can connect with those forces and work together with them. You might like to take a break in between turning compost heaps, sit quietly nearby and give yourself over to asking what this material wants, what is it saying to you, how does it relate to you?

Learn to work with nature, not just with its physical components, but with its spiritual qualities. You will find that not only does your garden feed your body with nourishing, tasty food, but that your soul will be satisfied, and that a deep well-being will be the result of every visit and every task that you do there.

Site Assessment Check List

Site assessment – information gathering

Physical base: Geology, soil types, depth, pH, organic matter, fertility, building sand, building clay, workable stone

Topography: gradients, key-lines, drainage, landscape

Climate: temperatures, rainfall, snow, winds, frost incidence, extremes, humidity

Microclimates: niches, sheltered spots, aspect, sun traps, frost pockets, exposed slopes

Water: springs, streams, ponds, water-table, flood risk, quality, quantity, catchment potential, marshes

Vegetation: communities, weeds, list all plants, edges, domestic plants, rare or endangered species, timber resources, existing crops

Animals: list all types, wild, domesticated, insects, wildlife corridors, rare or endangered species, habitats

Fire: risk of forest fire, use of fire to clear land, history, seasonality

Access: people, vehicles, roads, tracks, conditions, materials delivery, commuting possibilities

Existing structures: type and use, energy efficiency, retrofitting, extension, demolition, reuse of materials

Services: sewage, water, electricity, telephone

The site itself: boundaries, views, building sites, privacy, sacred spots, history, zones

Legal aspects: rights of way, building regulations, ownership, freehold, leasehold, preservation orders, future planning constraints

Locality: existing wider community, neighbours, schools, shops, pollution, history

Which questions have we forgotten?

Book List

This book is not an academic work, so though I do refer to books and articles at various places in the text, I have avoided detailed references and footnotes. This gives you the opportunity to look up things here for yourself.

I have divided the booklists into the chapter divisions, in order to make it a little easier for you to locate the books you are looking for. Some books clearly lend themselves to several chapters, but I tried to avoid repeating references. It's not such a bad thing to have to hunt through book lists, especially annotated ones; you never know what your eye might come across that wasn't quite what you were looking for, but nevertheless opened up something. I consider every book in the list a valuable contribution to my thinking about these subjects and I hope that the ones you read will contribute something to yours.

Chapter 1   The Story of the Global Ecovillage Network

Bhave, Vinoba. 1994. *Moved by Love*. Green Books, UK. *Just a great book, I read it for fun, and found out by chance that Vinobe was decades ahead of us. Read it, and get to know one of the great people of the twentieth century, the successor of Mahatma Gandhi.*

Carson, Rachel. 1965. *Silent Spring*. Penguin, UK. *The classic. What do I need to write about this? If you haven't read it, read it! If you've read it, then you know what all the fuss is about!*

Fike, Rupert. ed. 1998. *Voices From The Farm*. Book Publishing Company. Summertown, TN, USA. . *In this book members of The Farm talk about their community and how it changed over the years. These are authentic accounts of Ecovillage life as it is lived. Read it and get to know one of the most interesting alternative communities of the 1970s.*

Gilman, Diane and Robert. 1992. *Eco-villages*. In Context Institute. PO Box 11470 Bainbridge Island, WA 98110 USA. *The first formulation of the Ecovillage idea. Full of great definitions and insight. This report set the tone and direction of GEN.*

Global Ecovillage Network (GEN) – Europe. 1998. *Directory of Ecovillages in Europe. The ultimate travel guide. Maybe a little outdated now, but provided us with lots of new friends and places to stay when we drove from Israel to Norway in 2000, taking our time.*

Jackson, Hildur and Svensson, Karen. (eds). 2002. *Ecovillage Living.* Green Books and Gaia Trust, UK. *The best overview so far of the diversity and spread of Ecovillages, full of plans and pictures, and contributions from many of the leading activists and thinkers.*

Jackson, Ross. 2000. *And We Are Doing It!* Robert D. Reed Publishers. San Francisco. *Ross' story of how he made his way from international investment analysis to being one of the founders of the Ecovillage movement. The last chapter is a tremendous inspiration, a look into the future, what it might be like.*

Chapter 2   Patterns in Nature

Bell, Graham. 1992. *The Permaculture Way.* Thorsons, UK. *Written by my own teacher, I have a special regard for this book. Very readable, and with really good illustrations, it is a mine of useful information from a skilled practitioner*

Fukuoka, Masanobu. 1978. *The One-Straw Revolution.* Rodale Press, Emmaus, USA. *The book that swept the world in the seventies and helped create a new way of agriculture. Together with his* Natural Way of Farming *this is required reading for those who want to take Permaculture seriously.*

Holmgren, David and Mollison, Bill. 1978. *Permaculture One.* Transworld, Australia. *The first one, still a great inspiration, and full of really accessible graphics. Very empowering, even I can draw trees like Bill!*

Jackson, Wes. 1980. *New Roots For Agriculture.* Friends of the Earth, USA. *Throw away the plough, and get into natural farming! This is from the man who pioneered this idea in the Mid West. Read this book and change the way you think about farming.*

Lindegger, Max and Tap, Robert. 1986. *The Best of Permaculture.* Nascimanere, Australia. *A collection of articles from early copies of Permaculture magazines. Lots of gems in here, I have used several of the articles in teaching situations, with great success.*

Mars, Ross. 1996. *The Basics of Permaculture Design.* Candlelight Trust, Australia. *This book is the best short introduction that I have found yet. Clear, concise, well written and well illustrated. If you can only take one light book with you, take this one!*

Mollison, Bill and Slay, Reny Mia. 1991. *Introduction to Permaculture. Australia.* Tagari, Australia. *A really good boiled down version of the Designer's Manual. We used to give a copy of this book to each student of the design course in Israel.*

Mollison, Bill. 1979. *Permaculture Two.* Tagari, Australia. *Expands the ideas of the* Permaculture One. *Both these are worth reading to get the sense of how Permaculture has got to where it is today.*

Mollison, Bill. 1988. *Permaculture – A Designers' Manual.* Tagari, Australia. *Regarded by many as* The Bible! *It is thorough, with really good illustrations and diagrams, and contains enough information, experience and ideas to keep you busy for a long time. You can't really be a serious Permaculture designer without this book.*

Odum, Eugene P. 1963. *Ecology.* Holt, Rhinehart and Winston, USA. *Odum pioneered ecology as a science. For those of you who have got some way into Mollison, you will find many of the basic Permaculture ideas in Odum.*

Seamon, David and Zajonc, Arthur. Eds. 1998. *Goethe's Way of Science.* State University of New York Press, USA. *It was a great discovery for me to find that the basic idea of Permaculture had been around for quite a long time. For those who want to get deeper into the philosophical aspects, this is a must! Spend some time with Nigel Hoffman, reading his article on methodology.*

Sessions, George. ed. 1995. *Deep Ecology for the 21st Century.* Shambhala, London. *Probably the best all rounder for this subject. Lots of articles from lots of people, tracing how this philosophy arose, and a good collection of basic stuff from Arne Naess himself.*

Smith, Ken and Irene. 1975. *The Earth Garden Book.* Nelson, Australia. *A collection of experiences from 'back to the bush' freaks in Australia. The original seed bed from which Permaculture sprouted.*

Smith, Ken and Irene. 1978. *The Second Earth Garden Book.* Australia. Nelson. *Both these books describe various ways of gardening, gathering wild foods, building houses and managing small farms and homesteads. The material is based on experience, accompanied by crude drawings and fuzzy black and white photographs, and is a treasure trove of self-sufficiency advice.*

Suchantke, Andreas. 2001. *Eco-Geography*. Lindisfarne, New York & Floris, Edinburgh. *Here is looking at landscapes in a new way! I wish I had had this book when I was studying landscape geomorphology back in 1969! This is the best application I have come across, taking in geology, plants and animals and looking at the whole picture.*

Chapter 3   Modelling the Ecovillage: the Social Aspect

Christie, Nils. 1989. *Beyond Loneliness and Institutions*. Norwegian University Press, Oslo. *Nils is a professor of Criminology at Oslo University, and with a long-term connection to the Camphill movement in Norway. This is his sociological perspective of the Camphill phenomenon. Full of great anecdotes and insights, it has been translated into several languages, and is valuable as the view of an outsider looking in.*

Eno, Sarah and Treanor, Dave. 1982. *The Collective Housing Handbook*. Laurieston Hall Publications. *This is the collected wisdom from experience by a group of commune founders who had more than a decade of experience behind them when they wrote it. Though short, and with a lot of British specific information regarding legal models, it remains a book that I have often gone back to. The sections dealing with group dynamics and decision making methods are timeless and relevant.*

Ferguson, Ronald. 1998. *Chasing the Wild Goose*. Scotland. Wild Goose Publications. *The story of the Iona Community. As a Camphill member, this has a special significance because of the personal connection between the founder of Camphill, Karl König, and the founder of Iona, George Macleod. Get to know a completely different kind of community! Iona is a hybrid, a congregation, a kind of monastic order, an international movement, an ecumenical inspiration. Very difficult to pigeonhole (good for them!), but lots of great insights into people living and working together.*

Gorman, Clem. 1975. *People Together*. Paladin, UK. *An account of communes in England from the early 1970s. Good straightforward stuff.*

Houriet, Robert. 1971. *Getting Back Together*. Sphere, London. *In the late 1960s Robert Houriet traveled round communes on the east coast of the United States, and this is his story. For those who want to relax with some nostalgia for those good old days of long hair and back to the land, and read what life was really like, this is the book for those long winter evenings by the fire. Read it and enjoy it.*

Jackson, Hildur ed. 1999. *Creating Harmony*. Gaia Trust, Denmark. *Hildur has been a key person in the Ecovillage movement in Denmark, and internationally. She sees community as one way to explore and deepen our relationships to each other, and in this book she has collected the wisdom of many of the really experienced group dynamic and conflict resolution guides that are spread throughout the commune world. If you never have conflicts in your community, you don't need to read this book, just write to Hildur telling her the secret of your success. If you do experience conflict, then this book might give some pointers towards resolving them.*

König, Karl. 1990. *Man as a Social Being*. Camphill Press, UK. *A collection of lectures given by König in the last two years before his death in 1966. The first lectures explain in detail the analysis of society into its threefold spheres, and constitute some of the best explanations I have ever read. The second half of the book gives a thorough grounding in the Christian foundations of the Camphill movement.*

König, Karl. 1993. *The Camphill Movement*. Camphill Press, UK. *Two short essays by König about the threefold nature of Camphill, first published in the early 1960s. A great introduction, and stimulating reading.*

Luxford, Michael and Jane. 2003. *A Sense for Community*. Directions for Change, UK. *The result of several years of research and travel by two seasoned Camphill co-workers. Very much an insider book, it would be difficult for someone not familiar with Camphill life to understand, but for us Camphillers this is an invaluable insight into what is going on today.*

Platts, David Earl. 1996. *Playful Self-Discovery*. Findhorn Press, UK. *This book consists of a large selection of group dynamic games, with good notes on how to implement them, and how to follow them up in discussions afterwards. For me, this is a 'work' book, and gets used for many groups that I work with.*

Rees, William and Wackernagel, Mathis. 1996. *Our Ecological Footprint*. New Society, Canada. *With this book you can carry out your own Footprint analysis! This idea, that we can relate our lifestyle to the amount of land surface we need to sustain it, gives the lie to the held out promise that we can all be middle class, well off Americans. Read this and reduce your acreage!*

Schwartz, Dorothy and Walter. 1987. *Breaking Through*. Green Books, UK. *Walter and Dorothy spent a long time traveling the world and experiencing communes of different kinds. They are both established writers, Walter having a lifetime of writing for the* Guardian *newspaper, and Dorothy teaching creative writing. So you are guaranteed well written stuff. Combine this with their experiences and insights, and you get a winner!*

Chapter 4   House Design and Building Techniques

Borer, Pat and Harris, Cindy. 1997. *Out of the Woods*. Centre for Alternative Technology Publications/Walter Segal Self-Build Trust, UK. *A really thorough how-to book written by those who have done it. Lots of good illustrations and diagrams. Billed as a manual for those who want to build their own homes using natural materials and timber frame construction, it covers pretty much what you need. Highly recommended.*

Corson, Jennifer. 2000. *The Resourceful Renovator*. Chelsea Green, USA. *A really useful guide to re-using old building materials, taking each of the major materials in turn. Jennifer includes a number of real life examples to show how the ideas in the book really work out in practice.*

Day, Christopher. 1990. *Places of the Soul*. Aquarian/Thorsons, UK. *Christopher has a wide ranging experience designing buildings, and shows us how to create structures that reflect the organic. Buildings for human beings, softer and more in tune with our deeper needs. Lots of great drawings and examples.*

Harland, Edward. 1993. *Eco-Renovation*. Green Books, UK. *Probably one of the most useful books, as most of us already live in a house and would like to make it more environmental. Includes a useful check list with which you can plan your renovation. Also includes a very good resource list of places and organizations from the UK.*

Pearson, David. 1989. *The Natural House Book*. Gaia Books, UK. *This book really set a new tone for me in the realm of building. David presents us with wonderful pictures, and describes why we need a new set of building rules concerning materials, design and our whole approach to the idea of The House.*

Pearson, David. 1994. *Earth to Spirit*. Gaia Books, UK. *A continuation of his previous book, a collection of photographs which he collected from his architectural travels around the world. Put together with a great text which illuminates the pictures. The last section describes what is going on today, and you will meet some of the individuals who create the connection between natural house building, Permaculture and the Ecovillage movement.*

Chapter 5   Agriculture: Soil, Plants, Gardening and Farming

Appelhof, Mary. 1997. *Worms Eat My Garbage*. Flower Press, USA. *How about a worm farm in your coffee table in your living room? This is one of the wilder ideas in this great book on how to create soil from your garbage. This book contains everything you need to know about this, whether you're happy with a mini version in your living room, or if you want a large scale set up for your farm. Invaluable stuff for those who want good soil.*

Balfour, E. B. 1975. *The Living Soil.* Faber & Faber, UK. *The original account of the Haughley experiment which was the foundation of the British organic agriculture movement. Essential reading for anyone who wants to get to grips with the principles of the technique.*

Ball, D., and Davis, B., and Fitter, A., and Walker, N. 1992. *The Soil.* Harper Collins, UK. *The best book on soil I have come across. Lots of hard science and facts. Really detailed descriptions of composition, flora and fauna. Really gives you an insight into the life that goes on in the tiny crevices of our soil. My only complaint is that it devotes only two pages out of 190 to organic farming techniques! Don't be put off, though, it's worth getting to know all those millipedes, centipedes, nematodes and micro arthropods!*

Bell, Graham. 1994. *The Permaculture Garden.* Thorsons, UK. *A really good, concise book specializing in how to use Permaculture ideas in the garden. Great diagrams and drawings, and a real inspiration to get out there and start work!*

Bird, Christopher and Tompkins, Peter. 1975. *The Secret Life of Plants.* Penguin, UK. *You will be amazed at how plants behave. After reading this you'll never talk nastily to one again. This is seriously researched and might inspire you to carry out some simple experiments yourself.*

Cooper, David and Hobbelink, Henk and Velve, Renee. Eds. 1992. *Growing Diversity.* Intermediate Technology, UK. *This book was written to help grass roots development projects incorporate genetic resources activities into their programmes. It covers the world, and tells how it is down on the development farm.*

Douglas, Sholto. 1976. *Hydroponics.* OUP, UK. *A classic, written originally over fifty years ago, it describes what is called the Bengal System. Fascinating descriptions of experiments in Tanzania and Armenia, Calcutta and Florida. It even has futuristic plans for growing in outer space, on other planets and the moon!*

Facciola, Stephen. 1990. *Cornucopia.* Kampong, USA. *This is an amazing reference book, which you need to spend time getting to learn your way round, but it will be repaid a hundredfold. I just had tomatoes for lunch, and looked them up: more than 11 pages of varieties listed, with useful information about each one. He lists more than 3,000 species, the book is a homage to diversity.*

Fukuoka, Masanobu. 1985. *The Natural Way of Farming.* Japan Publications, Japan. *The companion book to* One Straw Revolution. *Fukuoka is one of the founders of the new revolution in agriculture, a towering genius who will go down in farming history as a true innovator. If you are at all interested in Permaculture, you need to read this book. Don't delay, scout round secondhand bookshops and get a copy.*

Harris, Dudley. 1978. *Hydroponics.* Sphere, London. *Straightforward introduction to mainstream hydroponics. Often regarded by permaculturalists as the very antithesis of what we are trying to achieve, nevertheless, in certain situations, it may well have relevance. This short book will get you going if you need it.*

Hart, Robert. 1996. *Forest Gardening.* Green Earth, UK. *Robert Hart was busy doing Permaculture long before he had heard about it. He brings in the vertical dimension by analyzing the different levels in a forest, from below the soil surface to the highest canopy. Another important aspect is the mix of different trees he puts together in order to maximize the output. A book based on real experience from someone who is out there doing it.*

Hyams, Edward. 1976. *Soil and Civilization.* John Murray, UK. *This gives the broad historical perspective to bear on how we treat our soils, and frankly, we don't have a very good track record. It seems that every place where we have practiced large scale plough agriculture, we have created serious soil erosion, in many places deserts and dust bowls. Read this as background material for Wes Jackson and Masanobu Fukuoka.*

Koepf, Herbert and Pettersson, Bo and Schaumann, Wolfgang. 1976. *Biodynamic Agriculture.* Anthroposophic Press, USA. *An accessible text book for the biodynamic farmer. A classic.*

National Academy of Sciences. 1975. *Underexploited Tropical Plants with Promising Economic Value.* Washington D.C. USA. *A list of over thirty plants which in the 1970s had not been used commercially. Some, such as* Quinua, Winged Beans *and* Jojoba, *have been brought into use, others still remain unused. The important principle here is that we should be open to developing new varieties. This book will open your eyes.*

Philbrick, Helen and John. 1980. *The Bug Book.* Garden Way, USA. *Real, practical stuff, the bulk of the book is a list of insects, the damage they cause and practical advice on how to get rid of them. Without chemicals or other harmful methods! Covers both ordinary organic methods and biodynamic.*

Pollan, Michael. 2001. *The Botany of Desire*. Random House, USA. *Not really a how-to book, but a great idea. We all think plants are so clever by developing mechanical techniques for spreading their seed, hooks to catch on passing sheep, sails to float them down the wind. How about their capacity to make themselves desirable to humans, who will then carry them around the world as attractive or useful parts of their culture? Pollan traces the spread of the apple, tulip, marijuana and potato and opens up ideas that are pretty wild. How smart are these plants? Can they really make themselves so attractive that we act as their servants in their conquest of the planet? Read this book in long wet winter evenings when you can't work on your garden, and be amazed!*

Prescott-Allen, Christine and Robert. 1983. *Genes from the wild*. Earthscan, UK. *Now twenty years old, and written before the present technology of genetic manipulation was an issue, this is still an informative and thorough introduction to where our agricultural genetic heritage comes from, and why we need to preserve it. It's short, concise and covers all the bases.*

Shewell-Cooper. 1974. *The Complete Gardener*. Collins, UK. *The Bible of the old-fashioned English gardener. Not so much explicit stuff on organics or any of this Permaculture stuff! We used ours to create a wonderful English country cottage garden, flowers, a little lawn, trees, hedges and lots of useful vegetables. Great stuff!*

Steiner, Rudolf. 1974. *Agriculture*. Biodynamic Agricultural Association, UK. *This is the foundation! A series of eight lectures given by Steiner in 1924 which forms the basis upon which biodynamic agriculture was developed. Unless you have a thorough grounding in anthroposophy, don't read this, go straight for the techniques. Once you experience how biodynamics really works, then this is the text, it will reveal all the secrets!*

Chapter 6   Water and Sewage

Browne, Will. 'From Waste to Wealth.' Article in *Resurgence* magazine No. 162. *This is a great sequel to the paper by Uwe Burka. And it has better maps!*

Burka, Uwe and Lawrence, Peter. *A New* 'Community Approach to Wastewater Treatment.' Informally circulated article. Obtainable from Oaklands Park Camphill Village, Newnham, Gloucestershire, GL14 1EF, England. Or from Watson Hawksley, Terriers House, Amersham Road, High Wycombe, Buckinghamshire, HP13 5AJ, England. *This must be ten or fifteen years old already, but still one of the gems in this field. Get it if you can! Detailed and scientific descriptions of how a Camphill Ecovillage solved its sewage treatment problem, and set a whole new trend in motion which subsequently spread throughout the Camphill movement. You don't need to reinvent the wheel, these people have already done it!*

Coates, Callum. 1996. *Living Energies.* Gateway Books, UK. *An account of the work of Schaumberger, the man who in his turn inspired the Schwenk team of father and son to go into water research. Wonderfully illustrated.*

Collis, John Stewart. 1972. *The Vision of Glory.* Charles Knight & Co, London. *This is a collection of articles and pieces by a great writer who died in the 1980s. Collis was finding patterns in nature when Mollison was still a kid, and writes about what he sees in wonderful prose. Hardly anyone seems to know about John Stewart, but he has been one of my great inspirations.*

Etnier, Carl and Guterstam, Björn. Eds. 1991. *Ecological Engineering for Wastewater Treatment.* Bokskogen, Gothenburg, Sweden. *A collection of papers given at the conference of the same name held at a college in Sweden. The breadth and scope is truly global, and this will give ideas for treating wastewater in most climatic conditions on the planet. Serious stuff, lots of tables, diagrams and academics.*

Hudson, Chris. 'Pond Systems and Natural Wastewater Treatment.' Article in Permaculture Magazine No. 8. *Good, stimulating article about the subject. Will get you thinking and inspired, but you will need more scientific details to set things up.*

Jenssen, P. D. and Skjelhaugen, O. D. *Local Ecological Solutions for Wastewater and Organic Waste Treatment.* Aas Agricultural University, Norway. *This is the result of several years of study and tests of the wastewater treatment facility at the Camphill village, Solborg, where I live. Serious, scientific stuff, and it led to the wider acceptance of these systems throughout Norway*

Ogden, Michael. 1992. 'Designing with Nature: Natural Systems for Wastewater Treatment.' Article in *Permaculture Drylands Journal*, Arizona, USA. Summer 1992. *A really good description of a system which lies somewhere between the open air Flowform pond and wetland process, and the Living Machine approach.*

Riegner, Mark and Wilkes, John. 'Art in the Service of Nature.' Informally circulated article. *Until John had Flowforms published (see below) this was the only real material I had on the subject. Luckily most of this has now been incorporated into his new book.*

Schwenk, Theodor and Wolfram. 1989. *Water – The Element of Life.* Anthroposophic Press, New York. *This is an account of the serious research done by the Schwenk team, looking at the way water behaves. The drop technique has shown itself to be amazingly sensitive to the slightest changes we make to the composition of water, and hints at water's capacity for memory.*

Schwenk, Theodor. 1996. *Sensitive Chaos*. Rudolf Steiner Press, London. *Schwenk was the inspiration and the teacher of John Wilkes, who developed the Flowform. This book is an invaluable guide to the magic of water and how it behaves.*

The Golden Blade. 1994. *Chaos, Rhythm and Flow in Nature*. Floris, Edinburgh. *Until last year it was hard to find stuff by John Wilkes about Flowforms. This is basically all I had in print, apart from odd photocopied diagrams and bits of informally circulated articles.*

Todd, John. 2001. 'Design Revolution.' Article in *Resurgence* magazine No. 207. July/August 2001. *The best succinct description of Living Machines and the ideas behind them I have come across.*

Wilkes, John. 2003. *Flowforms*. Floris, Edinburgh. *At last! The definitive book on this subject. If you are interested in water, how it behaves, its significance and its spiritual properties, then this is a must for you! The book also goes into detail how these properties are brought into play in a practical way, dealing with sewage treatment in various places.*

Chapter 7 Energy Sources and Alternative Technology

Baer, Steve. 1979. *Sunspots*. Cloudburst Press, USA. *This book may be a little old now, things have moved a long way, but it's a classic gem. Full of clear descriptions of practical things you can design, a few really wild ideas, and some great little short stories relating to radical use of solar energy.*

Baldwin, J. and Brand, Stewart. Eds.1978. *Soft-Tech*. Penguin, USA & UK. *An update to the Whole World Catalogue, concentrating on technology. Some really good articles and lots of product guides. Good stuff to get inspiration from.*

Boyle, Geoffrey and Harper, Peter. eds. 1976. *Radical Technology*. England. Undercurrents Publications. *This was one of the first comprehensive books on the subject to be published in England. The authors were involved with the magazine Undercurrents, which ran for several years, and the book contains wide ranging articles and lots of do-it-yourself stuff.*

Congdon, R. J. ed. 1977. *Introduction to Appropriate Technology.* Rodale Press, USA. *A wide-ranging book from the era when appropriate technology was on the up and up. I've used it a lot for references to things I couldn't find in other places, and for good solid background information.*

Rostvik, Harald. 1991. *Solenergi.* Sun-Lab Forlag, Norway. Also available in English as *Solar Energy. Wonderfully produced, full of clear pictures and diagrams. Takes you through solar energy from the basic facts, with lots of real life examples from around the world. Full of technical details, written by an internationally acclaimed expert.*

Schaeffer, John. Ed. 1994. *Solar Living Sourcebook.* Chelsea Green, USA. *Ten years old, and superseded now by more up to date publications, it still stands as a good introduction, with lots of text on basic technology, as well as a product guide.*

Chapter 8   Alternative Economics

Douthwaite, Richard. 1996. *Short Circuit.* Green Books and Lilliput Press, Dublin. *This is for me the best book so far on alternative economics. Long, detailed, serious and well written, by a real expert in the field. Lots of real life examples are given, mostly from the British Isles. Richard looks at energy and food supplies as well as the financial side of things, and the last chapters are about how we need to change our attitudes; how all these other things, like our economic systems, are reflections of how we think.*

Douthwaite, Richard. 1999. *The Ecology of Money.* Green Books, UK. *Can't be more concise than this! In just over 70 pages Richard tells us how money is produced, how we can create new money systems, and how we can run several systems side by side to create a stable economy. I can't recommend this book enough.*

Girardet, Herbert. 1999. *Creating Sustainable Cities.* Green Books, UK. *Because so many of us live in town, we need to find ways of improving things where we are. Herbert is serious, is taken seriously, and this is one of the best short versions of how we might go about greening our towns and cities.*

Groh, Trauger and McFadden, Steven. 1997. *Farms of Tomorrow Revisited.* Biodynamic Farming and Gardening Association, USA. *The book of my choice when it comes to Community Supported Agriculture. This is an expanded reprint of the first book they wrote, and is based on real life experience. Anyone wanting to get into CSA should look at this book first. Why not learn from the experience of others?*

Hayter, Teresa. 1981. *The Creation of World Poverty*. Pluto Press, UK. *A short, clear and concise book showing how the spread of colonialism and capitalism has created a gulf between rich and poor. As relevant today as it was when first published. It is essential that we understand how the system works before we begin to tinker with it. This book helps you understand.*

Henderson, Hazel. 1978. *Creating Alternative Futures*. Perigee Books, USA. *This may be more of historical interest today. Hazel saw into the future, consulting the oracle of then present day trends, and she saw that there is a possibility of creating an alternative, what she called a 'counter economy.' Present day trends have deepened and become more serious in the last quarter of a century, but the counter economy has not only developed, but established itself. It's great to read those who prophecy!*

Kanovsky, Eliyahu. 1966. *The Economy of the Israeli Kibbutz*. Harvard University Press, USA. *An old, out of date and pretty dry monograph, but a treasure trove for those interested in an academic view of the Kibbutz collective, its ideological ancestors, structure and economy, from a time before Israel and the region were torn apart in 'politically correct' opinions.*

Kennedy, Margrit. 1995. *Interest and Inflation Free Money*. Seva International, USA. *A short book, just over a hundred pages, one of the first I read about alternative economics, which actually spelt out systems which have been used, which are in use, and which can be implemented. My copy is now well thumbed and full of pencil marks underlining important bits. I reread most of it nearly every time I need to introduce alternative economics.*

Meron, Stanley. 1993. *Kibbutz in a Market Society*. Yad Tabenkin, Israel. *The Kibbutz created a new type of internal and between-Kibbutz type of economy, which over the years became absorbed into the national economy of Israel. Not without a lot of pain, which is still going on today. For those interested in how an alternative society and economy interfaces with a conventional one, this is your book! Written by an expert, insider, economist, researcher.*

Naughton, Tony. 1981. *Work Aid*. Commonwealth, UK. *When we established our own worker's co-operative, this was one of the books that we valued most, together with David Wright's* Co-operatives and Community. *Tony's book is an easy-to-read guide to setting up in business, taking you through all those boring old things like taxation, marketing, planning and keeping accounts. Our Louth Wholefood Co-operative is still in business today, over twenty years later!*

Porritt, Jonathan. 1984. *Seeing Green*. Basil Blackwell, UK. *Jonathan was at the first Findhorn conference on Ecovillages, in 1995, providing the political angle on how to transform society. This book is an early statement of the Green Party in England, giving a vision of how to get society transformed by politics. Good, rousing stuff, read it and become motivated!*

Schumacher, E. F. 1975. *Small Is Beautiful*. Harper & Row, UK. *This is one of those rare books that gave a new direction to the way we see the world, and which galvanized large numbers of people to action. At last, economics as if people mattered. If you haven't read it, make up for lost time and do so. If you've read it, then you know what I'm talking about.*

Sommerlad, Elizabeth. 1985. *Rural Land Sharing Communities: An Alternative Economic Model?* Bureau of Labour Market Research, Australia. *This came from the time when Bob Hawke was interested in trying alternative models for getting the Australian society and economy moving. It's pretty dry stuff, but has interesting snippets from the communities studied. The recommendations are interesting too, should national governments encourage people to form alternative communities? What a great question!*

Wright, David H. 1979. *Co-operatives and Community*. Bedford Square Press, UK. *This was of great value to us when we established a worker's co-operative in the early 1980s in England. Together with Tony Naughton's* Work Aid *we got the enterprise off the ground, and it's still operating, over twenty years later! This book concentrates on the legal ground rules and constitution.*

Chapter 9   Design Hands-On

Alexander, Christopher. 1977. *A Pattern Language*. OUP, New York. *This is one of the great books on architectural planning to have come out in the last few decades! It takes a couple of hours of concentrated work to come to grips with, and then your eyes open and you will never forget it! Over two hundred patterns are described, beginning with bioregions, and coming down to such details as where to put a shelf. No planner should be without one.*

Bobrow, Edwin. 1998. *Ten Minute Guide to Planning*. Alpha, New York. *Clear, concise and to the point, this book will take you through the stages in getting a plan together. It actually takes a bit more than ten minutes, but don't let that deter you. Straightforward and conventional, but it gives what you need to know for presenting your plan to those who need to approve it or support it.*

Bransford, John and Stein, Barry. 1984. *The Ideal Problem Solver.* W.H. Freeman, New York. *A great little book looking at the world of problems and how we solve them. Not explicitly dealing with either Permaculture or Ecovillages, but nevertheless of great value. Read it and be inspired!*

Buzan, Barry and Tony. 2000. *The Mind Map Book.* England. BBC Worldwide, UK. *Tony Buzan has registered the word Mind Mapping as a trademark, and made it his mission to spread the idea. Simple to learn, and has tremendous potential in unlocking us from straight or linear thinking. Worth getting into.*

Clark, Paul and Freeman, Julian. 2003. *Design.* Silverdale Books, UK. *A short little book on design, lots of illustrations and examples, pretty straight stuff, what design students will get to know when they study the basics. Good to refer to and dip into.*

Cousineau, Phil. and Zelev, Chris. eds. 1997. *Design Outlaws on the Ecological Frontier.* Knossos, USA. *The book of the film* Ecological Design — Inventing the Future. *(The Ecological Design Project, 1994) which itself is one of the great inspirational films about modern ecological design. The book is based on interviews with designers, and contains many gems of ideas and opinions.*

de Bono, Edward. 1969. *The Five-Day Course in Thinking.* Penguin, UK. *De Bono is a wonderful inspiration in getting us to think differently, laterally as he calls it. Release your creativity by doing some of the simple exercises he gives in this book.*

de Bono, Edward. 1971. *The Dog-Exercising Machine.* Penguin, UK. *By asking children to design a machine to exercise a dog, de Bono collected a number of widely varying designs. This he then sorted, and presents here as an analysis of design, illustrating different ways of approaching a design brief. You'll learn a lot about how we think from this.*

Jones, H. P. and Williams, Howard. 1972. *Physical Basis of the British Isles.* Macmillan, London. *This is actually a reprinted edition of a book I used when I was at school. Work your way through this, and you will know how to use maps. Based on the British Ordnance Survey map system, it will teach you to read and analyse topographical maps of any place in the world. Open up a new way of reading in your life!*

Morrow, Rosemary. 1997. *Earth User's Guide to Permaculture, Teacher's Notes.* Kangaroo Press, Australia. *This was an invaluable book for me when I began teaching design courses. Morrow is a well known Permaculture teacher in Australia, and this is her course, presented for other teachers. You could take the book and work through it with a group, and hey presto, you have a design course! If you are based in Australia and Vietnam, this is fine. For me I had to do some adaptation to the climatic and cultural areas I found myself in.*

Papanek, Victor. 1991. *Design for the Real World*. Thames & Hudson, London. *This book is really about forty years old, but still contains great ideas, fresh from the first burst of radical ecological thinking. Papanek is one of the first radical ecological designers, way ahead of Permaculture. The book is as relevant today as it was when it was first written.*

Register, Richard. 1987. *Ecocity Berkeley*. North Atlantic Books, California. *I came across this book when I first got involved in GEN, and it opened my eyes to the fact that Ecovillages were not just about tiny rural enclaves, but that the ideas of Permaculture and the Ecovillage movement were just as relevant to the city scene. This is a great little book, looking at a real life example, and suggesting an ecological scenario stretching many decades ahead. Great illustrations, great ideas. Most of us live in cities, let's start where we're at!*

Steiner, Rudolf. 2002. *Finding the Greater Self*. Rudolf Steiner Press, UK. *Steiner didn't only write heavy duty books on anthroposophy, he also wrote books of meditations and prayers. If you agree with me that design is the closest activity to the divine, then you may as well get real and start praying! I found the short verse I used in the introduction to* Ecovillages *in this book. You will find plenty more gems if you spend some time with it.*

Periodicals

This list cannot really be exhaustive. It consists of what I read regularly, plus a few other things I've come across. I have a theory that while most daily newspaper and TV/radio media concentrates on the bad things in the world, I can get a positive view by reading specialist magazines. You can start with these, but you will probably build up your own, unique set.

CALL
Editor: Anton Marks
Kvutsat Yovel, PO Box 3791
Migdal Ha'Emek, Israel
anton@kvutsatyovel.com

Camphill Correspondance
Editor: Peter Howe
Glasshouse College, Wollaston Road
Amblecote, Stourbridge
W. Midlands DY8 4HF, England
Tel: 01384-399 475
peterh1@beeb.net

Communities
Editor: D Leafe Christian
1025 Camp Elliott Road
Black Mountain, NC 28711, USA
Tel: 828-652-8517
communities@ic.org

Ecologist
Editor: Zac Goldsmith
Ecosystems Ltd
Unit 18 Chelsea Wharf, 15 Lots
Road, London SW10 OQJ
England
Tel: 01795414963
belinda@theecologist.org

Landsbyliv
Editors: JM Bang and Dag Balavoine
A forum for those who live and are
engaged in the Norwegian Camphill
villages. Only for those who read
Norwegian! (As co-editor I have to
give this one a plug!)
Solborg Landsby
3520 Jevnaker, Norway
Tel: 03213 3456
Fax: 03213 2020
landsbyliv@camphill.no

The Last Straw
Editor: Peter Bane
The International Journal of Straw
Bale and Natural Building, HC 66
Box 119 Hillsboro
NM 88042, USA
thelaststraw@strawhomes.com

New Scientist
Editor: Jeremy Webb
Global science and technology weekly
151, Wardour Street,
London W1F 8WE, England
enquiries@newscientist.com

Permaculture Activist
Editor: Peter Bane
PO Box 1209
Black Mountain, NC 28711, USA
Tel: 828-669-6336
Fax: 828-669-5068
pcactivist@mindspring.com

Permaculture Magazine
Editor: Maddy Harland
Permanent Publications
Hyden House Ltd
The Sustainability Centre, East Meon
GU32 1HR, England
webweaver@permaculture.co.uk.

Positive News.
Editor: Shauna Crockett Burrows
No. 5 Bicton Enterprise Centre
Clun, SY7 8NF, England
Tel: 01588-640 022
Fax: 01588-640 033
office@positivenews.org.uk
www.positivenews.org.uk

Resurgence
Editor: Satish Kumar
Ford House, Hartland, Bideford
Devon EX39 6EE, England.
Tel: 01237-441 293
Fax: 01237-441 203

Organizations

This is an area where I am certain to be out of date by the time the book goes to press. There are so many organizations out there. I will give a list of some of the ones I have come across, but you will need to do your own searching. It seems that the best place is the internet. In addition I really recommend going through the smaller stuff at the back end of many magazines, small ads, classifieds and so on. Amazing how much information gets spread that way too! If you want to be really pro-active, you can put in a small ad yourself.

• Biodynamic Agriculture Organizations

Australia:
Biodynamic Agricultural Association
PO Box 54, Bellingen, NSW, 2454
Tel: 02-9665 0566
Fax: 02-9665 0565
poss@midcoast.com.au
www.biodynamics.net.au

Egypt:
Bio-Dynamic Association
3 Belbes Desert Road, POB 1535
Alf Maskan, 11777 Cairo
Tel: 02-656 4154
Fax: 02-656 7828
EBDA@sekem.com

Germany:
Demeter-Bund e.V.
Brandschneise 1
64295 Darmstadt
Tel: 06155-8469-0
Fax: 06155-8469-11
Info@Demeter.de
www.demeter.de

Italy:
Demeter Associazione per la Tutela della Qualitá
Biodinamica in Italia, Strada Naviglia 11/A, 43100 Parma, Italy
Tel: 0521-776962
Fax: 0521-776973
demeter.italia@tin.it
www.demeter.it

Netherlands:
Vereniging voor Biologisch Dynamische Landbouw en Voeding
Postbus 236
3970 AE Driebergen,
Tel: 0343-531740
Fax: 0343-516943
Info@demeter-bd.nl
www.demeter-bd.nl

Norway:
Debio, 1940 Björkelangen
Tel: 6386 2670
Fax: 6385 6985
kontor@debio.no
www.debio.no

USA:
Biodynamic Farming and Gardening
Association, Inc., 25844 Butler
Road, Junction City, OR 97448
Tel: 541-998-5691
Fax: 541-998-5894
biodynamic@aol.com
www.biodynamics.com

UK:
Biodynamic Agricultural Association
Painswick Inn, Stroud, GL5 1QG
Tel/Fax: 01453-759 501
office@biodynamic.org.uk
www.biodynamic.org.uk

International: www.demeter.net

• Bruderhof

The Bruderhof Foundation
Farmington PA 15437, USA
www.bruderhof.com

• Camphill Network

The Camphill Movement is very dispersed, every country is autonomous.
You can get addresses from the international directory, and Britain has the
largest number of communities:

The Camphill Movement
Botton Village, Danby, Whitby,
YO21 2NJ, UK
Tel: 01287-660 871
Fax: 01287-660 888
www.camphill.org.uk

The Association of Camphill
Communities, Gawain House,
56 Welham Road
Norton, Malton
YO17 9DP, UK
Tel: 01653-694 197
Fax: 01653-600 001
info@camphill.org.uk

• Communal Studies Association

Kathleen M. Fernandez
POB 122, Amana
IA 52203, USA
www.communalstudies.org

• Diggers and Dreamers

Publishes occasional directories, only
for Great Britain:

D&D publications
PO Box 1808, MK18 3RN, UK

• Eurotopia

This is the best guide to European
communities, updated and reissued
every few years:

Ökodorf Sieben Linden
38486 Poppau, Germany
Tel: 039000-51235
Fax: 039000-51232
eurotopia@gmx.de
www.eurotopia.de

• Fellowship for Intentional Community

Route 1, Box 156, Rutledge
MO 63563, USA
www.ic.org

• Global Ecovillage Network

They have an enormous website, and are split into three regions:

GEN-Europe
Rosa-Luxemburgstr. 89,
14806 Belzig, Germany
Tel: 033841-44766
Fax: 033841-44768
info@gen-europe.org
www.gen-europe.org

Ecovillage Network of the Americas
Albert Bates
The Farm Ecovillage Training Centre
PO Box 90, Summertown
TN, 38483-0090, USA
Ecovillage@thefarm.org
www.gen.ecovillage.org

Global Ecovillage Network
(Oceania & Asia) Inc.
Lot 59 Crystal Waters Village,
65 Kilcoy Lane, Conondale,
Qld 4552, Australia
Tel: 07-5494 4741
Fax: 07-5494 4578
lindegger@gen-oceania.org

• ICSA

International Communal Studies
Association, Yad Tabenkin
Ramat Efal 52960, Israel
Tel: 03-534 4458
Fax: 03-534 6376
rsoboly-t@bezeqint.net
www.ic.org/icsa/

• Kibbutz organizations

Kibbutz Lotan,
Hevel Eilot 88855, Israel
Tel: 08-635 6968 or 05-2392 2046
Fax: 08-635 6827
ml-lotan@zahav.net.il
www.kibbutzlotan.com

• Organic farming groups

Community Supported Agriculture
of North America Inc.
Indian Line Farm, 57 Jugend Road
Great Barrington, MA 01230, USA
csana@bcn.net

• Permaculture

Norwegian Permaculture Association
Secretary: Jan Martin Bang
Solborg Camphill Village
3520 Jevnaker, Norway
Tel: 04812-9653 or 03213-3051
Fax: 03213-2020
jmbang@start.no

Index

Flowforms

The Rhythmic Power of Water

A. John Wilkes

Water is not only fundamental to life but is essential for the cycles and changes in nature. John Wilkes argues that water is the universal bearer of the character we put into it. For this reason the way we treat water is of crucial importance to our health, and to the well-being of our planet.

Working with his remarkable invention, the Flowform, Wilkes has uncovered hidden secrets of the world of water, and at the same time created an artform of great beauty. His lifetime of applied research into rhythms and water, fully revealed in this book for the first time, has startling implications for such topical issues as farming and irrigation; food production and processing; water treatment and recycling; and health and cosmetic products.

This ground-breaking book is lavishly illustrated to show both the beauty of the Flowform and the wide range of its applications.

Floris Books